Festivals and Celebrations

Festivals and Celebrations

A Global Cultural Odyssey

Rafeal Mechlore

WSM Publisher

CONTENTS

INDEX 1

INTRODUCTION 3

Chapter 1 17

Chapter 2 34

Chapter 3 57

Chapter 4 71

Chapter 5 89

Chapter 6 103

Chapter 7 119

Chapter 8 137

Chapter 9 151

Chapter 10 177

Chapter 11 195

Chapter 12 212

INDEX

Introduction

1. Defining the importance of festivals and celebrations in culture
2. The universal human impulse to celebrate
3. Overview of the book's exploration of diverse festivals around the world

Chapter 1: The Essence of Festivals
1.1 What are festivals and celebrations?
1.2 The role of traditions and rituals
1.3 Festivals as expressions of cultural identity

Chapter 2: The Science of Celebration
2.1 Psychological and sociological aspects of celebrations
2.2 The impact of celebrations on well-being
2.3 The science of shared joy and community bonding

Chapter 3: Religious Festivals
3.1 An exploration of major religious festivals (e.g., Diwali, Easter, Eid, Hanukkah, and Christmas)
3.2 The significance of these festivals in various faiths
3.3 Rituals, symbols, and stories associated with religious celebrations

Chapter 4: Seasonal Festivals
4.1 Festivals tied to the changing seasons (e.g., Spring and Autumn Equinox, Solstices)
4.2 Agricultural festivals and the celebration of nature
4.3 How seasonal festivals vary by region and climate

Chapter 5: Cultural Festivals

5.1 An in-depth look at culturally specific celebrations (e.g., Chinese New Year, Carnaval, Holi)
5.2 Cultural festivals as windows into the customs, values, and art of a community
5.3 The globalization of cultural festivals

Chapter 6: Music and Dance Festivals
6.1 The power of music and dance to transcend language and borders
6.2 Iconic music festivals (e.g., Woodstock, Coachella, Samba Fest)
6.3 How music and dance festivals have evolved over time

Chapter 7: Food and Culinary Festivals
7.1 Exploring the world of culinary celebrations (e.g., Oktoberfest, Thanksgiving, Diwali)
7.2 The role of food in cultural identity and celebration
7.3 Food festivals as reflections of local agriculture and cuisine

Chapter 8: National and Independence Day Celebrations
8.1 The importance of national identity and independence
8.2 The blending of historical remembrance and contemporary celebration

Chapter 9: Carnival and Mardi Gras
9.1 The history and cultural significance of Carnival and Mardi Gras celebrations
9.2 The role of masks, costumes, and parades
9.3 Global variations of these lively festivals

Chapter 10: Future Trends in Festivals
10.1 How globalization and technology are reshaping festivals
10.2 The sustainability and eco-consciousness of future festivals
10.3 Predictions for the future of global celebrations

Chapter 11: The Challenges and Controversies
11.1 The tension between tradition and modernity
11.2 Cultural appropriation and respect for traditions
11.3 Environmental and social issues in festival organization

Chapter 12: Preserving and Documenting Festivals
12.1 The importance of cultural preservation
12.2 Efforts to document and protect endangered festivals
12.3 The role of museums and institutions in preserving festival heritage

INTRODUCTION

The desire to rejoice is a profound and ubiquitous urge that has been present in humanity for a very long time. Festivals and other forms of public celebration have been an integral part of human existence for the entirety of recorded human history and across the great majority of the surface area of our planet. These communal manifestations of joy, reflection, and solidarity are not limited by geographical limits, linguistic barriers, or cultural norms. They serve as a thread that connects each of us to one another and to the rich tapestry of the human experience that we all have in common.

The book "Festivals and Celebrations: A Global Cultural Odyssey" is an epic journey into the very core of this innately human need to celebrate. This book is a witness to the many and varied ways in which we celebrate life, spirituality, the changing of the seasons, culture, music, and our shared identity as a group. It is an investigation into the core of what it is that makes us human, which is the yearning to congregate with others and rejoice.

This world tour will take you to some of the most remote and exotic locations on the planet, including the crowded streets of Rio de Janeiro's Carnival and the peaceful beauty of the Japanese Cherry Blossom Festival. This book is an investigation of the kaleidoscope of festivals and celebrations that mark the passage of time, repeat the cycles of nature, and represent the spirit of cultures from all over the world.

Our adventure starts with the fundamental aspects of festivals, including what they are and what they stand for. We go deep into the center of these festivities, illuminating their fundamental components and illuminating the function that they serve within our culture. These are not merely events; rather, they are significant representations of culture, tradition, and individuality.

In the next chapters, we will explore the complexities of many religious celebrations, which will lead us on a journey through the spiritual and symbolic rituals that define communities all over the world. These celebrations bring mankind closer to its spiritual origins, and they do it in a variety of ways, from the dazzling colors of Diwali to the profound meanings of Easter, Eid, Hanukkah, and Christmas.

Festivals that take place throughout the year provide us the opportunity to investigate the ways in which culture, agriculture, and the natural world are intertwined.

As we learn more about the equinoxes, solstices, and other astronomical events, we are able to appreciate the exquisite way in which other civilizations have synchronized their celebrations with the seasonal changes in the natural world. Our lives and the rituals we observe are imprinted with an enduring feeling of continuity thanks to the cycle of the seasons.

The hypnotic spectacle of the Chinese New Year and the vibrant energy of Carnaval are just two examples of the ways in which cultural festivals showcase the fascinating diversity of the world's numerous peoples. These festivals highlight the significant cultural expressions that play a role in the formation of the identities of communities all over the world. They teach us the beats of life, the flavors of culture, and the strength that can be found in variety despite its many facets.

The chapters that are devoted to music and dance festivals are a beautifully cohesive investigation into the ways in which art, rhythm, and melody may cross national boundaries and linguistic barriers. We travel to renowned events such as Woodstock, Coachella, and Samba Fest, gatherings where people come together to celebrate life through the shared experiences of music, rhythm, and dance.

Festivals devoted to food and the culinary arts transport our taste buds on a journey across the globe. Dishes such as paella, sushi, tamales, and baklava are examined in order to provide light on the complex cultural tapestry that is reflected in their flavors. Food is transformed into a statement of identity and a monument to the art of culinary production through the course of these festivals, which highlight the cultural richness of cuisine in its various forms.

Celebrations on Independence Day honor the sprit of nations, representing the yearning for sovereignty as well as the unifying pride that is carved into history. We travel to well-known festivals in countries like the United States and France, such as the Fourth of July in the United States and Bastille Day in France. These festivities capture the spirit of the nations they honor by combining traditional mourning with contemporary revelry.

Both Carnival and Mardi Gras are exciting celebrations that feature parades, costumes, and masks that are brightly colored and elaborately designed. These festivals are taking place all over the world and serve as a monument to the emancipatory power of celebration. We feel the exhilaration of both Carnival and Mardi Gras as we go from the vibrant streets of Rio de Janeiro to the colorful center of New Orleans.

Discovering how globalization, technology, and sustainable practices are transforming festivities presents a tempting challenge for those interested in the future of festivals.

We contemplate the ever-changing nature of these occurrences and think about the part they will play in the years to come as we think about the future. As we set sail on a voyage of prognostication and imagination, we picture a future in which celebrations will continue to bring people together regardless of physical distance or cultural background.

In the section under "Challenges and Controversies," we will take some time to focus on the difficult problems that contemporary festivals and celebrations are required to address. This chapter explores the ethical considerations that go into making our celebrations what they are, delving into everything from the conflict that arises between tradition and modernity to the pressing problems of cultural appropriation and environmental concerns.

Our journey comes to an end with a contemplation on the critical significance of maintaining these extraordinary customs and documenting them for future generations. It is crucial that we preserve the diverse patterns of human celebration in light of the fact that the world is changing at such a rapid rate. It is imperative that the enduring legacy of our cultural history be protected so that subsequent generations can admire and gain knowledge from it.

It is more than just a book; "Festivals and Celebrations: A Global Cultural Odyssey" provides a window into the very essence of what it means to be human. This book is an investigation into the joys, hopes, and dreams that we all share as members of the same global community. This book is your passport to the universal language of joy. It does not matter whether you are an avid traveler, an armchair adventurer, or simply someone who wishes to have a greater understanding of our world; this book is for you. This is an invitation to celebrate our common humanity as well as the rich tapestry of holidays and rituals that bind us all together.

1. **Defining the importance of festivals and celebrations in culture**

    Festivals and other types of festivities retain a significant place in human society, and their significance transcends national boundaries, linguistic barriers, and periods of history. They are not merely occurrences, but rather stand for an essential component of the life of a human being. Celebrations and festivals play a significant role in who we are as a people, how we feel about the community we live in, and how we are connected to the past, the present, and the future. During the course of this investigation, we dive into the significant significance of festivals and celebrations in culture, providing light on why they are important and how they define our communal identity.

    The inborn desire that all humans share to party and have fun

    The realization of a fundamentally human want, namely the yearning for festivity, is essential to gaining a proper appreciation for the significance of holidays and other occasions for public celebration. This want is not restricted in any way by culture, region, or the passage of time; rather, it is a common thread that runs through all of humanity. Humans have always been able to find a reason to join together and rejoice, whether it be through the elaborate rituals of tribal tribes in the past or the spectacular spectacles of modern global events.

There are many different reasons to celebrate, and these reasons draw from a vast variety of human experiences. Personal milestones include events such as births, weddings, and graduations. The spiritual connection and refreshment that can be found via participation in religious celebrations. Observing the changing of the seasons, as well as the solstices and equinoxes, is an important part of the seasonal festivals that people participate in. Festivals of culture honor the unique history, customs, and artistic expression of a community. The founding of a nation and its history are celebrated on each country's respective national holiday. Festivals of music and dance bring people together through the unifying power of rhythm and melody. Festivals dedicated to the culinary arts highlight both the pleasures of eating and the art of cooking.

Manifestations of a Cultural Sense of Self

Festivals and other forms of celebration play an important role in conveying a sense of cultural identity. They serve as mirrors that reflect the values, beliefs, histories, and customs of a community. These festivities capture the collective memory of a group of people by expressing the memories and experiences that they have in common with one another.

For instance, the national day of a nation is more than just a date on the calendar; rather, it is an embodiment of the nation's history and the fight for independence. The Fourth of July in the United States, Bastille Day in France, and Canada Day in Canada, to name a few examples, are national holidays that honor the founding of nations as well as the values of liberty and independence. People are reminded of the hardships and goals that have defined their identity through the use of these festivities, which generate a meaningful connection between the past, the present, and the future.

Celebrations of various religions are excellent examples of how culture can be powerfully expressed. They unite people from different cultures in the celebration of their common religious and spiritual experiences and beliefs. Diwali in Hinduism, Christmas in Christianity, Eid in Islam, and Hanukkah in Judaism are not only religious observances but also cultural celebrations that carry the history of these faiths by transmitting their tales, values, and hopes. These holidays are known as the Festival of Lights.

Festivals of a community's culture, such as the Chinese New Year, Carnival, or Holi, are excellent opportunities to see the community's artistic and creative expressions, as well as its customs. These festivals shed light on the distinctive traits that characterize a culture and offer insights into those traits. For instance, the multicolored lanterns, dragon dances, and intricate symbolism of the Chinese New Year all display the deeply ingrained customs and symbolism of the

Chinese culture.
The Importance of Celebrations, Both Socially and Emotionally
Festivals and other forms of public celebration play an important part in the psychological and social makeup of a society. They provide a sense of belonging and connection, bringing together individuals and communities in experiences that are shared of joy, reflection, and unity. The joy of a wedding and the gravity of a religious service are two examples of the strong feelings that might be prompted by celebrations. They make possible the venting of feelings and the formation of connections between individuals in a safe environment.

According to research in psychology, festivities are associated with higher levels of happiness and well-being. They make it possible for people to take a break from the monotony of day-to-day existence and savor the pleasures of specific moments in their lives. The common experiences that occur during times of celebration help to foster a sense of togetherness, which in turn helps to strengthen social relationships and lessen feelings of isolation.

Festivals and celebrations provide a common platform for people to join together, regardless of
their differences, in a society that is frequently marked by separation and hostility. For instance, in the midst of the jubilant mayhem of a music festival, people from a variety of different countries and backgrounds share a shared interest in music. People from all over the world come together to communicate their spirituality and religion during the solemnity of a religious ceremony, breaking down barriers such as language and country of origin in the process.

The Craft of Joyous Occasions
Not only are celebrations ways for cultures to express themselves, but they are also a type of art. They require meticulous planning, design, and inventiveness on the part of the creator. The art of celebration is most apparent in the layout of the rooms, the selection of the decorations, the composition of the music and dancing, and the cooking of the unique delicacies. These components weave together to create a fabric that is rich in both beauty and significance.

Take, for instance, the ornate design of a Mardi Gras float, the eye-catching costumes of Carnival, or the vibrant rangoli patterns of Diwali.

All of these are examples of intricate designs. These creative aspects are a crucial component of the celebration; they enrich the occasion as a whole, and they make an indelible mark on those who take part in it as well as those who only observe it.

In addition, celebrations frequently contain rites and customs that have been carried on from generation to generation. People are able to feel a stronger connection to their cultural history via the practice of these rituals because they act as a link between the past and the present. For the Jewish holiday of Hanukkah, the custom of lighting the menorah and for the Christian holiday of Christmas, the tradition of giving gifts, both hold great cultural and historical significance. These customs are a demonstration of how culture has persisted through the ages and how traditions have been kept alive.

Exchange of cultures and an understanding of the world

Festivals and celebrations, in today's increasingly interconnected globe, serve as vehicles for the interchange of cultural ideas and the promotion of global understanding. People from all over the world are given the chance to meet one another, discuss the customs of their home countries, and learn new perspectives on the varied and fascinating cultural backgrounds of those around them.

Cultural festivals, in particular, are conduits through which one can better comprehend and appreciate the myriad forms that human culture can take. People who take part in or attend cultural festivals from various regions of the world receive insights about the customs, art, and traditions of such cultures. These insights can be beneficial in a variety of contexts. This kind of experience cultivates empathy, respect, and admiration for the rich tapestry that is people all across the world.

Examples of the power of cultural interchange include the Rio Carnival, Woodstock, and the Notting Hill Carnival. Other examples include the Notting Hill Carnival. These events draw attendees and participants from all over the world, resulting in a melting pot of musical styles, dances, and artistic manifestations. They serve as a reminder that the language of celebration is global and transcends the spoken words that are used to express it.

In Harmony with Our Differences

The ability of festivals and celebrations to commemorate both unity and diversity is one of the most amazing characteristics of these types of events. They highlight the distinctive aspects of a culture while simultaneously putting an emphasis on the similarities that all human experiences share. Despite the fact that they celebrate our differences, they emphasize our common humanity.

Think about the festivities that take place on the night before the new year. People get together in communities big and small all around the world to say goodbye to the old year and hello to the new one. Even while the precise rituals and practices may differ from one nation to the next, the overarching themes of introspection, revitalization, and optimism are shared by all cultures. People from all walks of life get together to celebrate the new year on New Year's Eve because they share the desire to begin the coming year with a clean slate.

The multiplicity of festivities in multicultural countries, such as the United States and Canada, is a reflection of the heterogeneity that exists within the society as a whole. Participants hailing from a variety of cultural traditions join forces to take part in one another's respective celebrations. The cultural fabric of these countries is enriched as a result, and the principles of inclusivity and diversity are given a boost as a result of this as well.

A Representation of the Ideals and Values Upheld by Society

Festivals and other types of festivities serve another purpose, which is to act as mirrors that reflect the common values, goals, and aspirations of a society. They address not just the historical aspects of culture but also the modern worries and hopes, and as a result, they frequently personify the values and dreams of the community in which they are situated.

For instance, issues over the environment are gaining a larger and larger presence in today's celebrations. A growing number of celebrations and events are embracing environmentally responsible approaches in order to reduce their waste and their negative effects on the environment. This exemplifies the worldwide commitment to responsible and sustainable practices for the environment.

In recent years, several celebrations have integrated social and political messages, addressing problems like as human rights, equality, and justice. This trend is expected to continue in the coming years. Messages of hope, unity, or opposition can be conveyed through artistic manifestations during these events, which can serve as a platform for societal transformation. For instance, the AIDS Memorial Quilt is not only a beautiful piece of artwork but also makes a profound and moving message about the toll that the epidemic has had on human life. This quilt was made in reaction to the AIDS pandemic.

Festivals and celebrations are more than simple get-togethers; rather, they are a testimony to the core of what it means to be human. They have the power to bring us together in times of happiness, introspection, and harmony, thereby overcoming barriers and across national boundaries. Festivals are potent ways for cultures to express themselves, bringing the torch of history and legacy with them as they do so. They act as a mirror that reflects our core beliefs, our goals, and the experiences that we have in common.

Festivals and celebrations offer a universal language that speaks of joy, optimism, and solidarity in a world that is defined by diversity and division. They serve as a timely reminder that, despite our many distinctions, we are all connected by the common thread of our humanity. These gatherings represent not only an art form but also a kind of cultural interaction and a reflection of the ideals held by society. They are, in a very straightforward sense, a celebration of life itself.

2. **The universal human impulse to celebrate**

The desire to celebrate is inherent to every single living human being. It is a thread that has been woven into the very fabric of our existence, and its reach extends across borders of culture, language, and time. Celebration is an essential component of the human experience. This is true whether one is partaking in a jubilant wedding, a somber religious ritual, a cultural festival, or even a straightforward birthday party. The purpose of this investigation is to shed light on why we celebrate, how it links us, and the significance it bears in our lives by delving into the profound essence of the universal human drive to party.

The Concept of Celebration in Relation to the Human Condition

Celebration is an activity that is present in all different types of societies and cultures. Even if the reasons for celebrating can be very different, the act of celebration is something that all humans do. Humans have always been able to find a reason to join together and rejoice, and this has been true from the earliest civilizations to the most modern societies.

The need to commemorate special occasions is ingrained in our make-up as social beings. We have an innate need to be part of a community and to have experiences in common with one another. Celebrations provide an opportunity for people to get together and share in the delight of the occasion, as well as a timely reminder that we are not traveling this life's path alone.

The Response of Celebration to the Major Milestones in Life

The act of commemorating major junctures in one's life is frequently cited as one of the primary drivers of celebration. There are many different life events that need to be commemorated with a party, including but not limited to birthdays, anniversaries, graduations, and marriages. These occurrences serve as signposts indicating change and development in the life of an individual, and they carry a special significance for those who are directly engaged.

The commemoration of significant anniversaries has multiple functions. It gives people the opportunity to recognize and appreciate the changes and accomplishments that have occurred in their life. It presents an opportunity to convey one's appreciation and joy to the individuals who have contributed to the achievement of these milestones. In essence, commemorating these landmark occasions helps us form enduring memories that link us to our history and invigorate us for the years to come.

The Role of Celebration in Establishing Spiritual Connections

The inherent desire of humans to rejoice is inevitably going to manifest in a variety of contexts, including religious and spiritual gatherings. These festivities are more than just a way to celebrate personal milestones; rather, they are a statement of faith, dedication, and a connection to the spiritual world. Festivals of many religions offer a setting in which followers can commune with one another and rededicate themselves to their faith.

Sacred stories and reenactments frequently serve as the focal points of religious gatherings. For instance, Easter in Christianity is a celebration that remembers Jesus's resurrection, whereas Diwali in Hinduism is a festival that honors the triumph of light over darkness. These celebrations create a sense of continuity with a person's faith while also connecting individuals to the spiritual traditions that have played a role in the formation of their identities.

Observance as a Form of Reconnection with Nature

The connection to one's surroundings in the natural world is yet another aspect of the fundamentally human urge to celebrate. The changing of the seasons, the solstices, the equinoxes, and the agricultural cycles are all marked by various festivities that are timed to coincide with the cycles of nature. These kinds of festivities have been ingrained in human culture for many generations.

Celebrations of the changing seasons frequently include rites and customs that pay homage to the natural rhythms of the year. The Midsummer festivals in Scandinavia, for instance, are held to mark the day that is the longest of the year. These festivities are a method of expressing thanks for the earth's richness and reflect the profound connection that humans have with the world in which they live.

As a Form of Cultural Expression, Celebrations

Festivals are rich representations of the common human drive to rejoice, and different cultures have their own unique ways of doing so. The identity of a community, its beliefs, and the traditions it upholds are all reflected in these events. Festivals of culture shed light on the singular aspects that are responsible for the formation of a culture and provide a glimpse into the traditions, aesthetics, and history of a society.

One of the most astonishing things about cultural festivals is the amount of variety that can be found there. Every culture has its own special occasions for celebrating, complete with distinctive symbols, rites, and ways of expressing themselves. For instance, the calm and contemplative Hanami, which is celebrated during the cherry blossom season in Japan, is a striking contrast to the exuberant and vibrant Carnival that is held in Brazil.

The myriad of cultural festivities put on display the intricate pattern of human civilization as well as the myriad of ways in which different communities express themselves in their own unique ways.

Joy as a Universally Spoken Language of Celebration

Festivals of music and dance are living proof that joy can be communicated via any form of expression. Through the force of rhythm, melody, and the artistic expression of its participants, these events bring together people from a wide variety of backgrounds. The joy that can be experienced via music and dancing is not limited by linguistic or national boundaries.

Music festivals are becoming increasingly popular all around the world, as evidenced by the fact that events like Woodstock in the 1960s, which was a celebration of music and peace, attracted tens of thousands of young people. Woodstock became a symbol of an entire generation's desire to enjoy and come together as a result of the exhilaration, unity, and countercultural attitude that characterized the event.

The Art of Celebrating Through Cooking

Festivals dedicated to food highlight both the art of cooking and the joys that food can bring to the palette. These festivals give attendees a taste of culture by displaying the distinctive flavors and culinary customs of a variety of locations around the country. People have long come together to celebrate over shared meals and traditions, and food has always played an important role in these gatherings.

Festivals centered around food highlight the significance of food in cultural identity. Paella in Spain, sushi in Japan, tamales in Latin America, and baklava in the Middle East are not simply foods; rather, they are cultural expressions unique to their respective countries. The practice of culinary arts can serve as a conduit to better comprehend and value the richness and variety of human cultures.

The Festivities Serve as a Mirror Image of Our National Identity

Celebrations of a nation's national and independence days are an expression of that nation's collective identity and pride in its history. These festivities are held to recognize the values and concepts on which nations are built as well as to memorialize major historical events, highlight significant landmarks, and commemorate the birth of countries.

For instance, the independence and liberty of the United States of America are commemorated on July 4th, often known as Independence Day.

The assault on the Bastille and the beginning of the French Revolution are both commemorated on July 14, which is known as Bastille Day in France. These national holidays combine commemorating historical events with celebrating the here and now, so creating a synthesis of the past and the present.

A Party That Is More Like a Spectacle Made Up of Masks and Parades

Celebrations of Carnival and Mardi Gras are spectacular extravaganzas that flood the streets with masquerade masks, elaborate costumes, and parades. People are able to shed their mundane selves and embrace a spirit of liberation and merriment thanks to the fact that these holidays give them the chance to do so.

There is significant meaning behind the wearing of masks during Mardi Gras and Carnival. It enables people to shed the roles they are accustomed to playing and adopt a new identity for themselves. Parades, which are a public display of creative creation and a show of community spirit, are also a part of these events. The streets are transformed into a bright and surreal world through the use of floats, costumes, and performances.

The Celebration Serves as a Mirror for the Values and Aspirations of Society

Festivals and other forms of community celebration frequently serve as a mirror for a society's core beliefs, hopes, and ideals. Messages of a social and political nature can sometimes be incorporated into celebrations, in addition to the honoring of customs and traditions.

For example, in recent years, a number of festivities have shifted their focus to incorporate eco-consciousness and sustainable practices as central themes. This indicates a growing global commitment to the responsibility of protecting the environment. Green techniques are increasingly being used by festivals and events, with the goals of avoiding waste and lowering their overall impact on the environment.

Messages of a social or political nature are sometimes included at festivities. During these events, messages of hope, unity, or opposition could be conveyed through various artistic expressions. The AIDS Memorial Quilt is both a beautiful piece of artwork and a powerful message about the toll that the disease has had on human life. It was made in reaction to the AIDS pandemic. This demonstrates the potential of celebration as a platform for social change and activism, and it is a tribute to that power.

3. **Overview of the book's exploration of diverse festivals around the world**

The book "Festivals and Celebrations: A Global Cultural Odyssey" takes the reader on an enthralling excursion around the world, delving into the myriad of festivals and celebrations that dot our planet. This book provides a comprehensive overview of the myriad ways in which human society expresses itself via celebrations. It sheds light on the rich history of celebrations, the cultural relevance of celebrations, and the profound ways in which celebrations connect us to our common humanity.

The book is more than just a list of celebrations; rather, it is a colorful tapestry representing the spectrum of human experience, as seen through the prism of merriment. It is an adventure through time and space that invites readers to travel the continents and investigate the rituals, customs, and joyful expressions that define communities and build our global culture. This book is an odyssey.

The Festival Experience in Chapter 1 Introduction to Festivals

The voyage starts with an investigation of the fundamental nature of celebrations. In this chapter, we explore deeper into the nature of celebrations and what it is about them that makes them so important to the human experience. Our perspective of celebrations is shaped in part by the customs, rites, and experiences that we share with one another; we investigate this relationship. It is here where we lay the groundwork for the ensuing investigation of various celebrations that take place all around the world.

The science of celebration is covered in Chapter 2

The scientific and psychological components of celebrations are investigated in depth beginning with the second chapter of the book. It investigates the effect that celebrations have on our health and happiness, the sense of community that they help to cultivate, and the function that shared joy plays in the consolidation of social relationships. This chapter sheds light on the emotional and psychological relevance of celebrations and emphasizes the power that celebrations have to improve the quality of our lives.

Festivals Celebrated by Religious Groups in Chapter 3

Celebrations that are held in accordance with a particular religion are among the most profound examples of human joy. This chapter offers a comprehensive analysis of the most significant religious holidays celebrated by a variety of faiths all around the world. We examine the spiritual importance, rituals, and legends that are related with the many religious celebrations, such as the bright Diwali in Hinduism, the Easter festivities in Christianity, the festive mood of Eid in Islam, the symbolic Hanukkah in Judaism, and the cheerful spirit of Christmas. These celebrations range from Hinduism to Christianity to Islam to Hanukkah to Christmas.

The Holidays Celebrated Throughout the Year

Festivals that take place during specific times of the year have a strong connection to the natural world and the passage of time. This chapter will take us on a tour of the many different festivals that are associated with the changing of the seasons, solstices, and equinoxes. As we investigate the agricultural holidays, spring and autumn equinoxes, and the different ways civilizations around the world commemorate the changing seasons, these festivals provide an opportunity to reflect on the link between humans and environment.

Festivals of Different Cultures, Chapter 5

Festivals of culture are lively manifestations of a people's identity and their heritage. This

chapter presents a comprehensive investigation into the various regional and community-specific festivities that are rooted in their respective cultures. We delve into the diverse world of cultural holidays, beginning with the entrancing Chinese New Year and progressing all the way to the lively Carnaval in Brazil and the colorful Holi festival in India. Each festival is a demonstration of the cultural customs, philosophies, and artistic expressions of the communities who celebrate it.

Festivals of Music and Dance are Discussed in Chapter 6

The ability of music and dance to communicate with one another regardless of language barriers and geographical boundaries is the primary focus of this chapter. We travel the world in search of the most famous music and dance festivals, investigating the cultural significance of these events, the musical styles that best characterize them, and the remarkable opportunities for personal growth that they provide. We dig into the tremendous impact that music and dance have had on our lives, as well as the festivals that celebrate them, beginning with the illustrious Woodstock festival and moving on to the appeal of modern-day Coachella and ending with the enticing rhythms of Samba Fest.

Food & Culinary Festivals is the topic of Chapter 7

The preparation of food has long played an important role in human celebrations, and this role reflects both cultural identity and the art of cooking. In this chapter, we set out on a voyage across the world of food and culinary festivals, embarking on a gastronomic adventure along the way. We take pleasure in the aromas and tastes of foods from all over the world, such as the hearty delicacies of Oktoberfest, the vast feasts of Thanksgiving, the subtle flavors of Diwali, and the sweet indulgences of Chocolate Fest. These festivals provide attendees a chance to get a sense of culture by presenting the culinary customs and delectable meals that are characteristic of communities all around the world.

Celebrations of the Nation's Birthday and Independence Day are Detailed in Chapter 8

Celebrations of national and independence days occupy a special place in the hearts of nations since they mark the passage of their historical journeys and the ideals on which they were established. This chapter provides an in-depth look at key national festivities, such as Bastille Day in France and Independence Day in the United States of America. We bridge the gap between historical remembering and modern celebration by investigating the customs, symbolism, and cultural importance that are held within these events.

Mardi Gras and Carnival are Discussed in Chapter 9

Both Carnival and Mardi Gras are spectacular events that take place throughout the year and fill the streets with parades, costumes, and masks. In this chapter, we will dig into the history, cultural significance, and captivating traditions of these vivacious events. We experience the joy, creative exuberance, and the art of celebration that define these festivities, whether we are in the vivid streets of Rio de Janeiro's Carnival or in the exuberant heart of New Orleans during Mardi Gras.

Future Trends in Festivals is the Topic of Chapter 10

In this chapter, the book takes a step into the future, investigating how globalization, technology, and sustainability are transforming the landscape of festivities all over the world. We take a look at the changing face of festivals, the role that technology plays in both the planning and execution of these events, and the increasing emphasis placed on environmental stewardship. As we examine the future through the lens of celebration, we think about the part that these happenings will play in the years to come and the trends that will determine how they will develop.

The Challenging Debates and Contentious Issues of Chapter 11

There are always going to be difficult situations and contentious debates surrounding celebrations. In this chapter, we discuss the difficult challenges that contemporary festivals and celebrations have to overcome in order to remain relevant. We dive into the ethical considerations that define our celebrations, discussing topics such as the conflict that arises between tradition and modernity, as well as critical concerns about cultural appropriation and the influence that festivals have on the environment.

The Preservation of Celebrations and Their Documentation is Covered in Chapter 12

The last chapter focuses on preservation as its primary topic. In light of the fact that the world is undergoing rapid transformation, it is of the utmost importance that we preserve the diverse array of human celebrations for future generations to admire and gain insight from. We investigate the critical significance of documenting and conserving these unique practices in order to protect the enduring legacy that is our cultural history.

The final chapter of the book offers some final thoughts on the unfolding of the global cultural voyage. The book "Festivals and Celebrations: A Global Cultural Odyssey" is more than just a compilation of anecdotes about different types of celebrations; rather, it is an exploration of the human experience and a testament to the strength of happiness and unity that binds us all together. It is an invitation to explore the global language of celebration, to embrace our shared humanity, and to discover beauty in the diversity of cultures and traditions that beautify our globe.

Chapter 1

The Essence of Festivals

The human spirit is expressed in a way that is both universal and everlasting via the celebration of festivals. They have the capacity to bring communities together in exuberant celebration and are imbued with the cultural significance and profound symbolism of the occasion. Festivals hold a particular place in the hearts of people all over the world. Whether it is the bright brilliance of Diwali in India, the exuberant music of Carnival in Brazil, the holy rituals of Easter in Christianity, or the tranquil beauty of the Japanese Cherry Blossom Festival, people all over the world celebrate festivals in their own unique ways. In this investigation into the fundamental nature of festivals, we get to the bottom of what it is that makes these events so important to the lived experience of humans.

1. **The Opening Statements**
   Festivals are not the same as other types of events. They are the aggregate manifestations of a culture's traditions, identity, and history. Festivals capture the entirety of the human experience by denoting significant moments, establishing a connection to our history, and motivating us for the future. Festivals, at their core, are essentially a celebration of humanity, our common ideals, and our goals.
2. **The Instinctive Drive in Every Person to Have a Good Time**
   The need to celebrate is a human instinct that is shared by all people and is recognized as the driving force behind the creation of festivals. This impulse is not limited by any particular culture, geographic location, or period of time. Festivals are not specific to any one society or era, but rather they are universal expressions of joy, introspection, and unity. They are the ties that bind us to one another and to the rich tapestry of the human experience that we have all had in common.

3. **The Importance of Customs and Practices**
   Numerous celebrations are built on years of accumulated custom and observance. They serve as the foundational cultural skeleton upon which celebrations are formed. The lighting of candles, the exchanging of gifts, the preparation of traditional dishes, and the donning of certain costumes are only some examples of the kinds of things that might constitute rituals. These traditions act as a link to the past, bridging the gap between us and the generations that came before us as well as the stories that have helped to shape our cultural identities.

4. **Commemorating Important Milestones in Life**
   The act of commemorating major junctures in one's life is frequently cited as one of the primary drivers of celebration. There are many different life events that need to be commemorated with a party, including but not limited to birthdays, anniversaries, graduations, and marriages. These occurrences serve as signposts indicating change and development in the life of an individual, and they carry a special value for everyone concerned. The commemoration of significant life events serves multiple purposes: it enables individuals to recognize and appreciate the transitions and achievements that have occurred in their lives, it enables individuals to express gratitude to the people who have been a part of these milestones, and it enables individuals to create enduring memories that connect us to our past and inspire us for the future.

5. **The Role of Festivity in Establishing a Spiritual Connection**
   Celebrations that are observed in accordance with a religion offer something very special and meaningful. These festivities are more than just a way to celebrate personal milestones; rather, they are a statement of faith, dedication, and a connection to the spiritual world. Festivals of various religions provide believers with an opportunity to commune with one another, recommit themselves to their faith, and feel a closer connection to the divine.
   This section examines significant religious holidays celebrated by a variety of faiths around the world, illuminating the spiritual meaning behind these events as well as the rituals and stories associated with them. Whether it be the luminous Diwali in Hinduism, the Easter celebrations in Christianity, the festive atmosphere of Eid in Islam, the symbolic Hanukkah in Judaism, or the joyous spirit of Christmas, these festivals are not only religious observances but also cultural events that carry the legacy of these faiths by conveying their stories, values, and hopes. For example, Diwali in Hinduism is a festival that honors the victory of good over evil.

6. **Festivities as a Means of Reconnecting with Nature**
   Celebrations that take place throughout the year are inextricably linked to the natural environment and the passage of time. They do this by recording the solstices, equinoxes, and the agricultural calendar, which shows that they are aware of the natural cycles that occur. These events offer a window of time in which

to consider the connection that exists between humans and the natural world. Gratitude for the earth's bountiful resources is frequently expressed through the rites and customs that are practiced in conjunction with annual festivals, which are often timed to coincide with the ever-shifting patterns of the natural world. This section examines a variety of seasonal festivities, including Midsummer festivals in Scandinavia, the lively feasts of the spring and autumn equinoxes, and the varied ways in which different cultures around the world commemorate the changing of the seasons. As a result of these celebrations, we gain a deeper understanding of the fundamental link that exists between humans and the world in which they live.

7. **A Kaleidoscope of Identity Through the Lens of Cultural Festivals**
Festivals of culture are lively manifestations of a people's identity and their heritage. The one-of-a-kind qualities that distinguish one culture from another are highlighted and celebrated during these events, which also provide a glimpse into the traditions, aesthetics, and history of the community. In this part of the article, we will delve into the ever-changing world of cultural festivals by going on a journey through culturally significant events that are held in many parts of the world and communities.

    Each holiday is a testament to the cultural traditions, values, and art of the communities that celebrate it. From the fascinating Chinese New Year to the energetic Carnaval in Brazil and the vivid hues of Holi in India, each festival is a testament to the people who celebrate it. We investigate the value of cultural festivals, the tales they convey, and the ways in which they connect people to their cultural history in order to better understand their own identities.

8. **Music and Dance: The International Sign Language of Joyful Occasions**
Festivals of music and dance are a monument to the fact that celebration can be communicated through any language. Through the force of rhythm, melody, and artistic expression, they bring together individuals from a variety of different backgrounds. Participants and viewers alike are brought together by an unseen bond that is forged through the joy of music and dancing, which is unaffected by obstacles such as language or nationality.

    This section will take readers on a journey around the world to famous music and dance festivals, where they will learn about the historical significance of these events, the musical genres that define them, and the remarkable experiences that they offer. We dive into the tremendous impact that music and dance have had on our lives as well as the festivals that honor them, beginning with the renowned Woodstock festival that represented an entire generation's drive to celebrate and join together, moving on to the appeal of modern-day Coachella, and ending with the irresistible rhythms of Samba Fest.

9. **Gastronomic Celebrations: A Savory Treat for the Senses**
Festivals dedicated to food highlight both the art of cooking and the joys that

food can bring to the palette. These festivals give attendees a taste of culture by displaying the distinctive flavors and culinary customs of a variety of locations around the country. People have traditionally gathered around shared meals and rituals as a way to celebrate, and food has always been an integral element of these occasions.

In this section, we set out on a voyage across the world of food and culinary festivals, embarking on a gastronomic adventure along the way.

We take pleasure in the aromas and tastes of foods from all over the world, such as the hearty delicacies of Oktoberfest, the vast feasts of Thanksgiving, the subtle flavors of Diwali, and the sweet indulgences of Chocolate Fest. These festivals not only offer a chance to partake in gastronomic delights but also serve as a window into cultural traditions and the finer points of the culinary arts.

10. **Festivities Honoring the Nation's Birthday and Declaration of Independence: The Pride of Nations**

    Celebrations of national and independence days occupy a special position in the collective consciousness of nations. These festivities are held to recognize the values and concepts on which nations are built as well as to memorialize major historical events, highlight significant landmarks, and commemorate the birth of countries. This section provides an in-depth look at key national festivities, such as Bastille Day in France and Independence Day in the United States of America.

    We investigate the customs, symbols, and cultural importance that are associated with these many events. Celebrations on national and independence days bridge the gap between historical commemoration and modern exuberance, reflecting the collective identity and pride of a nation in the process.

11. **Carnival and Mardi Gras: A Global Exploration of Costumes and Processions**

    Celebrations of Carnival and Mardi Gras are spectacular extravaganzas that flood the streets with masquerade masks, elaborate costumes, and parades. People are able to shed their mundane selves and embrace a spirit of liberation and merriment thanks to the fact that these holidays give them the chance to do so. In this part of the guide, we dig into the history, cultural significance, and fascinating traditions of these vivacious events.

    We experience the joy, creative exuberance, and the art of celebration that define these festivities, whether we are in the vivid streets of Rio de Janeiro's Carnival or in the exuberant heart of New Orleans during Mardi Gras. We investigate the function that masks and parades play in these events, focusing on how they enable individuals to transform their identities and play roles that are not often associated with them.

12. **The Pivotal Aspects of Upcoming Celebrations**

    The book takes a giant leap into the future with this chapter, which examines

how globalization,
technology, and sustainability are transforming the landscape of festivities. We take a look at the changing face of festivals, the role that technology plays in both the planning and execution of these events, and the increasing emphasis placed on environmental stewardship.

As we examine the future through the lens of celebration, we think about the part that these happenings will play in the years to come and the trends that will determine how they will develop. The dynamic quality of our environment, as well as the malleability of human celebration to conform to shifting norms and expectations, will be reflected in the core of upcoming celebrations.

13. **Difficulties and Debates: The Complicated Aspect of Festivities**

    There are always going to be difficult situations and contentious debates surrounding celebrations. In this section, we discuss the difficult challenges that contemporary festivals and celebrations need to overcome in order to remain relevant. We dive into the ethical considerations that define our celebrations, discussing topics such as the conflict that arises between tradition and modernity, as well as critical concerns about cultural appropriation and the influence that festivals have on the environment.

    This part encourages readers to ponder the intricacies of celebration, to wrestle with the challenges surrounding cultural sensitivity, environmental responsibility, and the ever-changing landscape of tradition and innovation, and to reflect on these issues.

14. **Preservation and Documentation: Protecting the Inheritance of Festivities**

In light of the fact that the world is undergoing rapid transformation, it is of the utmost importance that we preserve the diverse array of human celebrations for future generations to admire and gain insight from. In this section, the crucial significance of documenting and conserving these extraordinary traditions is examined. By doing so, we can guarantee that the enduring legacy of our cultural history will be protected.

In this article, we discuss the part that museums, archives, and digital documentation play in the process of maintaining the spirit of celebrations and the narratives they convey. To ensure that future generations can connect with their cultural heritage and comprehend the significance of festivities over the course of human history, the preservation of traditions is the critical component that must take place.

At the end of the book, a celebration of the heart of festivals as a celebration of humanity itself serves as the theme. The book "Festivals and Celebrations: A Global Cultural Odyssey" is more than just a compilation of anecdotes about different types of celebrations; rather, it is an exploration of the human experience and a testament to the strength of happiness and unity that binds us all together. It is an invitation to explore the global language of celebration, to embrace our shared humanity, and to discover beauty in the diversity of cultures and traditions that beautify our globe.

As we get to the end of our journey, we pause to consider the cultural journey that has taken place across these pages all around the world. We celebrate the human instinct to congregate, to mark milestones, to connect with the divine, and to acknowledge our connection to the natural world. In addition, we recognize the importance of celebrating the natural world's relationship to us. We accept music and dance as a universal language, the different flavors of culinary festivities as a universal language, and the pride of nations as a universal emotion.

In addition, we are aware of the difficulties and debates that are associated with holding festivals in the present era, which requires us to take into consideration the moral and ecological implications of our gatherings. Last but not least, we acknowledge the significance of preservation and documentation in securing the heritage of our festivities. This is done to ensure that future generations will be able to appreciate and gain knowledge from the diverse fabric that is human culture.

Festivals, in all their guises and manifestations, boil down to a celebration of life in and of itself. It is a mirror of the human spirit, the values that we share, and the goals that we aspire to achieve. The ability to join together as a community, to find happiness in the presence of others, and to celebrate the significant moments and passages in our lives is exemplified by the existence of festivals. They are a vivid statement of our culture and identity as well as a reminder of the splendor and variety that characterizes our world, and as such, they are a celebration of humanity.

1.1 What are festivals and celebrations?

Celebrations and festivals have been around for a very long time, and they continue to be timeless and universal manifestations of human culture and the human experience. They highlight key milestones in our lives, connect us to our cultural and religious heritage, and generate a sense of solidarity and joy among communities. They serve as vibrant touchpoints in the tapestry of our lives. These occurrences are of the utmost importance, as their influence extends beyond the confines of space and time and brings together the myriad strands that make up our common humanity. In this investigation, we look deeper into the nature of festivals and celebrations, including what they are, why they are significant, and the diverse shapes they take across different cultures and customs.

What Gives Festivals and Celebrations Their Character

Festivals and celebrations are not simply get-togethers or social activities; rather, they are manifestations of the aspiration of the human spirit to participate in a communal outpouring of happiness, appreciation, and introspection. They are a monument to the human drive to record milestones, find meaning in the world, and connect with one another, but at their heart, they are a celebration of life.

These occurrences exemplify the cultural and emotional complexity of our lives, and they represent a universally experienced aspect of being a person that is not bound by time or location.

A Common and Shared Part of the Human Experience

The need to commemorate special occasions is profoundly ingrained in the essence of humans. It is an instinct that is shared by everyone everywhere, regardless of their history, culture, or country. Celebrations have always played an important role in the history of humanity, whether they were practiced in ancient societies or contemporary ones. Festivals are demonstrations of joy and unity that connect people all over the world. They are not restricted by geographical borders or cultural differences.

In the earliest civilizations, festivals were held to mark the changing of the seasons, abundant harvests, and the cycle of life and death. These festivals are said to represent the origin of the universal human experience of celebration. The human yearning to connect with the natural world and find meaning in the cosmic rhythms that regulated their life was the impetus behind the celebrations that date back thousands of years.

Religious celebrations came into existence when communities progressed and arranged themselves according to commonly held ideas and values. These sacred rituals allowed people to recognize the supernatural forces that ruled their existence while also uniting communities in their shared religious beliefs. They also provided a space for individuals to engage in spiritual introspection and devotion. Religious holidays are an essential part of the human experience of connecting with the divine. Whether it is the solemn observances of Easter in Christianity, the exuberant festivities of Diwali in Hinduism, or the meditative month of Ramadan in Islam, each of these celebrations plays an important role.

Putting Milestones in Life on Display

Festivals and celebrations serve a number of purposes, one of the most important of which is to celebrate critical milestones in one's life. There are many different life events that need to be commemorated with a party, including but not limited to birthdays, anniversaries, graduations, and marriages. In the life of an individual, these occurrences stand in for defining periods of change, growth, and transition, and they carry with them profound personal meaning.

Not only do we acknowledge and appreciate the changes and accomplishments in our own lives when we celebrate life's milestones, but we also express gratitude for the individuals who have been a part of these milestones in our lives. Festivals are a means to celebrate the familial and social connections that have played an important role in the development of our path.

They imprint on our minds enduring memories that link us to our history and provide motivation for our lives to come.

Take, for example, the festivities around a wedding. Marriage brings together not only two people but also their families, cultures, and customs from both sides of the family tree. A wedding represents the start of a new period in a couple's life together, and the celebration that surrounds it acts as a happy send-off into this new part of life. These landmarks are not just significant on an individual level; they also have cultural and societal significance, representing the norms, values, and expectations of society as a whole.

The Role of Celebration in Establishing Spiritual Connections

Due to the fact that they are intricately connected with spirituality, religion, and devotion, religious festivals present a one-of-a-kind opportunity for celebration. These celebrations are more than just a way to celebrate personal milestones; rather, they are an expression of the faith of the community as well as a renewal of its spiritual commitment. Festivals of many religions provide believers with an opportunity to congregate with one another and make a common connection with the divine.

Religious celebrations are frequently distinguished by the observance of rites and customs that are imbued with profound theological import. For instance, the Christian holiday of Easter serves to remember the resurrection of Jesus, which is considered to be one of the most significant events in Christian theology. The practices associated with Easter, such as the lighting of lights and the symbolic breaking of bread, are potent demonstrations of faith and provide a connection to a higher spiritual plane.

Diwali, also known as the Festival of Lights, is a significant holiday in Hinduism. It celebrates the victory of light over darkness as well as the triumph of virtue over evil. The occasion is marked by the burning of oil lamps, the trading of sweets, and the exploding of fireworks. These ceremonies are not just culturally significant but also profoundly spiritual; they provide people with a medium through which they can commune with the divine and recommit themselves to their religious beliefs.

Religious celebrations build a connection between the human experience and the supernatural by giving people the opportunity to pray, meditate, and show their devotion to a higher power. These festivities are not only about the rituals and customs that have been passed down from generation to generation; rather, they are about the communal spiritual experience that serves to bond a community together.

Observance as a Form of Reconnection with Nature

Celebrations of the changing seasons have strong ties to the natural world and the cycles that it follows. The changing of the seasons, the solstices, the equinoxes, and the agricultural cycles are all celebrated at these events. They offer a setting conducive to introspection regarding the connection that exists between people and the natural world. The ceremonies and customs that are observed during festive times of the year frequently include expressions of gratitude for the bountiful resources provided by the earth and are synchronized with the ever-shifting patterns of nature.

A great number of ancient civilizations held annual festivals to commemorate the passage of time according to the agricultural calendar. These celebrations frequently corresponded with the times of planting and harvesting, and they served as a show of appreciation for the food that provided for the sustenance of communities. Midsummer festivals, for example, were held in Scandinavia and honored the summer solstice, which is the longest day of the year. These festivals also marked the peak of the summer season. People joined together to celebrate the lengthening of the daylight hours, take part in various activities, and think about the bounty of the natural world.

Themes related to rebirth and renewal were frequently integrated into seasonal festivals as well. For instance, the vernal equinox is connected to the beginning of a new life cycle as well as the flowering of plants and flowers. Festivals featuring themes of rebirth and expansion were common ways that various cultures marked the passage of time throughout this time.

These celebrations are meant to provide as a gentle nudge in the direction of remembering the profound connection that humans have with the wider world. They are a manifestation of the human desire to discover significance in the natural world and to pay homage to the reoccurring patterns that rule life on Earth.

Festivals of Culture: A Mirror of Who We Are as a People
Festivals of culture are lively representations of a community's sense of self, its values, and the traditions it holds dear. These festivals provide an opportunity to share one's culture's customs, arts, and heritage with others, in addition to providing a window into one's culture's heritage, art, and artifacts. The distinctive qualities that characterize a culture and its people are highlighted in a festival's celebration of that culture.

One of the most astonishing things about cultural festivals is the amount of variety that can be found there. Every culture has its own special occasions for celebrating, complete with distinctive symbols, rites, and ways of expressing themselves. As an illustration, one of the most important holidays in Chinese culture is the Spring Festival, which is also known as the Chinese New Year.

As the beginning of the lunar new year, it is celebrated with get-togethers of friends and family, feasting, performances of dances including dragons and lions, and the giving and receiving of lucky red envelopes.

Carnaval is a celebration that takes place in Brazil in the days leading up to Lent. It is known for its vibrancy and exuberance. The exquisite costumes, vibrant parades, and lively samba music have made it one of the most famous festivals in the world. The festival is a demonstration of the passion that the Brazilian people have for music, dance, and the artistic expression of their ideas.

The coming of spring is marked with an explosion of color and merriment at the Holi festival, which is held in India. People congregate in the streets to engage in the practice of throwing colored powders and water at one another, which results in the creation of a colorful show. The event is a celebration of the triumph of virtue over evil as well as the coming of warmer weather and renewed vigor.

Each community's history, morals, and customs are displayed in the various cultural festivals that are held throughout the year. These festivities provide a glimpse into the ways in which individuals engage with their cultural history by showcasing the art, music, and cuisine that define a culture. Festivals of other cultures may be a great source of pride and identity, as well as a useful reminder of the diverse and complex fabric that is human culture.

Celebrations in the form of music and dance festivals have become a global phenomenon

Festivals of music and dance are a monument to the fact that celebration can be communicated through any language. Through the power of rhythm, song, and artistic expression, these gatherings bring together individuals from a variety of different backgrounds. Participants and viewers alike are brought together by an unseen bond that is forged through the joy of music and dancing, which is unaffected by obstacles such as language or nationality.

Festivals of music and dance frequently contain performances from a wide variety of genres and styles, thereby reflecting the cultural and artistic diversity that exists all across the world. Take for example the illustrious music festival that took place in Woodstock, New York, in 1969. It was a metaphor of the drive of an entire generation to get together, celebrate love and peace, and take pleasure in the music that embodied their time period. Woodstock was more than simply a music festival; it was a cultural event that reflected the beliefs and ideals of an entire generation.

Festivals such as Coachella have evolved into cultural symbols in the modern era, particularly within the music and arts scenes.Coachella is a music festival that takes place every year in the state of California. The festival has a broad lineup of bands and artists, which draws attendees from all over the world. The festival provides guests with an all-encompassing experience of music, art, and culture, which contributes to the development of a sense of community and connection among those who attend.

Festivals of music and dance are not restricted to any one specific culture or style of music or dance. They rejoice in the exhilaration of creative expression, the exhilaration of movement, and the capacity of music to elevate the spirit of the human being. These festivals foster an environment of communal celebration, bringing people together to share in the joy of appreciating the aesthetic value of creative expression.

Festivals of Cooking Are Like a Banquet for the Senses

Celebration among humans has traditionally revolved heavily around the consumption of food. People are brought closer together through the celebration of shared meals and traditions, and it represents both cultural identity and the art of cooking. Festivals dedicated to food and drink honor the joys of the palate while also providing an opportunity to sample a variety of cultures and flavors from around the world.

Food festivals are an opportunity to sample a wide variety of delectable meals that are representative of a variety of cultural traditions. Consider the world-famous beer and food celebration known as Oktoberfest, which is hosted in Munich, Germany. The event is a celebration of Bavarian culture and includes a range of substantial meals and beers, such as sausages, pretzels, and sauerkraut. The Oktoberfest is a celebration of the Bavarian love of food, wine, and the company of others, and it serves as a tribute to this passion.

Another holiday that places a considerable emphasis on food is Thanksgiving, which is mainly celebrated in the United States. Thanksgiving is a time when friends and family get together to celebrate the harvest with a feast that often consists of roasted turkey, stuffing, cranberry sauce, and pumpkin pie. The holiday of Thanksgiving is a celebration of the traditions and values of American families, as well as the significance of being thankful.

Not only are lights and fireworks used to celebrate Diwali in India, but a large variety of sweets and munchies are also consumed during the holiday. Traditional Indian desserts such as gulab jamun, jalebi, and barfi are included among these delectable offerings. The cuisine plays an important role in the celebration, as it brings members of the community and families together to take part in the festivities and enjoy the happiness that the festival brings.

Festivals of food allow participants to investigate their cultural identities through the medium of their taste buds. They give guests the opportunity to sample the flavors and ingredients that characterize the cuisine of a particular location. Food is more than simply something to eat; it is also a reflection of culture and history, and culinary festivals offer the chance to taste the culinary treasures that are associated with different cultures.

Celebrations of our Nation's Birthday and Declaration of Independence: The Pride of Nations

Celebrations of national and independence days are important events that honor the birth of nations and remember important historical milestones. National and independence day celebrations are held on the same day. These celebrations have a strong connection to the identity of a nation, as well as its values, ideals, and the path it has taken throughout its history. They bridge the gap between historical remembrance and modern exuberance, reflecting the collective identity and pride of a nation as a whole in the process.

One of the most well-known examples of a national celebration is the one that takes place in the United States on July 4th and is known as Independence Day. This event celebrates the adoption of the Declaration of Independence in 1776, which declared independence from British domination. The day is commemorated with fervent displays of national pride, including parades and fireworks displays, as well as barbecues. Reflection on the nation's history, ideals, and the principles established in the Declaration of Independence is encouraged during this time for all citizens of the United States of America.

In a similar vein, the French commemorate the beginning of the French Revolution and the storming of the Bastille in the year 1789 with a prominent national holiday known as Bastille Day. Parades, fireworks, and a robust emphasis on the nation's shared sense of purpose are the hallmarks of today's festivities. The long legacy of the French Revolution and the ideals of liberty, equality, and fraternity are commemorated annually on the holiday known as Bastille Day.

The purpose of national and independence day celebrations is not limited to commemorating past events; rather, they represent an opportunity for a country to articulate its core beliefs and its aspirations for the future. These events are meant to serve as a reminder of the values upon which a nation is formed, as well as the significance of civic engagement and pride.

A Guide to the Wonderful World of Carnival and Mardi Gras Masks and Parades

Celebrations of Carnival and Mardi Gras are spectacular extravaganzas that flood the streets with masquerade masks, elaborate costumes, and parades.

People are able to shed their mundane selves and embrace a spirit of liberation and merriment thanks to the fact that these holidays give them the chance to do so. They are characterized by artistic expression, an abundance of creative enthusiasm, and an environment of celebration.

One of the most well-known festivals that takes place all over the world is the Rio de Janeiro Carnival in Brazil. It is known for its lively parades, which are accompanied by samba music and colorful costumes. The festival provides its attendees with the opportunity to become a part of a larger-than-life spectacle by donning elaborate costumes and masks that give them the freedom to play a different role than they normally would and adopt new identities.

Another well-known festival is Mardi Gras, which takes place in New Orleans and is noted for its raucous parades, extravagant masquerade balls, and the custom of tossing beads and other gifts to the masses. Before the somber season of Lent begins, the time of Mardi Gras is spent partying and indulging in excess.

The celebrations of Carnival and Mardi Gras provide a sense of liberation from the restraints of day-to-day existence, in addition to presenting a one-of-a-kind opportunity for creative expression. They make it possible for individuals to take part in a bigger creative performance and to completely submerge themselves in a world filled with masks, costumes, and parades.

The Core of Upcoming Occasions to Celebrate

Festivals and celebrations have evolved alongside the planet as a whole. The character of future festivities will be formed by globalization, technological advancements, and an increasing dedication to being environmentally responsible. People from all over the world travel to participate in festivals because they can find something going on there that speaks to their interests and ideals.

The impact of technology has also had a transformative effect on the organization of festivals and the way attendees experience them. People from all over the world are now able to connect with worldwide celebrations because to the proliferation of streaming platforms, social media, and other digital technology. Festivals are no longer restricted to certain geographic areas; instead, they can be experienced digitally, which enables people to take part in the festivities from any point in the world.

A growing dedication to preserving the environment and being environmentally responsible is reflected in the trajectory of the future of festivities. The environmental effect of many festivals is being mitigated in a variety of ways, including the implementation of trash reduction programs, the use of renewable energy sources, and environmentally friendly business practices.

The essence of forthcoming celebrations will increasingly incorporate a focus on the responsible and sustainable management of the surrounding environment.

The Complicated Aspect of Festivities, Including Difficulties and Controversies

Festivals and celebrations, despite the fact that they bring people together and are a source of joy, are not exempt from the difficulties and debates that might accompany them. Celebrations in the modern age frequently face the challenge of reconciling traditional elements with more contemporary elements. As cultures shift and develop, issues arise regarding the continued usefulness of particular traditions and the extent to which they require modification.

Festival organizers are obligated to confront the complicated problem of cultural appropriation. It is the practice of members of one culture adopting or imitating aspects of another culture, most of the time without knowing or respecting the cultural context of the element being adopted or imitated. This problem calls into question the authenticity and respect that festivals are expected to demonstrate when displaying aspects of different cultures.

Another important worry is the effect that events have on their surrounding environments. Large-scale events have the potential to leave a considerable ecological footprint, both in terms of the amount of energy consumed and the amount of garbage generated. In order to conserve the world, festivals have a responsibility to investigate and implement measures that will lessen their negative effects on the natural environment.

The safeguarding of the celebratory tradition through preservation of artifacts and documentation

In light of the fact that the world is undergoing rapid transformation, it is of the utmost importance to preserve the diverse array of human celebrations for future generations to admire and gain wisdom from. The processes of preservation and recording are both essential components of this process of safeguarding.

When it comes to maintaining the heritage of past festivities, museums, archives, and digital recording all play an essential part. Festival objects, costumes, and historical records can be displayed in museums because to the space these establishments provide. People are given the opportunity to connect with the history and cultural significance of festivals thanks to these institutions.

The histories of festivals, as well as any documentation of them, are saved in archives for future generations to read. They store images, videos, written descriptions, and historical records that might provide light on the cultural and social aspects of the celebrations that took place in the past.

The capturing of festivities in digital format is becoming an increasingly significant step in the preservation process. Festivals are now able to be recorded and distributed to audiences all around the world thanks to advances in digital technology. People may access the sights and sounds of festivals from any location thanks to online platforms and archives, which provides a medium for cultural exchange and understanding.

1.2 The role of traditions and rituals

A community or society's traditions and rituals play an essential part in the formation of its cultural identity, the development of a sense of belonging within its members, and the maintenance of its collective memory. They are the threads that are woven into the fabric of culture, and they provide a framework for social interaction, spiritual connection, and the transmission of values from one generation to the next. Culture is the fabric that is woven from the threads. Traditions and rituals, which have their origins profoundly ingrained in the past, serve as a bridge between the intricate pattern of history and the modern terrain of human existence. Their roots are deeply ingrained in the past.

Observance and Maintenance of Cultural Identities

The continuation of customs and observances is essential to the protection of a culture's identity. They stand for the traditions, behaviors, and ideas that constitute a community's way of life and determine its identity. These cultural markers are frequently handed down from one generation to the next, acting as a guiding light for continued existence and a wellspring of communal pride.

Individuals are able to reassert their connection to their cultural heritage when they behave in a manner consistent with long-standing customs and take part in rituals. The participation in these rituals gives members of the community a sense of belonging and helps them develop a common identity. They serve as a living repository of the history, values, and collective experiences of a community, ensuring that the core of the culture is preserved even as time passes by.

Values and beliefs are passed down through generations.

The passing down of morals and convictions from one generation to the next is one of the most important functions that can be performed by traditions and rituals. Younger members of communities are instilled with a sense of responsibility and cultural awareness as a result of the transmission of their communities' guiding ethical principles, moral codes, and societal standards through the use of these activities.

Oftentimes, traditions and rituals take on the role of educational instruments, communicating significant cultural teachings as well as fundamental life skills in a way that is both concrete and experiential. They provide as a framework for gaining a knowledge of the societal roles, interpersonal interactions, and ethical standards that are upheld within the community. Individuals are able to internalize the values and beliefs that serve as the basis of their cultural identity when they participate in these acts.

Maintaining a unified and consistent cultural identity

By encouraging a feeling of shared history and legacy, traditions and rituals are a significant factor in the maintenance of a culture's continuity as well as its cohesiveness. They serve as a gathering place for people of the community, allowing them to come together to memorialize significant events, seasons, or achievements while also celebrating them. These common experiences foster a sense of togetherness and solidarity, which in turn contributes to increased social cohesiveness and mutual comprehension.

Individuals fortify their relationships with one another and the social links that bind them together by taking part in communal rituals and sustaining common traditions. This type of collective participation helps to cultivate a sense of community and belonging, transcending the distinctions between individuals and helping to cultivate a collective identity that brings people together under a shared cultural roof.

Expression of a Connection to One's Emotions and Spirituality

In many cases, a community's traditions and rituals act as channels via which its members can express their spiritual and emotional relationships with one another. They offer a framework for interacting with the divine, seeking spiritual guidance, and cultivating a sense of reverence for the sacred in one's daily life and practices. The fabric of a community's customs and rituals is frequently anchored by religious observances, rites of passage, and other forms of religious and spiritual rites and ceremonies.

Individuals show their dedication, thanks, and regard for the spiritual forces that create their worldview through the use of these rituals as a means of communication. They derive comfort from the spiritual connections that these practices cultivate and the feeling of purpose that they establish in their lives, which allows them to find peace in the routine that these activities provide.

Changes in Seasons and the Lifecycle Are Marked By This

Within a community, traditions and rituals mark the passage of time, both in terms of the passage of the seasons and the passage of key lifecycle events.

Individuals are better able to negotiate the passage of time, record transitions, and recognize the cyclical pattern of life with their assistance. Whether it is the celebration of harvest festivals, the observance of religious holidays, or the remembrance of life milestones like as birth, coming of age, marriage, and death, customs and rituals give a systematic framework for remembering these significant occasions in a person's life.

Individuals are able to discover meaning and purpose in the ups and downs of life thanks to the seasonal and lifecycle changes that are marked by these markers. People are able to anticipate and get ready for the transitions that define their personal and social journeys thanks to the sense of continuity and predictability that they provide.

Support for the Preservation of Cultural Traditions and Diversity

The preservation of cultural history and the celebration of cultural variety are both significantly aided by the practice of traditions and rituals. They provide as a prism through which individuals can understand the complex tapestry of human experience, which encompasses a variety of different cultures, behaviors, and beliefs in a variety of different communities. Communities may embrace the beauty of cultural pluralism and develop an environment of tolerance and mutual respect when they do so by recognizing and honoring the many traditions and rituals that exist within their midst.

Fostering an awareness and understanding of other cultures through the practice of traditions and rites contributes to the preservation of cultural heritage and diversity. It fosters an environment of cultural interchange and intercultural discussion, which contributes to the enrichment of the social fabric, and it encourages individuals to investigate and participate in a variety of cultural practices.

The protection of cultural artifacts that cannot be touched

In order to successfully protect intangible cultural assets, traditions and rituals are absolutely necessary. They preserve the tales, folklore, musical traditions, and oral histories that are the foundation of a community's cultural identity. Communities safeguard the continuation of their distinctive cultural expressions and artistic legacies by preserving the intangible aspects of their heritage and passing them down from generation to generation.

Communities are able to demonstrate their inventiveness, inventiveness, and artistic prowess through the practice of maintaining their intangible cultural legacy through the practice of customs and rituals. It brings to light the significance of cultivating and protecting cultural manifestations that both identify the essence of a people and contribute to the richness of the cultural fabric that exists across the globe.

1.3 Festivals as expressions of cultural identity

1. Traditional Practices and Practices that Have Been Passed Down Festivals frequently center on traditional practices and customs that have been handed down from generation to generation. These traditions are necessary components of a culture's identity because they embody the historical foundations, moral standards, and religious convictions of the civilization. These cultural observances, such as the burning of lamps during the festival of Diwali in India or the sharing of a Thanksgiving feast in the United States, serve as cultural touchpoints that connect individuals to their ancestry.

2. **Creative Expressions:** Festivals offer a stage upon which the creative expressions of a culture can be presented to an audience. Festivals showcase the inventiveness and skills of a community via various forms of art, including music, dance, visual arts, and crafts. Examples of creative forms that are closely connected with cultural identity include the samba rhythms of Rio de Janeiro's Carnival and the complex designs of Rangoli during Diwali. Neither of these are just performances.

3. Food is an essential component of any culture, and festivals frequently contain a culinary feast that represents the culinary traditions of the community being celebrated. These feasts highlight the flavors, components, and methods of preparation that characterize the cuisine of a particular country. For example, the dish paella, which is associated with Spain's La Tomatina celebration, and

mooncakes, which are associated with China's Mid-Autumn celebration, are both examples of culinary traditions that serve as symbols of cultural identity.
4. **Traditional Attire and Costumes:** During festivals, attendees may frequently be seen dressed in traditional garb and costumes that have deep roots in the culture being celebrated. These clothes are more than just articles of clothing; rather, they serve as symbolic representations of the identity of a civilization. These costumes are a visual monument to cultural pride, whether it is the vivid saris worn during Holi in India or the elegant kimonos of Japan's Gion Matsuri. Both of these festivals take place in India and Japan.
5. **Folklore and Oral Traditions:** Festivals frequently include oral traditions such as storytelling, tales, and folklore that are significant to the narrative of a community. Parades, performances, or rituals are all excellent vehicles for the transmission of these tales, which help to pass on the knowledge, history, and moral principles of a society. Celebrations like New Orleans' Mardi Gras, which is steeped in rich mythology and symbolism, are prime instances of how folklore and oral storytelling play a significant role in the event's overall experience.
6. **Symbols and Icons of Culture:** Festivals frequently include symbols and icons of culture that are immediately recognizable and have a significant significance. These graphical expressions of cultural identification might take the form of anything from national flags to regional emblems, and they all serve the same purpose. For instance, the beautiful peacock feathers that are worn during India's Krishna Janmashtami and the Chinese dragon dance that is performed during China's New Year are examples of cultural symbols that are immediately connected with the celebration of these particular holidays.

Chapter 2

The Science of Celebration

Celebration is something that has always been deeply ingrained in the human psyche and has taken many forms throughout human history, including those that are cultural, religious, and societal. A sense of belonging, identity, and community are all fostered via the participation in celebrations, which play an important role in human existence. These celebrations might range from ancient ceremonial events to contemporary gatherings. The goal of the field of study known as the "science of celebration" is to get an understanding of the significant effects that community celebrating may have on both the well-being of individuals and the cohesiveness of societies by delving into the complex interplay that exists between the disciplines of psychology, sociology, and cultural anthropology. This investigation into the science of celebration sheds light on the mental, emotional, and social processes that lie behind the human propensity for honoring momentous events and accomplishments.

Celebration's Origins Can Be Traced Back to Evolution

Discovering the adaptive value of celebration behaviors requires delving into the evolutionary roots of those activities. Evidence from anthropology suggests that early humans participated in community rituals and celebrations in order to strengthen social links, establish group cohesion, and commemorate significant milestones in their evolution. These behaviors not only strengthened interpersonal relationships, but they also reaffirmed cultural norms and shared values, which helped to cultivate a collective identity, which is essential for surviving in harsh and unpredictable situations. The evolutionary origins of celebratory behaviors that are engrained in human civilizations throughout time and geographical borders are highlighted by the fact that cohesive groups have a greater chance of surviving.

The Neurobiological Processes Involved in Rejoicing

Research in the field of neuroscience sheds insight on the neurological underpinnings of joy, happiness, and community bonding by illuminating the complex interaction that exists between festive experiences and the functions of the brain. During celebratory events, various parts of the brain, including the prefrontal cortex, amygdala, and nucleus accumbens, become active, according to studies that utilize neuroimaging techniques. The activation of certain neurotransmitters, such as dopamine and endorphins, is correlated with increased levels of euphoria and a strengthening of the good emotional states that are linked with celebratory events. The neurobiological dynamics of celebration provide light on the important role that the brain's reward system plays in molding human behavior and facilitating social interactions.

Implications for a Person's Psyche When Engaging in Festive Activities

The substantial impact that celebration has on an individual's well-being, emotional resilience, and psychological flourishing can be better understood by investigating the psychological elements of celebration. Psychologists highlight the therapeutic value of festive experiences as a means of relieving stress and anxiety, as well as fostering a sense of optimism and hope. The development of pleasant emotions through participation in communal celebrations strengthens psychological resilience, improves coping mechanisms, and facilitates the development of adaptive responses to the obstacles of everyday life. In addition, celebrations are effective methods for bolstering one's sense of self-worth, cultivating a sense of accomplishment, and developing a constructive self-concept, all of which contribute to an improved sense of psychological well-being as well as an increased level of overall life satisfaction.

The Importance of Commemorative Rituals in a Sociocultural Context

The value of commemoration rituals extends far beyond the individual psychological advantages they provide, and they play a crucial part in the formation of collective identities, cultural legacy, and social cohesiveness. The rich fabric of human history can be preserved through the use of celebrations as vehicles for the transmission of cultural values, historical legacies, and historical customs from one generation to the next. Festivals, ceremonies, and other commemorative traditions build a sense of belonging and solidarity among members of a community by symbolizing the community's shared beliefs, customs, and collective objectives. In addition, celebratory events foster a spirit of inclusivity and mutual respect, both of which are essential for the development of varied and harmonious communities. This is because celebratory events promote social integration, intergroup harmony, and cross-cultural understanding.

Implications for the Current Era and Prospects for the Future

Given the myriad of complexities and unpredictability that face modern civilizations, the science of celebration takes on an even greater significance in today's setting. There is a huge amount of untapped potential for improving mental health, social cohesion, and cultural resilience that can be unlocked by incorporating scientific findings into the planning, design, and execution of celebratory initiatives. Future endeavors in the science of celebration can leverage advances in technology and interdisciplinary research to facilitate evidence-based approaches to optimize the psychological and sociological impact of communal festivities. This will result in the promotion of holistic well-being and the development of a more cohesive and compassionate global community.

The study of celebration provides a multi-faceted prism through which one can gain a better understanding of the complex interplay that exists between human intellect, emotion, and the sociocultural dynamics of human societies. This multidisciplinary field sheds light on the profound relevance of communal rejoicing in supporting individual well-being and society harmony by untangling the evolutionary, neurological, psychological, and sociocultural roots of celebratory rituals.

In a world that is always changing, the secret to cultivating resilient communities, safeguarding cultural heritage, and developing a shared sense of joy, solidarity, and collective purpose lies in embracing the transformative power of celebratory interventions that are guided by scientific study.

2.1 Psychological and sociological aspects of celebrations

Celebrations are something that may be found in any human culture. These celebrations, which can range from birthdays and marriages to religious holidays and national festivals, are significant on both a psychological and a sociological level. They have a significant impact on our life, having a formative effect on our feelings, relationships, and communities. In the course of this investigation into the psychological and sociological components of celebrations, we will delve into the individual and collective dimensions, shedding light on how these communal traditions effect human behavior and the structures of society.

Celebrations: Some Considerations From a Psychological Perspective
Wellness in Emotional Aspects:

Feelings of joy and contentment are inextricably bound up with festivities. They make it possible for people to feel joy, enthusiasm, and excitement by providing a venue for those emotions. All aspects of a celebration—the planning of it, the event itself, and the happy recollections it leaves behind—contribute to an increase in a person's sense of emotional well-being. Research in the field of positive psychology has demonstrated that savoring pleasant experiences, such as those that occur during celebrations, can increase one's overall happiness and the degree to which they are satisfied with their life.

Connecting with Others:

People from many walks of life, including family, friends, and members of the community, frequently congregate for celebrations. Creating a sense of social connection requires activities such as getting together, exchanging stories, and honoring core beliefs in common. These connections with other people provide a meaningful impact on an individual's psychological well-being. Because having a solid support system can act as a buffer against the stress and misfortune that life throws at us, celebrations play an important role in both the formation and maintenance of these connections.

A feeling of one's own identity and of belonging:

The holding of celebrations is essential to the process of identity building. They frequently center on storylines from a person's culture, religion, or nation that serve to strengthen that person's sense of belonging to a group.

Participating in these events can serve to validate an individual's identity and give one the impression of being a part of something that is far bigger than themselves. This helps to foster a feeling of purpose and meaning in one's life, both of which are essential components of psychological health.

Relaxation Techniques:

Celebrations offer a welcome diversion from the daily grind and a welcome opportunity to relax. Endorphins are the body's natural painkillers and stress relievers. The production of endorphins can be triggered by engaging in activities such as dancing, singing, or even just having casual conversations with loved ones during a festive occasion. These endorphins work against the stress hormones, which leads to a decrease in anxious feelings and an overall improvement in one's mental condition.

Recollections that are fond:

Celebrations frequently result in the formation of enduring memories. These recollections are recorded in one's autobiography and contribute to the formation of one's sense of identity. Significant life events have a way of sticking in people's memories, and such memories can be a source of positive reinforcement when they are needed the most.

Increased Resistance to Breakdowns:

The capacity to persevere in the face of adversity, also known as psychological resilience, can be improved by engaging in rewarding activities. Celebrations operate as a reservoir of pleasant feelings and memories, which can be drawn upon in times of difficulty. This reservoir can be replenished by celebrations. Because of this increased resilience, individuals are better able to deal with the difficulties of life.

A Look at Some of the Sociological Aspects of Festivities

Maintaining Social Cohesion:

Celebrations have the power to bring people together as a society. They bring individuals together who come from a variety of different backgrounds, allowing for the transcendence of differences and the development of a sense of unity. In multi-ethnic civilizations, the celebration of a variety of festivals has the potential to foster tolerance and understanding, ultimately making a contribution to the cohesiveness of the society.

Protecting Our Cultural Heritage:

Traditions and ideals of a culture can be passed on from one generation to the next through the medium of celebrations. They serve as a forum for the preservation of cultural traditions and encourage the continuation of the rituals, customs, and activities that define the identity of a particular community. In the absence of celebrations, cultural legacy runs the risk of being lost over time.

Building Up the Community:

Participation from everyone is typically required during celebrations. Cooperation and coordination are not only required for the event itself, but also for the preparations and the decorations. This part of the celebration, which focuses on establishing community, has the potential to contribute to the establishment of a sense of shared purpose and responsibility that goes beyond the celebration itself.

Exchange on Both the Economic and Social Fronts:

Celebrations are frequently accompanied by the giving and receiving of presents, meals, and many kinds of services. These transactions have repercussions, both economically and socially. Celebrations have the potential to increase sales and jumpstart economic activity for enterprises. Giving gifts to others and sharing possessions can help establish social relationships and foster a sense of reciprocity among individuals.

Rituals of Society:

Rituals and deeds having significant meaning are frequently performed during celebrations. By reaffirming commonly held principles and standards, these practices have a significant and long-lasting effect on society. For instance, the societal expectation of a lifelong commitment between two individuals is reaffirmed during the ceremony that marks the beginning of a marriage. A sense of regularity and stability is provided by rituals, which function as social anchors in a community.

The Resolution of Conflict:

In many cases, celebrations present an opportunity for the resolution of disagreements and the promotion of reconciliation. In the context of the holidays, for example, get-togethers with one's family might act as a platform from which to confront and rebuild damaged relationships. The joyous environment has the potential to alleviate stress and stimulate open conversation.

Identifying Oneself and Being Included:

People are given the opportunity to express who they are and to take part in the culture of the group during celebrations, which can be inclusive. This is of utmost significance for underrepresented groups, many members of which may experience feelings of exclusion. A sense of social justice and equality can be fostered via celebrations that are inclusive and recognize individuals and groups.

Interaction of Psychological and Sociological Processes

The emotional and social sides of celebrations are tightly connected with one another. The psychological health of an individual makes a contribution to the state of mental health in a society as a whole. People who are content with themselves and have a strong mental fortitude are more likely to participate in social activities and make a constructive contribution to the communities in which they live. In turn, society, through its cultural, social, and economic structures, provides the framework for celebrations to occur and influences the psychological well-being of individuals. These structures make up the social fabric.

The psychological benefits of social connection and identity affirmation, which are acquired from celebrations, help to highlight the relevance of sociological issues.

In consequence, social cohesion and the maintenance of cultural traditions have the potential to generate an atmosphere that is conducive to the experience of positive psychological outcomes. The reciprocal nature of the relationship between the person and society is brought into focus by this interaction.

Celebrations are about much more than just having a good time in the moment. They are profoundly ingrained in both the human mind and the institutional frameworks of society. The emotional and social dimensions of celebrations are inextricably intertwined, and their effects can be felt not just at the individual level but also at the level of society as a whole. We are gaining a deeper knowledge of how celebrations shape our lives, how they bring people together, and how they contribute to the construction of a better and more connected world as we continue our investigation of the significance of these events.

2.2 The impact of celebrations on well-being

The practice of holding celebrations is deeply ingrained in human history, culture, and society. They play an important part in the way our lives are experienced on an emotional, psychological, and social level. Celebrations have the capacity to bring about feelings of happiness, develop social relationships, and generate enduring memories. This is true not just of personal milestones such as birthdays and weddings but also of cultural and religious events. This in-depth investigation will look into the fascinating and multifaceted topic of how festivities affect one's well-being.

This is a topic that has captured our interest for good reason. We will investigate the effects of celebrations on a variety of psychological, emotional, social, and even physiological factors, shedding light on the fundamental ways in which these events influence our overall health and happiness.

The Effects of Celebrations on a Person's Psyche
Joy and other favorable feelings:

The very nature of a celebration is to bring about feelings of happiness. They provide a reprieve from the monotony of everyday life, allowing people the opportunity to indulge in joy and other uplifting feelings for a short period of time. In addition to contributing to an increase in one's overall emotional well-being, the act of looking forward to a festive occasion, participating in the gathering, and reflecting on the happy feelings it evokes all individually contribute to this effect. Research in the field of positive psychology has demonstrated that enjoying happy experiences, such as those that occur during celebrations, can increase one's level of overall pleasure and overall contentment with life.

Relaxation Techniques:

The release of tension that might result from celebrations is common. The celebrations, the feeling of belonging, and the enjoyment of social contacts all contribute to a reduction in the levels of stress experienced. Endorphins are the body's natural painkillers and stress relievers. Dancing, singing, and spending quality time with loved ones are all activities that have been shown to induce the production of endorphins.

The alleviation of stress not only contributes to an improvement in mental well-being but also has beneficial implications for physical health.

Self-Respect and an Optimistic Concept of Oneself:

During celebrations, accomplishments and significant steps are frequently recognized.

Individuals are encouraged to recognize and honor their own growth and development by celebrating personal accomplishments such as graduating from school or advancing in their careers. These festivities help lead to increased feelings of self-esteem as well as a more positive concept of one's self. They serve as a gentle nudge in the direction of one's own potential and the ability to achieve one's goals.

Resistance to fracturing:

The capacity to persevere in the face of adversity, also known as psychological resilience, can be improved by engaging in rewarding activities. Celebrations help an individual's resilience by virtue of the fact that they are happy and memorable experiences. The joyful feelings and social networks that are developed through participation in celebrations act as resources that enable individuals to better deal with the difficulties of life.

Recollections that are fond:

Memories that last a lifetime are forged at celebrations. These recollections are recorded in one's autobiography and contribute to the formation of one's sense of identity. Significant life events have a way of sticking in people's memories, and such memories can be a source of positive reinforcement when they are needed the most. The capacity to access and relive happy memories is a potent instrument for preserving one's mental health and well-being.

Wellness in Emotional Aspects

Emotional well-being and psychological health are inextricably linked, however the former emphasizes the individual's emotional experience more than the latter does. Celebrations play an important part in improving a person's emotional well-being by generating moments of happiness, joy, and other positive emotions. The act of celebration itself, as well as the events that come along with it, can have a positive impact on an individual's entire emotional state.

Celebrations are a good way to keep in mind the great aspects of life, even when confronted with challenging circumstances. They make it possible for people to feel a wide spectrum of emotions, from excitement and joy to love and gratitude, and everything in between. This emotional richness adds to increased emotional well-being as well as a life that is more rewarding.

The Effects of Celebrations on Society

Connecting with Others:

Family, friends, and people of the community will frequently congregate during festivities to celebrate. Creating a sense of social connection requires activities such as getting together, exchanging stories, and honoring core beliefs in common. These relationships with other people make a substantial impact on an individual's mental health. Because having a solid support system can act as a buffer against the stress and misfortune that life throws at us, celebrations play an important role in both the formation and maintenance of these connections.

A Feeling of Complementarity:

The narratives of a culture, a religion, or a nation can often have strong influences on celebrations. They give individuals a feeling of belonging to a specific group or community that they are a member of. Participating in these events can serve to validate an individual's identity and give one the impression of being a part of something that is far bigger than themselves. This feeling of belonging is absolutely necessary for leading a happy and healthy social life.

Building Up the Community:

Participation from everyone is typically required during celebrations. Cooperation and coordination are not only required for the event itself, but also for the preparations and the decorations. This part of the celebration, which focuses on establishing community, has the potential to contribute to the establishment of a sense of shared purpose and responsibility that goes beyond the celebration itself. Communities that take the time to gather together and celebrate typically find that they are better able to work together and find solutions to problems that they face in common.

The Resolution of Conflict:

Celebrations offer a window of opportunity to work through differences and advance efforts toward reconciliation. In the context of the holidays, for example, get-togethers with one's family might act as a platform from which to confront and rebuild damaged relationships. The joyous environment has the potential to alleviate tensions and promote open communication, both of which can ultimately contribute to the resolution of problems.

Identifying Oneself and Being Included:

People are given the opportunity to express who they are and to take part in the culture of the group during celebrations, which can be inclusive. This is of utmost significance for underrepresented groups, many members of which may experience feelings of exclusion. A sense of social justice and equality can be fostered via celebrations that are inclusive and recognize individuals and groups.

Rituals of Society:

Rituals and deeds having significant meaning are frequently performed during celebrations. By reaffirming commonly held principles and standards, these practices have a significant and long-lasting effect on society. For instance, the societal expectation of a lifelong commitment between two individuals is reaffirmed during the ceremony that marks the beginning of a marriage. A sense of regularity and stability is provided by rituals, which function as social anchors in a community.

Exchange on Both the Economic and Social Fronts:

Celebrations are frequently accompanied by the giving and receiving of presents, meals, and many kinds of services. These transactions have repercussions, both economically and socially. Celebrations have the potential to increase sales and jumpstart economic activity for enterprises. Giving gifts to others and sharing possessions can help establish social relationships and foster a sense of reciprocity among individuals.

A Look at the Effects of Celebrations on the Body
Relaxation Techniques:

There is a strong correlation between the psychological and emotional repercussions of celebrations and their physiological effects as well. An increase in the release of endorphins and a decrease in the levels of stress hormones like cortisol are both common effects of celebratory behavior. The reduction in stress has immediate repercussions for physical health, including the lowering of blood pressure and the improvement of immunological function.

Wellness in terms of one's body

Social activities are generally a part of celebrations. These activities can either be strenuous (such as dancing, athletics, or games) or relaxing (such as picnics or sitting). Participating in active pursuits at times of celebration makes a positive contribution to one's overall physical well-being and assists individuals in maintaining a healthy way of life.

Duration of life:

The positive effects that celebrations have on people's social and emotional lives can lead to longer and healthier lives. There is a correlation between having a healthy mental state and having a robust social support network, which has been related to enhanced longevity. Celebrations have the potential to assist in the formation and strengthening of these factors, which can lead to a life that is both longer and more satisfying.

A Look at the Sociological Effects of Celebrations
Protecting Our Cultural Heritage:

Traditions from a culture can be kept alive through the practice of holding celebrations. They are times when communities reflect on their past, consider their core values, and observe their traditional practices. In the absence of celebrations, cultural legacy runs the risk of being lost over time. These gatherings serve as a connection point for people of different generations, facilitating the passing down of traditional wisdom and customs.

Maintaining Social Cohesion:

Celebrations have the power to bring people together as a society. They bring individuals
together who come from a variety of different backgrounds, allowing for the transcendence of differences and the development of a sense of unity. In multiethnic civilizations, the celebration of a variety of festivals has the potential to foster tolerance and understanding, ultimately making a contribution to the cohesiveness of the society.

Building Up the Community:
Celebrations are frequently used as a driving force in the process of constructing and fortifying communities. Having a sense of belonging can be cultivated via the shared experience of organizing and taking part in a celebration. Communities that come together to celebrate are more likely to work together on a variety of projects, address concerns that are common to all members, and offer assistance to their constituents.

The Resolution of Conflict:
As was just discussed, celebrations may be a helpful tool in the process of conflict resolution since they provide a forum for open and constructive conversation. In the context of the holidays, for example, meetings of the family can frequently serve as occasions to confront and mend broken relationships, which adds to the overall harmony of the family as well as the community.

Rituals of Society:
Celebrations frequently incorporate cultural or religious rites with the purpose of reinforcing the
community's standards and values. These rituals not only serve as reminders of what a society regards to be significant, but they also contribute to the preservation of social order and stability.

Identifying Oneself and Being Included:
Celebrations encourage inclusivity by giving people a forum in which they may share who they are and be acknowledged for their place within a broader group. This helps people feel like they belong. This inclusiveness is vital for minority groups that may feel marginalized, and it helps develop a society that is more just and equal.

Exchange on Both the Economic and Social Fronts:
Celebrations have the potential to stimulate economic activity, which in turn can help to enhance local economies. This might happen when there is an increase in tourism, sales of goods and services, and other types of spending during celebrations and festivals. The promotion of community cooperation and reciprocity through economic trade at times of celebration has the additional effect of having social implications.

The Interaction of Phenomena Associated with Psychological, Emotional, Social, and Physiological Aspects of Festivities
Celebrations have a significant impact on an individual, both psychologically and emotionally, and this helps contribute to the person's overall sense of health and happiness. These aspects include contentment, a reduction in stress, increased self-esteem, the ability to bounce back from negative experiences, and the formation of pleasant memories.

In addition, festivities have sociocultural repercussions that are not limited to the local community but rather affect society as a whole. A social connection, a sense of belonging, the development of a community, the peaceful resolution of conflicts, and the cultivation of a common identity are all examples of social elements.

The psychological and emotional impacts of celebrations are intricately connected to the effects that festivities have on one's body. The alleviation of stress and the accompanying release of endorphins that occur during celebrations have direct repercussions on one's physical health as well as their general well-being. In addition, the active pursuits that are customarily connected with festivals assist to the maintenance of a healthier way of life. In addition, the sense of community and the social relationships that are created throughout the course of celebrations can lead to a life that is both longer and more satisfying.

The way in which these many parts of festivities interact with one another underlines the connection of individual well-being and the cohesiveness of society. Celebrations have the potential to act as a conduit between an individual and their community, between one person's joy and the enjoyment of the group as a whole.

The Importance of Festivities in a Variety of Different Societal and Cultural Contexts

Differences Across Cultures:

There can be a large amount of variation amongst cultures with regard to the manner in which celebrations are carried out, as well as the customs and rituals that are observed. In some cultures, particular celebrations may place an emphasis on collective values, while in others, they may place more of an emphasis on individual achievements. The manner celebrations are carried out in different countries, as well as the meanings attached to those festivities, can have an effect on the health of the people living in those societies.

The social setting:

Celebrations are able to acquire new meanings and significance depending on the social context in which they are held. For instance, celebrations may have a more pronounced impact on social cohesiveness in a community with a strong sense of community, but in a society with a stronger emphasis on individualism, festivities may be regarded as opportunities for personal delight. Celebrations can contribute to well-being in a variety of ways, some of which are influenced by the social norms and values that prevail in a given setting.

Importance From a Religious and Spiritual Perspective:

Celebrations hold a place of religious or spiritual importance in many different cultural traditions. These festivities frequently foster a sense of belonging to a religious or spiritual community, which contributes to the mental and emotional health of those who identify with these beliefs. A sense of purpose and a connection to a higher power can be gained via the participation in the spiritual parts of festivities.

Globalization and the Celebrating of Differences in Cultures:

Celebrations that encompass more than one culture are becoming more widespread in today's globally interconnected society. Holidays such as Christmas and

Halloween, for instance, have been appropriated by a variety of different civilizations all around the world and given their own unique twists. These festivities provide one-of-a-kind opportunities for individuals to encounter a variety of cultural and social circumstances, which may help individuals' overall well-being by widening their viewpoints and contributing to their overall development.

The influence that festivities have on people's mental and physical health is varied and runs deep in human history, culture, and society. The existence of celebrations in our lives has an effect on not only our psychological and emotional well-being but also our social and physiological well-being as well. Joyful moments are produced during celebrations, which also serve to enhance and develop social interactions and communal ties.

When we have a better understanding of the enormous impact that celebrations have on both the well-being of individuals and of society as a whole, it will be easier for us to approach the various events that occur in our lives. Not only do they offer the chance to feel joy and happiness, but they also help to develop solidarity and social cohesiveness among those who participate. Celebrations, in all of their myriad guises and throughout all of the world's myriad civilizations, play an essential part in the process of making the world a more harmonious and fulfilling place.

2.3 The science of shared joy and community bonding

A major component that helps to reinforce the links that exist within a community is joy that is shared, which is typically experienced through communal festivals and festivities. These shared experiences of joy are profoundly ingrained in the human experience and play an important role in the development of a sense of belonging, cooperation, and social cohesion. The field of study known as the science of shared joy and community bonding investigates the psychological, social, and neurological underpinnings of how the experience of joy in a group context affects both the individuals who participate in the experience and the community as a whole. During this investigation, we will look into the mechanisms and effects of joy that is shared, as well as its evolutionary roots, its psychological underpinnings, and its significant role in the process of community formation.

The Evolved Roots of Community Bonding and Laughter Shared Across Species

It is essential to investigate the evolutionary origins of phenomena like as community bonding and shared joy in order to have a complete understanding of the science behind these phenomena. The emergence of strong social relationships and group cohesion as a strategy for survival was a defining characteristic of the evolution of humans. It was found that when members of a group discussed their positive feelings and experiences with one another, it helped strengthen the group's sense of togetherness and cooperation, which in turn increased their odds of surviving and reproducing.

Survival of the Group and Working Together:

In ancient times, human beings banded together to establish groups and communities for the purposes of mutual defense and resource distribution. Cooperation was essential for the early human populations in order to successfully hunt, gather, and fend off predators. The group would celebrate happy events like fruitful harvests or fruitful hunts as a way to strengthen their sense of unity and their commitment to a common goal.

The Establishment and Maintenance of Social Norms:

Celebrations and times of shared delight served, too, as a means of reinforcing a group's preexisting social norms and values. By participating in the festivities together, individuals demonstrated their commitment to adhering to these norms, which helped to the cohesiveness and cooperation of the group. In essence, the group's shared happiness served as a social glue, further strengthening their sense of identity and unity.

The Resolution of Conflict:

Conflicts and disputes were unavoidable in groups that were rather close-knit. The pleasant feelings that are connected with celebrations help to reduce tensions and encourage open conversation, which can frequently serve as a method for the resolution of conflicts that have been shared in joy. In this setting, celebrations played an important role in preserving social harmony and were therefore essential.

The adaptive advantages of gathering together as a group to celebrate happy events are highlighted by the evolutionary roots of shared joy and community connection. These mechanisms continue to play an important part in human societies in the modern world, helping to develop a sense of belonging as well as social cohesiveness.

Mechanisms of Psychological Happiness in Communal Settings

The intricate interaction of psychological systems that affect people on an individual level as well as the communities in which they live is what makes joy contagious.

These mechanisms contribute to emotional well-being, develop social relationships, and create a sense of identity and belonging in addition to providing a sense of community.

The Mirror Neuron System:

Activation of mirror neurons is one of the primary neurological factors that contribute to the feeling of shared joy. These neurons become active whenever we do an action as well as if we watch another individual performing the same action. When we see other people experiencing happiness, the mirror neurons in our brains light up. This triggers a neurological resonance that enables us to empathize with them and connect with the feelings they are experiencing. This brain resonance makes it easier for joy to spread among a group of people.

Feelings Can Easily Spread:

Emotional contagion is the phenomena in which members of a group "catch" the feelings that are being experienced by other members of the group. When one member of a group is filled with happy, it has the potential to rub off on the other members

FESTIVALS AND CELEBRATIONS

of the group and produce an atmosphere of contagious joy. This phenomena can be witnessed in a variety of different social settings, ranging from religious gatherings to sporting events.

The Theory of Social Identity:
According to social identity theory, individuals classify themselves and others into social groups based on shared qualities, values, and experiences with other members of those groups. Celebrations and times of delight shared by a community help to fortify a sense of social identity by drawing attention to the shared histories, experiences, and ideals that unite its members. This, in turn, increases a person's sense of belonging to the group as well as their sense of who they are inside the group.

Feelings of happiness and general well-being:
The release of good emotions such as happiness, enthusiasm, and thankfulness can be triggered by experiencing delight that is shared with others. These happy feelings have a significant influence on the well-being of an individual, contributing to a stronger sense of happiness, life satisfaction, and overall psychological health.

Enhanced Personal and Social Connections:
The social relationships that exist within a society are strengthened when joy is shared. The happy feelings that are felt during collective celebrations help to form enduring memories and strengthen interpersonal ties. These improved social relationships contribute to an individual's overall emotional well-being by providing a support system upon which they can rely in times of need and thereby providing a support system for others.

The Effects of Happiness on Society When It's Shared
The experience of joy that is shared has a tremendous effect on society, since it can change the dynamic of communities and cultures. It promotes the transmission of cultural values and traditions, as well as a sense of belonging, encourages social collaboration, and helps develop a sense of community.

Protecting Our Cultural Heritage:
During celebrations, cultural values, traditions, and historical narratives are frequently passed down from generation to generation. Communities maintain their cultural history by participating in joyful activities together. This helps to ensure that significant rituals and beliefs are passed down from one generation to the next. This preservation is absolutely necessary in order to keep a feeling of communal identity alive.

Integration into Society:
Individuals from many walks of life can come together to celebrate and celebrate together, which is beneficial to social integration. Celebrations serve as a unifying factor, helping people to look past their differences and foster a sense of solidarity in the process. In multiethnic societies, the joy that people enjoy with one another helps to cultivate tolerance and understanding, which in turn contributes to social cohesion and harmony.

Resilience of the Community:

The resiliency of a community can be strengthened when joy is shared. Communities that have shared experiences and triumphs are better prepared to support one another in times of difficulty because they have been through those experiences and celebrations together. When people get together to celebrate happy times, they form relationships that give them a sense of collective power and the ability to triumph over adversity.

The concept of Social Capital:

Within communities, the social relationships that are cultivated via the experience of shared joy contribute to the buildup of social capital. Trust, reciprocity, and the pooling of resources are all examples of aspects of social capital that are essential to the efficient operation of communities. The formation and upkeep of these social networks, which, in turn, contribute to the community's overall well-being, are significantly aided by the participation of individuals in various types of celebrations.

The importance of Festivities in the Formation of Community

Celebrations, whether they are cultural, religious, or secular in nature, play an essential part in the process of community bonding via the shared experience of joy.

These gatherings provide a structure for individuals to come together, celebrate their experiences in common, and cultivate stronger social connections with one another.

Observances of Cultural Traditions:

Communities are afforded the opportunity to celebrate their cultural identities by participating in cultural celebrations such as Chinese New Year, Diwali, and Mardi Gras, amongst others. These festivities serve as a focal point for individuals to come together, reinforce the values and rituals that define their cultural group, and exhibit the pride that they have in their cultural heritage.

Festivities Associated with Religion:

Celebrations of faith, such as Christmas, Eid, and Hanukkah, hold a special place in the hearts and minds of members of religious communities. Believers are able to develop a stronger feeling of community through gatherings like these, in addition to having the opportunity to proclaim their beliefs. Strong connections are formed between members of a faith community through the participation in communal religious rituals and celebrations.

Celebrations at the National Level:

Celebrations at the national level, such as Independence Day or Bastille Day, contribute to the development of a sense of national solidarity and identity. These events serve to inspire citizens to congregate in order to celebrate the history and core values of their country. Patriotism and a sense of allegiance to one's country are strengthened by participation in national celebrations.

Celebrations of a Personal Nature:

FESTIVALS AND CELEBRATIONS

The importance of personal festivities, such as birthdays, weddings, and graduations, in the
formation of community bonds cannot be overstated. These gatherings provide chances for people's families and friends to get together and commemorate the significant life moments and accomplishments of particular people. Celebrations of a person's life help to strengthen the support network that exists within their social group.

Festivities Tailored to a Particular Community:
Reunions of college alumni and neighborhood block parties are only two examples of the kinds of gatherings that are exclusive to particular communities or groups. These gatherings aim to reinforce the links that already exist within these communities, fostering a sense of belonging while also promoting cooperation.

The Neuroscience Behind the Happiness of Others
Research in the field of neuroscience gives light on the brain mechanisms that are responsible for shared joy and the effect that it has on community bonds. Studies using neuroimaging techniques have demonstrated that the feeling of joy and other pleasant emotions activates particular brain areas and neurotransmitter systems that play an important role in the formation of bonds and other social connections.

The Points and Prizes Method:
During times of intense happiness, some regions of the brain, known collectively as the reward system, become active. These regions include the prefrontal cortex and the ventral striatum. The processing of rewards and the reinforcement of virtuous behaviors are under the purview of this system. Dopamine and other neurotransmitters are released in people's brains when they share a joyful experience together; these neurotransmitters help people feel more pleasure and contentment.

Oxytocin and the Formation of Social Bonds:
Oxytocin, sometimes known as the "love hormone" or the "bonding hormone," is a chemical that is secreted into the bloodstream as a result of social interactions and emotional experiences. Oxytocin, which fosters trust, empathy, and social bonding, is released when two or more people experience joy together. This hormone helps individuals feel more emotionally connected to one another, which in turn promotes stronger social cohesiveness within a society.

Mirror neurons and the development of empathy:
Empathy and being able to comprehend the feelings of others depend heavily on something called mirror neurons. Individuals have a sense of emotional resonance when their mirror neurons fire as a result of witnessing the happiness of their contemporaries during times of celebration. This brain resonance is a fundamental component in the experience of joy that is shared, and it also contributes to an enhanced sense of communal belonging.

Emotional Contagions That Are Uplifting:

The activation of mirror neurons is a key factor in the psychological phenomenon known as
emotional contagion, which refers to the transmission of feelings from one person to another. When individuals join together to celebrate, the joy that one person feels can rapidly become contagious and spread throughout the group, resulting in a happy experience that is common to all members of the gathering.

The Importance of Joy in Shared Experiences, Both Socially and Culturally
Promoting an Attitude of Inclusivity:
By creating a setting in which people from all walks of life can congregate and rejoice together, shared pleasure contributes to the promotion of inclusiveness. Because it fosters a sense of belonging and acknowledgment within the greater community, this inclusion is particularly important for underrepresented groups, which are often excluded from it.

The Reiteration of Core Cultural Values:
In particular, cultural festivities serve to reaffirm a community's commitment to upholding its values, practices, and traditions. These gatherings act as a repository of cultural information, ensuring that these beliefs and practices will be passed down to subsequent generations.

In the sake of fostering tolerance and comprehension:
Celebrations of other cultures bring people closer together and help build tolerance and understanding between those of different backgrounds. People are given the chance to recognize, value, and respect the customs and principles held by others, which, in the end, contributes to the development of a society that is more peaceful and welcoming to those of all backgrounds.

Improving One's Social Capital :
Within communities, the social relationships that are cultivated via the experience of shared joy contribute to the buildup of social capital. This social capital is a vital resource for communities because it enables them to collaborate, support one another, and more effectively solve difficulties that are common to all communities.

Encouraging Participation in Group Activities:
The experience of joy that is shared is frequently the impetus for group endeavors and undertakings that benefit the community. Communities that come together to celebrate are more inclined to work together to solve problems, make positive changes, and participate in endeavors that are beneficial to the community as a whole.

Putting an Emphasis on the Significance of Unity:
The significance of maintaining unity within a community is highlighted when joy is shared by its members. It is a useful reminder that individuals are interconnected parts of a bigger whole and that the combined power of those individuals may triumph over adversity and difficulties.

The Importance of Neuroscience in the Study of Community Bonding and the Experience of Shared Pleasure

The field of neuroscience has been of critical importance in elucidating the processes underlying communal happiness and social connection. The study of neural processes and the development of tools for imaging the brain have both contributed significantly to our understanding of the biological underpinnings of social experiences.

Emotional resonance and the Role of Mirror Neurons:

The breakthrough that was made in neuroscience was the identification of cells known as mirror neurons. These neurons are in charge of empathy and being able to comprehend the feelings that other people are experiencing. When we observe the emotional experiences of another person, our mirror neurons become active, resulting in the formation of a neural resonance that promotes emotional understanding and connection among members of a group.

The Neural Reward System consists of:

When it comes to the processing of rewards and pleasant feelings, the reward system of the brain, and in particular the ventral striatum and the prefrontal cortex, plays a pivotal role. This system is activated during celebrations and times of shared delight, which reinforces the pleasure associated with collective happiness and fosters the formation of social bonds.

The Oxytocin Connection and Trust:

Oxytocin is a hormone that is released during social interactions and emotional experiences. This hormone plays a crucial part in the development of trust and empathy in others. Oxytocin is released into the body when people share happiness, which strengthens social bonds and trust within a society.

Feelings Can Easily Spread:

Emotional contagion, or the phenomena in which people "catch" the emotions that are being exhibited by others, has been the topic of a great deal of research. The activation of mirror neurons and the contagious spread of happy feelings among members of a group are both necessary components of the emotional contagion that results from shared joy.

Reinforcement positif dans la société:

Positive social experiences, such as shared joy, have been proven to result in enhanced brain activity that is connected with feelings of reward and reinforcement, according to research carried out in the field of neuroscience. Through the use of positive social reinforcement, social relationships are strengthened, and a sense of community is fostered.

The Benefits of Happiness in Community for One's Psyche and Overall Well-Being

The impact that joy shared with others has on one's mental health and overall well-being is significant. It does this by encouraging happiness, producing happy memories, and developing social relationships, all of which contribute to an individual's emotional and psychological well-being.

Improved Capacity for Emotional Expression:

When someone else is happy, it contributes to our own feelings of contentment and mental health. An individual's mental state can receive a direct and positive impact from the happy feelings that are experienced during communal festivities. This can lead to an increase in general happiness as well as life satisfaction.

Recollections that are fond:

The formation of happy memories is frequently prompted by the experience of delight that is shared. These recollections are recorded as part of an individual's autobiography and contribute to the formation of that person's sense of identity. During trying circumstances, it can be helpful to recall and reflect on happy occasions in the past as a source of positive reinforcement.

Enhanced Personal and Social Connections:

The social relationships that exist within a society are strengthened when joy is shared. Celebrations foster long-lasting relationships, which are an essential source of emotional support because of the good emotions and support networks that are created during these occasions.

Resilience in Emotional Aspects:

Positive experiences, such as shared joy, help people develop psychological resilience, which can be defined as the capacity to bounce back after being challenged. Individuals are equipped with the emotional resilience necessary to effectively deal with the hardships of life when they participate in communal celebrations.

Relaxation Techniques:

The sensation of joy that is shared can frequently lead to a reduction in stress. Endorphins are the body's natural painkillers and stress relievers. The production of endorphins can be triggered by engaging in activities such as singing, dancing, or even just spending quality time with loved ones during celebrations. The alleviation of stress has positive effects, not only psychologically but also physiologically.

A Feeling of Complementarity:

Joy that is spread about helps to cultivate a sense of community within its members. When people join together to celebrate, they develop a greater sense of identity and purpose in their lives, both of which are necessary for psychological well-being.

The connection between the joy that is shared and the resiliency of the community

The ability of a community to survive and recover from adversity, whether it be in the form of a

natural disaster, economic strife, or social issues, is referred to as community resilience. Joy that is shared plays a vital role in building community resilience through a number of different methods, including the following:

Solid interpersonal connections:

The social relationships that exist within a society can be strengthened via the sharing of joy. In times of need, individuals are able to band together and offer support to one another thanks to the strong connections that exist between them. The psychological and social connections that are forged through the experience of shared joy serve as the basis for the community's capacity for resilience.

Improved Capacity for Social Capital:

Communities are gifted with a significant resource in the form of social capital when members of the community experience and share joy together. It gives them the ability to work together, pool their resources, and organize themselves more efficiently in the face of challenges. The ability of a community to heal and rebuild is bolstered as a result of this concerted effort.

Positivity in terms of the emotions: reserves

The happy feelings and memories that are formed when people come together to celebrate serve as emotional reserves for both individuals and communities. When confronted with difficult circumstances, one might tap into these reserves in order to keep a positive view and retain emotional resilience.

Communication in a Time of Crisis:

The connections and communication networks that are established through the sharing of joy make it easier to communicate effectively during times of crisis. Communities that come together to celebrate are frequently better able to share information, offer support, and organize their reactions to challenges.

Sense of Oneself and One's Place in the World:

A community's perception of itself and its role in the world is strengthened when its members experience joy together. This shared sense of identity has the potential to act as a unifying factor during trying times, encouraging individuals to band together and strive toward achieving shared objectives.

Resilience in Psychological Aspects:

Celebrations that encourage people to feel joy together are beneficial to the psychological resiliency of a community. Individuals are equipped with the tools necessary to better cope with the psychological stressors that are connected with crises through the good experiences and emotional support that are generated through celebrations.

The Influence that Festivities Have on the Integration of Society

A Sense of Belonging and Unity:

Individuals are more likely to feel connected to one another and that they belong when they participate in celebrations. individuals are able to more strongly confirm their shared identities and values when they get together to celebrate a tradition or event that they all have in common. This helps to enhance the connections that individuals have with one another.

Acceptance as well as comprehension:

Tolerance and understanding can be fostered via the participation of people from a variety of different backgrounds in celebrations. People will have the opportunity to learn about and understand the traditions and principles held by others, which will contribute to the development of a society that is more accepting of diversity and cohesive.

Increasing the Strength of Our Social Bonds:
People come together during celebrations to talk about the good times they've had and strengthen the social relationships that result. These connections provide a basis for cooperation, support, and collective action, all of which contribute to an increased sense of social cohesiveness.

Increasing One's Stock of Social Capital:
The social capital of a group or society can be increased through the holding of celebrations. Individuals and organizations are able to effectively work with one another and find solutions to common problems when they have social capital, which includes trust, reciprocity, and shared resources.

The Resolution of Conflict:
Celebrations are frequently an occasion for the resolution of conflicts and the reconciliation of differences. Gatherings of the family around the holidays, for instance, serve as a platform for addressing and mending broken relationships, which, in the end, contribute to harmony within the family and the community.

Values and Observances That Are Universal:
Celebrations are full of rituals and activities with symbolic meanings that serve to reinforce norms and values that are held in common. These traditions act as social anchors, bringing a feeling of consistency and predictability to a society. As a result, they foster social cohesiveness by offering this sense of stability and predictability.

Building Up the Community:
It takes a group effort to put on a celebration, from the initial planning stages to the actual celebration itself. This component of celebrations that involves collaboration helps to cultivate a sense of shared purpose and responsibility, which extends beyond the celebration itself and contributes to the formation of community.

Celebrations and the act of sharing joy are met with a number of challenges and criticisms.

The exclusiveness of:
There are times when celebrations are restricted to a select few, either on purpose or by accident. This exclusivity has the ability to turn off people who do not come from the same cultural, religious, or socioeconomic background, which can then lead to emotions of being excluded.

Consumption culture:
A great number of events have become more commercialized throughout time, with an emphasis placed on consumer purchasing. This change has the potential to overshadow the original intent of the celebration and contribute to the development of a culture that places an emphasis on materialism and excess.

Influence on the Environment:
Large-scale celebrations frequently have a considerable impact on the environment, including the production of an excessive amount of waste, the consumption of an

excessive amount of energy, and the polluting of the air. This may have a negative impact on the environment as well as the ability to support life.

Abuse of both alcohol and drugs in excessive amounts:

Some festivities are connected with excessive use of alcohol and other substances, which can result in a variety of undesirable outcomes, including issues relating to one's health as well as social issues.

The effects of Pressure and Stress:

For some people, celebrations can be a cause of stress, particularly when there are high expectations attached to the event or financial pressures that must be met in order to participate.

Loss of Respect for Tradition :

There are several instances in which festivities have developed to the point that they no longer have much of a connection to the traditions or cultural importance that they once did. This might lead to the gradual loss of cultural behaviors and values.

It is crucial for communities and individuals to be aware of these issues and criticisms and to work toward the creation of celebrations that are sustainable, connected with the values and objectives they hold dear, and inclusive of as many people as possible.

The celebration of life's milestones in the modern era: opportunities and challenges

Celebrations and times of joyous fellowship are met with a new set of obstacles and opportunities in the modern day. The manner in which people participate in and express themselves during festive occasions has been significantly altered as a result of globalization, technology advances, and evolving cultural norms.

The Obstacles

Commercialization: Many festivals have become more focused on consumer expenditure as a result of the trend toward commercialization. This commercialization has the potential to obscure the celebration's original intent and contribute to the development of a culture that values materialism and excess.

Isolation in Social Life The development of technology has, paradoxically, resulted in a rise in people's feelings of isolation in their social lives. During times of celebration, virtual interactions via social media and other forms of digital communication can sometimes take the place of actual, in-person encounters. This has the potential to lessen the feeling of shared joy and strengthen the bonds between members of the community.

Impact on the Environment: Parties that are held on a large scale frequently have a substantial effect on the environment, including excessive trash, increased energy use, and pollution. Celebrations in the modern era need to have a greater regard for the environment in order to address these concerns.

Disparities in economic circumstances might make it difficult for individuals to fully participate in and enjoy celebrations to the fullest extent possible. Some people are unable to feel included in celebrations because the costs associated with organizing or attending them, such as weddings or holidays, are out of their financial reach.

Occasions to seize:

Virtual Celebrations: Recent advances in technology have opened the door to the possibility of holding celebrations online, which enables people to communicate with their loved ones no matter where they live in the globe. These online gatherings have the potential to increase diversity and bring people together despite physical separation.

Celebrations are becoming more sustainable and environmentally friendly as more people become aware of the importance of addressing environmental concerns. People on an individual and community level are becoming more aware of the impact that their celebrations have on the environment and are implementing measures that aim to decrease waste and promote sustainability.

The concept of inclusivity is becoming increasingly prevalent in modern festivities, which are also placing a larger emphasis on diversity and being sensitive to different cultures. Efforts are being made by communities to make sure the festivities are approachable and inclusive of people of all different kinds of backgrounds.

Celebrations provide a window of opportunity for community engagement and bonding, which is especially important in light of the problems that modern life presents. People are becoming more aware of the significance of getting together in person to celebrate and create joyful moments that can be shared by everyone.

Globalization has made it possible for people from different cultures to share their celebrations and traditions with one another. A greater number of people from a variety of cultural backgrounds are becoming familiar with and taking part in celebrations that were previously foreign to them, which fosters more intercultural understanding and solidarity.

Chapter 3

Religious Festivals

Many billions of people all across the world look forward to religious festivals each year with excitement and anticipation. These holy and joyous holidays are intricately entwined with the customs and beliefs of a culture's religious community as well as the entirety of the human experience. Religious festivals, such as Diwali in India, Christmas in the Western world, Eid al-Fitr in the Muslim calendar, and Hanukkah in the Jewish faith, offer a profound insight into the human relationship with the divine, the togetherness of communities, and the preservation of cultural legacy. Diwali is a festival that celebrates the victory of good over evil. This in-depth investigation investigates the significance of religious holidays, delving into their historical and cultural origins as well as the myriad of ways in which people all around the world celebrate these occasions.

1. The Importance of Different Religious Celebrations
   Religious festivals, usually referred to as holy days or feast days, are celebrations of spiritual significance that are observed by many different religions and belief systems. These celebrations are distinguished by the performance of rites, the holding of ceremonies, and the convening of community meetings, all of which are intended to honor, memorialize, and communicate devotion to the divine. The significance of religious holidays extends far beyond the act of observing the religion that celebrates them; instead, these celebrations frequently play an important part in the psychological, social, and cultural well-being of both individuals and communities.
   Connection to the Spiritual World:
   The formation and reaffirmation of a spiritual connection is the primary purpose that drives participation in religious celebrations. Believers take use of these opportunities to strengthen their faith, ask pardon from the divine, and express thanks for the blessings in their lives. These holidays provide a planned

time for contemplation, meditation, and prayer, which helps to strengthen the connection with one's religious tradition.

Identifying One's Culture:

The cultural identity of a group or region is inextricably bound up with the celebration of several religious holidays. In doing so, they contribute to the maintenance and transfer of cultural legacy by reflecting the norms, principles, and practices of the particular group to which they belong.

Traditions in terms of dress, music, and dance, as well as cuisine, are frequently exhibited throughout the celebrations.

Integrity of the Community:

Celebrations of faith have a significant impact on the cohesiveness of the communities they serve. They make it possible for individuals to interact with one another, build their social links, and take part in shared experiences. The participants in these get-togethers have a stronger sense of cohesion and belonging as a result.

Regarding both morality and ethics:

The celebration of many different religious holidays is defined by an emphasis on moral and ethical conduct. They frequently encourage folks to embody compassion, charity, forgiveness, and justice in their day-to-day lives by conveying messages of these virtues and urging others to do the same.

Moments for Contemplation:

Many religious celebrations include set times for individuals to reflect on their lives and do self-analysis. They encourage believers to examine their behavior, ask for pardon for whatever faults they may have committed, and establish moral and ethical standards for their lives moving forward.

The Repeating Patterns of Life and Nature:

There are several religious celebrations that are intricately intertwined with the natural and seasonal cycles. They may mark the changing of the seasons, agricultural harvests, or celestial happenings, thereby strengthening humanity's connection to the natural world.

Instruction and the Passing Down of the Faith:

The passing down of one generation's faith to the next can best be accomplished through the celebration of various religious holidays. Through taking part in these festivals, children are able to get knowledge regarding their religion, traditions, and morals.

2. The Diverse Historical Origins and Rich Cultural Traditions Behind Religious Festivals

The history of religious celebrations extends back millennia, and the customs associated with them have developed over the course of time. These traditions have frequently been shaped by the geographical, cultural, and historical backdrop of the areas in which religious holidays are observed. The intricate fabric of

FESTIVALS AND CELEBRATIONS

human civilization is reflected in the rich variety of traditions that are brought together during religious celebrations.

Festivals Observed by Hindus

India, with its many different religious customs, is the location of a large number of Hindu celebrations. The Hindu Festival of Lights, known as Diwali, celebrates the triumph of light over darkness as well as the victory of knowledge over ignorance. The entrance of spring and the triumph of good over evil are celebrated at Holi, also known as the Festival of Colors. The nine-night festival known as Navaratri is a celebration of the goddess Durga, who is seen as the embodiment of the divine feminine force.

Festivals Observed by Christians

The Christian religion celebrates a number of important holidays throughout the year. One of the most well-known holidays, Christmas is a celebration of the birth of Jesus Christ and is characterized by the giving and receiving of gifts as well as the setting up of festive decorations. Easter is a celebration that remembers the resurrection of Jesus and places an emphasis on themes of redemption and fresh starts. The coming of the Holy Spirit upon the apostles is what the festival of Pentecost celebrates.

Festivals Observed by Muslims

There are two principal celebrations that occur on the Islamic calendar, and they are known as Eid al-Fitr and Eid al-Adha. The month-long fasting period known as Ramadan comes to a conclusion with the celebration of Eid al-Fitr, also known as the "Festival of Breaking the Fast." The Islamic holiday known as Eid al-Adha, also known as the "Festival of Sacrifice," commemorates the willingness of Ibrahim (also known as Abraham) to obey God's command and sacrifice his son.

Jewish holidays include:

The religion of Judaism celebrates a wide variety of holidays, each of which has its own unique importance. Pesach, also known as Passover, is a celebration that remembers when the Israelites were freed from their enslavement in Egypt. The miracle of the oil lasting for eight days in the temple is celebrated at Hanukkah, also known as the Festival of Lights. A day of fasting and repentance is observed on Yom Kippur, also known as the Day of Atonement.

Festivals Observed by Buddhists

The numerous subgroups that comprise Buddhism each celebrate their own unique holidays. The Buddhist holiday of Vesak, which is also known as Buddha Purnima, honors Siddhartha Gautama, the historical Buddha, by commemorating his birth, enlightenment, and death. Songkran, the Thai New Year, is celebrated with activities that involve making merit and taking part in water festivals.

Celebrations of Sikhism:

Sikhism, which was established in the 15th century by Guru Nanak, celebrates a number of different holidays. Vaisakhi, also known as Baisakhi, is a Sikh holiday that celebrates the establishment of the Khalsa, a society of warriors. Diwali, which is also celebrated by Sikhs, is an important holiday in the Sikh religion because it commemorates Guru Hargobind's freedom after being imprisoned.

Festivals Observed by Native Americans and Pagans

Indigenous and pagan traditions all throughout the world celebrate a broad variety of holidays that have some relationship to nature, the passage of the seasons, or the spiritual bond with the land. The Native American Powwow, the Celtic Beltane, and the African Yoruba festivals are a few examples of the many types of celebrations that fall within this category.

Holidays Celebrated for No Religious Reason

There are several areas that celebrate secular holidays that have significant cultural and historical meaning. For instance, the Carnival in Rio de Janeiro, Brazil, is famous for its lively and colorful parades, whilst the Chinese New Year, despite having its origins in cultural and astrological customs, has developed into a festival that is renowned all over the world.

Festivals of the Fusion:

The world is becoming more interconnected, and as a result, more and more festivals that celebrate the variety of different cultures and belief systems are appearing. These celebrations frequently incorporate aspects of a variety of ethnic traditions, which helps to promote unity and cross-cultural understanding.

3. Traditions of Festivities Celebrated During Religious Holidays

Religious celebrations are distinguished by the presence of a diverse array of celebratory customs, each of which has strong ties to the specific faith and culture they honor. These customs are illustrative of the variety and individuality that can be found in religious celebrations from country to country.

Traditions, Observances, and Events:

In many cases, the rituals and ceremonies that are practiced during religious celebrations are considered to be the most important parts of the event. These can take the form of prayers, blessings, processions, and other acts of worship that range in terms of their complexity and the significance of the symbols they use.

Various adornments:

Decorations appropriate for the occasion are always present at religious celebrations. These may take the form of bright banners, garlands, flowers, or lights, all of which have some sort of significant symbolic meaning. For instance, during the Christian holiday of Christmas, a Christmas tree and a nativity scene are shown, while during the Hindu holiday of Diwali, rangoli and lamps are displayed.

Both Fasting and Eating:

Both fasting and feasting are frequently practiced during religious celebrations.

As observed during the holy month of Ramadan in Islam, fasting can be a symbol of self-discipline, purification, or solidarity with those who are in need. The practice of feasting, on the other hand, is symbolic of abundance, joy, and participation in communal activities with others.

The arts of Music and Dance:

In many different religious celebrations, music and dancing play an essential part. Joy, commitment, and a sense of cultural identity are all conveyed via the practice of these art forms. For example, the ancient hymns and carols of Christmas, the Sufi whirling dance performed by the Mevlevi Order of Islam, and the elaborate classical dances performed during Indian festivals.

The Wearing of Clothes and Attire:

During religious holidays, attendees may frequently dress in unique garments and garb. The selection of these garments is based on the symbolic meaning of such garments, which may signify chastity, modesty, or cultural heritage. Pilgrims attending the Hajj in Islam wear white robes, and people attending Indian festivities wear colorful saris and turbans. Other examples include these.

Giving Presents:

Giving presents to one another is a tradition that is observed at many different types of celebrations. The meanings behind these presents could include love, benevolence, or something spiritual. This custom is demonstrated by the giving and receiving of gifts during the Christmas holiday, the giving of zakat during Eid al-Fitr, and the exchanging of sweets during the Diwali festival.

Deeds of Benevolence:

The practice of compassion and goodwill is frequently highlighted during religious holidays. These can include providing food for the needy, aiding those who are less wealthy, or engaging in volunteer work in the community. During the Hindu festival of Annakut, the Christian season of Lent, and the Jewish festival of Purim, people are known to perform deeds of generosity in similar ways.

The Way of the Pilgrim and Other Journeys:

Pilgrimages to holy sites or other places of historical or religious significance are an integral part of a number of different religious celebrations. Pilgrims set out on these kinds of treks in the hopes of achieving enlightenment on a spiritual level and satisfying the requirements of their religion. The most well-known examples of this are the journey to Mecca known as the Hajj in Islam and the Kumbh Mela in Hinduism.

4. The Effects of Religious Celebrations on a Global Scale

   Individuals, communities, and societies are all profoundly influenced by the celebration of various religious holidays. Their impact is not limited to the area of religious devotion; rather, it permeates all elements of life, including the cultural, economic, and social spheres.

The Economy in Relation to Tourism

Tourism and the economy of many communities are directly tied to the observance of several religious holidays. Festivals frequently attract visitors from all over the world, which results in a rise in the amount of business activity, jobs associated to tourism, and the sale of goods and services relevant to the festival.

The Exchange of Cultures:

The religious celebrations provide as a forum for the interchange of different cultures. Visitors who come from a variety of backgrounds are given the opportunity to learn about the norms, rituals, and beliefs of the community that is hosting them, which fosters intercultural understanding and tolerance.

Promotion of Regional Arts and Crafts

Crafts, textiles, and other artisanal goods made in the local community are frequently sold at festivals. These products bring attention to the one-of-a-kind artistic heritage of the area while also supporting the efforts of the region's artisans and crafters.

Dialoguing Across the Faiths:

Some religious celebrations encourage discussion and tolerance amongst people of different faiths. persons have the opportunity to learn about and develop an appreciation for religions different than their own during gatherings that are accessible to persons from a variety of religious traditions.

Maintaining Social Cohesion:

Festivals are great for fostering social cohesiveness because they bring people together to participate in shared experiences. People who come together to celebrate, eat together, and take part in activities that bring the community together tend to strengthen the bonds that bind them.

Protecting Our Cultural Heritage:

The continuation of many different religious celebrations is essential to the protection of cultural heritage. They have an important role in passing on values, practices, and traditions to subsequent generations, which is essential to guaranteeing that these things will continue to exist.

Philanthropy and charitable giving both:

Charitable deeds and philanthropic endeavors are frequently associated with celebrations. The less fortunate may get assistance in the form of food, clothing, or money assistance during these occasions, which contributes to the promotion of social welfare and justice.

Possibilities for Furthering One's Education:

Festivals are a wonderful educational resource because they provide participants with opportunity to learn about the history, art, music, and traditions that are linked with a particular culture or faith.

5. Difficulties and Debates Involved in the Observance of Religious Celebrations

The process of commercialization

The commercialization of religious holidays has the potential to obscure the value of those holidays on a spiritual level. An unhealthy obsession with consumerism and marketing can result in the worship of material goods and a diversion from the essential religious message.

Influence on the Environment:

Large-scale events, particularly those involving fireworks or large crowds of people, frequently have an effect on the surrounding environment by adding to pollution and waste. More and more people are being urged to embrace sustainability.

The exclusiveness of:

People who do not belong to specific religious or cultural groups may experience emotions of marginalization when they attend certain festivals because these celebrations may be restricted to members of those specific groups.

Tensions between Religions:

Religious celebrations have the potential to exacerbate existing interfaith tensions, misunderstandings, and confrontations in areas that are home to a wide variety of religious communities. It is critical to encourage respectful conversation amongst people of different faiths.

Concerns Regarding Safety:

Gatherings of a large number of people at religious celebrations can raise a number of safety issues, including the need for crowd control and security measures, as well as the possibility of accidents or stampedes. To protect the health and safety of the participants, taking appropriate precautions is absolutely necessary.

Appropriation de la culture:

The appropriation of religious and cultural aspects of festivals by outsiders, typically for the aim of making a profit, may be regarded as disrespectful or offensive by the communities that place a high value on these traditions.

The fundamentalist view of religion:

In some instances, religious celebrations can serve as a stage for religious fundamentalism or extremism, which can have detrimental repercussions for society as a whole.

It is vital to address these difficulties and debates while preserving the cultural and religious significance of these celebrations and promoting the positive features of those celebrations.

6. The Persistent Significance of Traditions Regarding Religious Holidays

The minds and emotions of people all across the world have a special spot reserved specifically for religious celebrations. These festivities are a monument to the wide diversity of human culture and belief systems, since they are characterized by their spiritual significance, cultural traditions, and communal gatherings.

Individuals have the opportunity to strengthen their cultural identities, establish community togetherness, connect with the divine, and participate in acts of charity and generosity as a result of these events.

Religious celebrations are held all over the world and play a significant part in fostering cultural interaction, communication between people of different faiths, and the conservation of cultural traditions.

It is crucial that we continue to celebrate and commemorate these holidays while also addressing the issues and controversies that they may provide as we continue to navigate a world that is becoming a more interconnected one. Doing so will allow us to promote a broader knowledge of the significance of religious holidays, as well as their ongoing legacies and the impact they have on the community on a worldwide scale.

3.1 An exploration of major religious festivals (e.g., Diwali, Easter, Eid, Hanukkah, and Christmas)

The social, cultural, and spiritual fabric of cultures all over the world is significantly strengthened by the observance of religious festivals. These gatherings, which have their origins firmly planted in religious dogma and cultural custom, offer a stage upon which communities can reminisce about pivotal moments in their history and communicate their allegiance to a higher power. Diwali, Easter, Eid, Hanukkah, and Christmas are the five most important religious holidays, and each one is distinguished by its own particular practices and meanings.

Diwali is:

Diwali, or the "Festival of Lights," is a significant holiday in the religions of Hinduism, Sikhism, and Jainism. It also goes by the name Deepavali. It is a festival that lasts for five days and takes place in either October or November. It celebrates the triumph of light over darkness as well as the triumph of good over evil. Diyas, also known as lamps, and other brightly colored decorations are commonly seen in both private and public areas. People go together to participate in grandiose firework displays and trade candies and presents with one another. During the occasion, families gather to engage in religious rites and to recite prayers addressed to Lakshmi, the Hindu goddess of wealth and prosperity.

Good Friday:

Easter, which celebrates the resurrection of Jesus Christ, is considered to be one of the most significant holidays in the Christian calendar. The celebration is traditionally held on the Sunday that immediately follows the first full moon that occurs after the spring equinox. The season of Lent, which consists of abstaining from food, praying, and thinking about one's life, comes before Easter. As part of the festivities, special church services, the decorating of Easter eggs, and the tradition of the Easter bunny delivering chocolate eggs are all part of the celebrations. Easter is a Christian holiday that celebrates the resurrection of Jesus Christ and the triumph of life over death.

The festival of Eid al-Fitr:

The Islamic holy month of fasting, Ramadan, comes to a conclusion with the celebration of Eid al-Fitr, which is also known as the "Festival of Breaking the Fast." Following the completion of one month of religious austerity and introspective endeavors, a moment of rejoicing and giving thanks is appropriate. Muslims get together to pray in large groups, greet one another, and celebrate by eating festive feasts with their families and friends. It is also a time for donating to those who are less fortunate by participating in the act of charity known as Zakat al-Fitr during this time. The Islamic holiday of Eid al-Fitr places an emphasis on the virtues of compassion, solidarity, and gratitude within the religion.

The festival of Hanukkah :

The Jewish holiday known as Hanukkah, often known as the "Festival of Lights," is a significant celebration that lasts for eight days and typically takes place in December. In the midst of the Maccabean Revolt against the Seleucid Empire, the Second Temple in Jerusalem was re-dedicated, and this holiday celebrates that event. An essential part of the Hanukkah celebration is the lighting of the menorah, a nine-branched candelabrum that represents the miracle of the oil that burnt for eight days when it was only supposed to last for one. Latkes and sufganiyot are two classic Jewish desserts that are deep-fried and filled with either jelly or custard. Other family traditions include playing games, singing songs, and eating traditional dishes.

Holiday Season:

Christmas is a significant celebration in the Christian calendar that is observed on December 25 to commemorate the birth of Jesus Christ. The Advent period, which anticipates the arrival of Christ and is commemorated by praying, abstaining from food, and performing acts of charity, is what distinguishes this time of year from others. The celebrations will involve putting ornaments on Christmas trees, trading gifts with one another, and singing Christmas carols. During special church services, feasts, and the exchange of traditional meals, families meet together to celebrate together. The essence of Christmas is love, peace, and goodwill toward all people, and it places an emphasis on the virtues of generosity, forgiveness, and reconciliation.

Within their individual faith communities, these important religious holidays help build togetherness, compassion, and a closer connection to the divine. This is because these celebrations contain tremendous cultural, spiritual, and social significance. They serve as a reminder of the traditions and ideals that have stood the test of time and continue to make people's lives better all around the world.

3.2 The significance of these festivals in various faiths

For believers all over the world, major religious holidays play an important role in their personal and communal life on multiple levels, including the spiritual, cultural, and social. Not only are these events times for worship and reflection, but they also serve as a means of expressing devotion, interacting with the community, and preserving cultural traditions. Diwali, Easter, Eid, Hanukkah, and Christmas are five of the most important religious holidays celebrated by people of different religions. Let's discuss the meanings behind these holidays.

Diwali is a festival that is celebrated by Hindus, Sikhs, and Jainists:

In Hinduism, Sikhism, and Jainism, the holiday of Diwali, often called the "Festival of Lights," is celebrated with a great deal of zeal and excitement. The triumph of light over darkness, the triumph of good over evil, and the triumph of knowledge over ignorance are the main themes of the Hindu festival of Diwali. The exact religious significance may differ from one of these traditions to another. In Hinduism, this day celebrates the triumph of Lord Rama over the demonic ruler Ravana and his subsequent return to Ayodhya. Because Guru Hargobind was freed from his incarceration during this time, it carries a special significance for Sikhs. It is the day that Lord Mahavira is said to have attained Nirvana, according to Jainism.

Diwali is a significant festival that invites people to engage in spiritual introspection, to pray to various deities, and to ask for blessings on their path to prosperity and well-being. In addition, it is a time when families get together to visit with one another, give and receive gifts, and enjoy festive meals. The lighting of diyas is meant to represent the eradication of one's spiritual ignorance and the enlightenment of one's inner self through the acquisition of heavenly knowledge. The festival of Diwali is significant because it symbolizes the triumph of light over darkness as well as the perseverance of good over evil.

Easter (in the Christian religion):

The celebration of the resurrection of Jesus Christ that takes place on Easter is fundamental to the Christian faith. It is a symbol of the triumph of life over death and of salvation for all of humanity, and it carries with it significant theological meaning. Following the gloomy season of Lent, which concentrates on Christ's sacrifice and humanity's need for redemption, the Christian liturgical calendar culminates with Easter as the celebration of the resurrection of Jesus Christ.

The Easter Sunday service is the most important act of worship that takes place during Easter. During this service, believers assemble to remember the resurrection of Jesus Christ. The Easter tradition of coloring eggs reflects the significance of the holiday by serving as a metaphor for the beginning of a new life and rebirth. The Easter bunny is a relatively new addition that has a more secular origin; yet, it serves to highlight the pleasure and rebirth that are linked with this holiday. The celebration of Easter highlights the virtues of faith and hope, as well as the promise of eternal life.

(Eid al-Fitr) in Islam:

The Islamic holiday of Eid al-Fitr, sometimes referred to as the "Festival of Breaking the Fast," is an important and significant celebration. It is the end of Ramadan, a month during which people fast, pray, and reflect on themselves and their lives. The importance of the holiday of Eid al-Fitr rests in the expression of thanks for having successfully completed the fast, as well as the spiritual purification and development that was accomplished throughout the month.

FESTIVALS AND CELEBRATIONS

On this day, Muslims gather at their local mosques for special prayers and sermons to reaffirm their faith and express gratitude for the spiritual support and direction they received during the month of Ramadan. Families and friends get together to share meals and trade presents as a way to highlight the festival's emphasis on the community nature of the event. Zakat al-Fitr is a practice that exemplifies the ideals that are emphasized on the holiday of Eid al-Fitr, such as compassion, unity, and the obligation to assist those who are less fortunate.

(Hanukkah, in Jewish tradition):
An important Jewish holiday known as the "Festival of Lights," Hanukkah celebrates the rededication of the Second Temple in Jerusalem as well as the miracle of the oil that was found in the temple's holy lamp. The celebration lasts for eight days, during which time participants are encouraged to contemplate the resiliency and faith of the Jewish people in the face of adversity.

An essential part of the Hanukkah celebration is the lighting of the menorah, with one candle being added to it each night. This is a representation of the miraculous nature of the oil that burnt for eight days straight despite the fact that there was only enough oil for one day. Traditional activities associated with Hanukkah include singing songs, eating delicacies cooked in oil, and playing games such as dreidel. The celebration emphasizes the necessity of keeping one's cultural and religious history, as well as the value of having faith and persevering through difficult times.

Christmas, in the Christian religion:
The birth of Jesus Christ is honored with the celebration of Christmas, which is one of the most well-known and extensively observed Christian holidays. The idea that Jesus is the Messiah and the Son of God, who came to deliver people hope, salvation, and the promise of eternal life, is the key to understanding the meaning of this text.

Beginning with Advent, a time of preparation and expectation for the birth of Christ, the holiday season of Christmas is a time for introspection and contemplation. The culmination of the holiday season is the celebration of Christmas Eve and Christmas Day, which typically includes attending church services, exchanging gifts, and decorating Christmas trees.

The Christian principle of love is reflected in the act of giving, which also represents the idea that Jesus is the greatest gift that God has given to humanity. Giving, forgiving, and making peace with one another are all emphasized as important virtues throughout the Christmas holiday, which reflects the love, peace, and goodwill attitude.

3.3 Rituals, symbols, and stories associated with religious celebrations
Tradition, spirituality, and the relevance of culture are all intricately woven into the fabric of religious festivities. These events are frequently characterized by a plethora of rituals, symbols, and tales, each of which carries a significant significance for the people who observe them. Within religious communities, these components serve the purposes of bolstering faith, educating members, and developing a sense of solidarity

and continuity. In the course of this investigation, we are going to look into the traditions, symbols, and tales that are related with the numerous religious festivities practiced around the world.

1. The Rituals That Are Performed During Religious Celebrations

A Sense of Spiritual Connection: The performance of rituals can help individuals feel as though they have a stronger spiritual connection to the divine. They frequently entail acts of worship, such as praying, meditating, or performing other responsibilities required by a particular religion.

The performance of rituals is an important part of maintaining cultural and religious traditions and ensuring their continuation from generation to generation. They take responsibility for ensuring that the traditions and principles of a specific faith are carried on from one generation to the next.

The performance of rituals is one way for groups to become closer to one another. They foster a sense of oneness and one goal among the participants through their activities. Participation in group activities and the exchange of experiences is common in rituals.

Transformation on a Spiritual Level Some rituals are performed with the intention of bringing about a change on a spiritual level. The act of baptism, which is central to the Christian religion, is meant to represent cleansing and a new beginning for the individual.

1. **The meaning of the Christian Mass**
   The celebration of the Eucharist, sometimes called the Mass, is one of the most important rites in Christianity. It is a celebration that remembers the Last Supper that Jesus shared with his disciples. Believers are encouraged to partake in the consecrated bread and wine that are served throughout the Mass. These elements represent Christ's flesh and blood, respectively. The Christian community receives spiritual sustenance and is brought closer together via the observance of this liturgy.
2. **Recitation of prayers in Islam:**
   The Friday prayer known as the Salat al-Jumu'ah is considered by Muslims to be the most important of their five daily prayers. Congregational prayers are held on Fridays at noon, and they are seen as a weekly opportunity for Muslims to come together for the purpose of worshipping collectively.
3. **The Diwali Puja, as Practiced in Hinduism**
   The unique prayer service known as a puja is performed in honor of Diwali, also known as the Festival of Lights. During these gatherings, families get together to worship to many deities, most commonly seeking the favor of Lakshmi, the

FESTIVALS AND CELEBRATIONS

goddess of wealth and prosperity. This ceremony is not complete without the lighting of diyas, the recital of aarti, and the sharing of gifts between participants.

4. **The Passover Seder, as Practiced in Judaism**

The Passover holiday, also known as Pesach, is honored with a meal known as a Seder. Participants read from the Haggadah, which is a text that narrates the account of the Exodus. This allows them to retell the story of how the Israelites were freed from their enslavement in Egypt. The unleavened bread (matzah) and the bitter herbs, both of which are included on the Seder plate, each have their own particular symbolic meaning.

II. The Significance of Symbols in Religious Ceremonies

Crucifixion and resurrection of Jesus Christ are represented by the cross, a major symbol in Christianity. The cross symbolizes both events. It is a symbol of salvation and life that endures forever.

The Crescent and the Star as emblems of Islam The crescent and the star are two emblems of Islam that are very well known. The star is meant to represent the direction that God provides, and the crescent moon is used to indicate the beginning of each lunar month in Islam.

Om is a sacred sound and symbol in Hinduism, and it is considered to be a representation of both the divine and the ultimate truth. It is said aloud during times of prayer and meditation.

In Judaism, the menorah is a candelabrum with seven branches that is used to symbolize the Temple that was located in Jerusalem. In order to remember the miraculous supply of oil that was discovered during Hanukkah, a menorah with eight branches is lit each night.

In Buddhism, the lotus blossom is considered to be a representation of both enlightenment and the attainment of purity. It is a representation of the path that leads from darkness to light.

Judaism's significance of the Star of David The Star of David, which is a star with six points, is a symbol of both Jewish identity and Judaism. It is commonly connected with the Jewish religion and can be seen displayed on the flag of Israel.

The Christian religion considers the dove to be a representation of the Holy Spirit as well as a symbol of peace. It is a symbol of the presence of God and the blessings he bestows.

III. Narratives Involved in Religious Festivities

The Christian celebration of Christmas centers on the Nativity Story, which recounts the birth of Jesus in Bethlehem. As told in the Gospels of Matthew and Luke, the narrative places an emphasis on the arrival of the Savior as well as the virtues of humility and love.

Jewish tradition observes the holiday of Passover as a way to remember when the Israelites were freed from their servitude in Egypt. The narrative of Moses liberating the Israelites from their slavery is at the heart of the celebration, which places an emphasis on following God's lead.

Diwali, a festival that is observed by Hindus, derives its origins from the Hindu epic literature known as the "Ramayana." It narrates the narrative of Lord Rama's victory against the demon king Ravana and his subsequent return to his kingdom victorious.

The Life Narrative of Muhammad, the Prophet of Islam: Both Eid al-Fitr and Eid al-Adha are connected to the life and teachings of the Prophet Muhammad in Islamic tradition. They serve as a constant reminder to Muslims of his exemplary life as well as the virtues of charity, sacrifice, and devotion.

The Life of Siddhartha Gautama, Also Known as the Buddha (Buddhism): Many Buddhist celebrations are centered on the life and teachings of Siddhartha Gautama, also known as the Buddha. The narrative of the Buddha's ascent to enlightenment and the establishment of the Four Noble Truths is at the heart of these ceremonies.

Jewish Tradition Relates the Story of Moses and the Ten Commandments: The Jewish ethical and moral values are grounded in the Ten Commandments, which were communicated to Moses at the foot of Mount Sinai. They play a pivotal role in a variety of Jewish ceremonies and festivals.

These tales are more than just anecdotes; rather, they are active components of the religious traditions. They offer direction, instructive morals, and a feeling of continuity with times gone by.

Celebrations of religious holidays are constructed on the foundation of rituals, symbols, and narrative. The purpose of these gatherings is to strengthen the believers' spiritual connection with the divine, to pass on important cultural and religious values, and to foster a sense of community. These aspects are the essence and driving force behind religious customs; they add depth to the lives of those who follow these traditions and ensure that the legacy of faith is preserved for future generations. Religious celebrations, when viewed in this light, become much more than a set of behaviors; rather, they become a reflection of the beliefs, hopes, and stories that define a faith and the people who practice it.

Chapter 4

Seasonal Festivals

Seasonal festivals have been an important part of human society for thousands of years. These celebrations commemorate crucial transitions in nature, agriculture, and the cosmic cycle. These festivities are intricately entwined with the rituals and customs of various cultures, the beliefs of various religions, and the cycles of the natural world. They serve as a manner of commemorating the changing of the seasons, expressing gratitude for the bounties of nature, and developing a sense of community and spiritual connection among participants. This in-depth investigation dives into the rich fabric of seasonal celebrations across a variety of cultural traditions, shedding insight on their historical origins, cultural significance, and modern expressions.

1. **The Importance of Holidays Celebrated Throughout the Year**
   Agricultural Accomplishments of Note:
   Many of the annual celebrations of the changing seasons are tied to significant agricultural activities like planting and harvesting, as well as the cycle of growth. During these celebrations, rituals and ceremonies are frequently performed with the goals of ensuring a prosperous harvest, expressing thanks to the soil, and seeking the earth's blessing on future agricultural activities.
   Heritage of the Culture:
   Festivals that take place throughout the year play an important role in the process of passing on ingrained knowledge and conserving cultural traditions from one generation to the next. They establish a sense of cultural continuity and identity by encapsulating the traditions, rituals, folklore, and culinary practices that are exclusive to a particular region or community.
   Connection to the Spiritual World:
   Festivals that take place during specific times of the year sometimes have a religious or spiritual significance, which serves to highlight the interconnectedness of humanity and the divine. They develop a closer connection with the sacred

and the natural environment by providing chances for spiritual reflection, acts of purification, and acts of devotion.

Integrity of the Community:
These celebrations act as a spur for the formation of communal bonds and contribute to the overall cohesiveness of the community. They establish a sense of belonging and common purpose among participants by bringing people together. Communities frequently participate in group events, celebrations, and feasts with the goals of strengthening social bonds and promoting better understanding between members of the community.

Renewal on a Cyclical Basis:
The cyclical nature of life, death, and rebirth is represented by various festivals that take place throughout the year. They offer folks a sense of hope, renewal, and the promise of new beginnings by reminding them of the fundamental state of perpetual change and regeneration that is present in the natural world.

2. **Holidays Celebrated Throughout the Year in Various Cultures**

Festivals held in the Spring
Celebrations held in the spring are meant to stand for rebirth, fertility, and the beginning of a new cycle of life. One such event is the Holi festival, which takes place in India and celebrates the entrance of spring with the use of bright colors and jubilant activities. The beginning of spring and the Persian New Year are both celebrated during the Nowruz holiday, which is held in a number of nations across the Middle East and Central Asia.

Festivals Observed on the Summer Solstice
Numerous societies hold festivals to commemorate the summer solstice, which is seen as a
time of plenty, light, and energy. Traditional dances, bonfires, and floral wreaths are a part of the Midsummer celebrations held in countries in Northern Europe and the Baltic region. These festivals mark the longest day of the year. The Incan sun god Inti is honored at the Inti Raymi festival, which takes place in the Andean regions of South America and coincides with the winter solstice in the Southern Hemisphere. The festival places an emphasis on the return of the sun's power and warmth.

Festivals Celebrate the Harvest:
The purpose of harvest festivals is to give thanks to God for a prosperous harvest and to enjoy the bountiful gifts that nature has bestowed upon us. One major example is the Thanksgiving holiday, which is celebrated in the United States of America and Canada. This holiday is known for its traditions include feasting, getting together with family, and expressing thanks. The conclusion of the winter solstice and the beginning of the harvest season are both commemorated by the festival known as Pongal in South India. This event pays homage to the sun god Surya and is celebrated with great passion.

Celebrations of the Autumnal Equinox:
The autumn equinox is a moment of equilibrium and transition since during this time there are equal amounts of sunshine and darkness. The Chinese Mid-Autumn Festival, also known as the Moon Festival, is celebrated with mooncakes, lanterns, and family reunions to symbolize the value of familial togetherness and the end of the harvest season. In Korea, the Chuseok holiday is a time for paying respect to ancestors, partaking in the exchange of traditional dishes, and commemorating the arrival of fall.

Celebrations of the Winter Solstice:
Festivals held around the time of the winter solstice celebrate the longest night of the year as well as the start of the slow return of daylight. In Northern Europe, the Yule holiday is celebrated with a feast, the adornment of evergreen trees, and the burning of candles to represent hope and light in the midst of darkness. These traditions are inherited from ancient Germanic customs and date back thousands of years. The Dongzhi Festival in China places an emphasis on maintaining a healthy balance between yin and yang. This festival is observed by the consumption of tangyuan, which are glutinous rice balls that symbolize the coming together of a family.

3. **Cultural Customs and Ceremonies Involved in Occasions Celebrated Throughout the Year**

Traditions Regarding Food Preparation and Consumption:
Seasonal celebrations are frequently accompanied by lavish feasts and long-standing culinary customs that put the spotlight on regional fare, time-honored delicacies, and treasured family recipes. For instance, the Thanksgiving meal in the United States is defined by roasted turkey, cranberry sauce, pumpkin pie, and other seasonal delights that reflect abundance and gratitude. Another example is the Christmas dinner in Europe, which is distinguished by Christmas pudding.

Performing Arts Including Dance and Music:
Festivals are brought to life with performances of traditional dance and musical recitals that reflect the artistic expressions and cultural heritage of the town. Agricultural activities, historical events, and seasonal shifts are frequently the subjects of the narratives conveyed by these performances. One example of a traditional springtime rite is the Maypole dance, which is performed in Europe. This dance is meant to represent fertility as well as the awakening of nature.

Offerings and Expressions of Gratitude in Rituals:
Many of the celebrations that take place during specific times of the year include rituals that entail expressing thanks, making offerings, and praying in order to seek blessings for a prosperous time of year. As a symbol of reciprocity and reverence for the natural world, these rites may involve the offering of fruits, grains, flowers, and incense to the gods or spirits.

Arts and Crafts: Decorative Arts and Crafts
Celebrations serve as a source of motivation for the production of works of ornamental art and craft, which are then used to embellish private residences, public areas, and ceremonial sites. The community's cultural aesthetics and artistic sensibilities are often reflected in these artistic manifestations through the use of seasonal motifs, brilliant colors, and traditional designs.

Processions and Parades for Ceremonial Occasions:
Many of the annual celebrations of the changing seasons include ceremonial processions, parades, and community meetings that call for the involvement of the local populace as well as religious and cultural organizations. During these processions, sacred items, effigies, or other symbolic representations of deities and historical characters may be displayed. This helps to build a sense of collective pride and communal identity among the participants.

4. **The Religious and Symbolic Importance of Observing the Various Annual Festivals**

There is both Light and Darkness:
There are a number of festivals that occur at the same time as the solstices or the equinoxes, and they emphasize the difference between light and darkness. Light is a symbol of hope, knowledge, and the triumph of good over evil. Candles, lanterns, and bonfires are all common ways that light is used to symbolize this concept. On the other hand, darkness is representative of ignorance, stagnation, and the requirement for one to have a spiritual awakening.

The Biological Clock:
The cycles of life, death, and rebirth that are intrinsic to the natural world are reflected in the seasonal celebrations that take place all throughout the world. The recurring patterns that are observed in nature, such as the passage of time and the development and decomposition of living things, can be interpreted as metaphors for the human experience.

Coexistence in Peace with Nature:
A significant number of the rites performed during seasonal celebrations highlight humanity's
link with nature as well as the necessity of maintaining ecological balance. People strive to reestablish harmony and balance with the natural world through the recitation of prayers, performance of rituals, and celebration of the changing of the seasons.

The principles of Gratitude and Reciprocity:
The expressions of gratitude and the spirit of reciprocity play an important role in the celebrations that take place throughout the year. These celebrations provide chances to acknowledge the treasures that have been bestowed onto the land, to express gratitude, and to acknowledge the responsibility that comes with taking care of the environment.

Respect for the Past and Obligation to Ancestors:
Ancestors, historical figures, and cultural heroes are frequently honored throughout the various celebrations that take place throughout the year. These rites serve the purpose of honoring the heritage of those who came before, taking strength and wisdom from the collective memory of a culture as well as the historical narratives of the past.

Components of Symbolism:
There is a wealth of metaphorical meaning packed into various symbols, such as the maypole, the harvest cornucopia, the Yule log, and the colorful rangoli decorations. They are symbolic of the perpetual rebirth of life, the bountiful nature of the soil, and the inextricable bond that exists between all forms of life.

5. **Contemporary Expressions of Seasonal Festivals and the Development of Their Origins**

Integration of Different Cultures and Diversity:
In a world that is becoming more interconnected, seasonal celebrations frequently include aspects from a variety of cultures, which results in the creation of one-of-a-kind fusion festivals that honor diversity. These gatherings encourage interaction and understanding amongst people of different cultures.

Respect for the Environment and Long-Term Sustainability:
A significant number of today's festivals place a significant amount of importance on eco-friendliness and environmental consciousness. Efforts are undertaken to lessen the amount of waste produced, lessen the influence that celebrations have on the surrounding environment, and educate attendees on the need of ecological preservation.

Celebrations that are Digital and Virtual:
The advancement of technology has led to the creation of digital and virtual versions of traditional celebrations during holiday seasons. Live-streamed events, virtual tours of cultural exhibits, and online community gatherings are all becoming more prevalent, enabling participants to attend from all over the world.

Celebrations that Include People of Different Religions and Faiths:
There is a growing movement toward interfaith and interdenominational celebrations of seasonal festivals in communities that are culturally and religiously diverse. These gatherings encourage religious tolerance and cooperation by bringing together people of all religions with the purpose of celebrating shared ideals.

Accessibility and inclusiveness both:
The community as a whole is invited to participate in the seasonal festivities that are held, and every effort is made to make sure that everyone may participate. These efforts might include making accommodations for people who have physical or mental impairments, making translated information available, and cultivating welcoming environments for people who come from a variety of backgrounds.

Throughout the millennia, annual festivals have been an essential component of the spirituality and culture of the human race. They serve as evidence of the unbreakable bond that exists between people and the natural world, and they lend support to the repetitive patterns of birth, aging, and death in the natural world. These festivities have profound roots in the cultural heritage, religious beliefs, and community traditions of their communities. They offer opportunity for expressions of appreciation, introspection, and rejuvenation.

Seasonal festivals continue to be a source of cultural enrichment, spiritual nutrition, and community cohesion in spite of the ongoing change and evolution that is taking place in the world. They serve as an everlasting reminder of the interconnection of all living things and the necessity of living in harmony with the land. The continuing significance of seasonal festivals acts as a reminder of our connectedness to one another as human beings and of the obligation we have to take care of the world that we live in at a time when globalization and technological progress are accelerating at an ever-increasing rate.

4.1 Festivals tied to the changing seasons (e.g., Spring and Autumn Equinox, Solstices)

The cultural, spiritual, and historical significance of festivals that coincide with the changing of the seasons, such as the Spring and Autumn Equinoxes and the Summer and Winter Solstices, dates back a very long time in many different communities all over the world. These astronomical occurrences indicate significant turning points in the course of the Earth's yearly voyage around the sun, and they serve as harbingers of the changing of the seasons. The veneration that various cultures have for nature, agricultural activities, and cosmic rhythms is reflected in the celebrations that are related with astronomical events. These celebrations have deep roots in the cultural legacy of various communities. This investigation dives deeper into the colorful tapestry of celebrations that are connected to the changing of the seasons, shedding light on the symbolic meanings, historical backgrounds, and modern manifestations of these events.

1. **The Spring Equinox: A Time to Celebrate New Beginnings and the Return of Spring**
   Nowruz, often known as the Persian New Year:
   The Persian holiday of Nowruz, whose name literally translates to "new day," is celebrated in conjunction with the vernal equinox. It is a holiday that is celebrated in the country of Iran as well as among communities of Persian heritage all over the world. Nowruz is the first day of the Persian New Year and marks the beginning of spring. This holiday celebrates the rebirth of nature as well as the victory of light over darkness. The Haft-Seen table, which is decorated with seven symbolic items representing rejuvenation, abundance, and good fortune, is what distinguishes the festival from other similar celebrations.

(Ostara, or the Wiccan Spring Festival)
The modern Pagan celebration of Ostara takes place around the time of the Spring Equinox, which is seen as a period when light and darkness are in equal parts. The celebration takes its name from the Germanic goddess Eostre, with whom it is associated, and Easter is celebrated in her honor. The celebration of Ostara places an emphasis on fertility, growth, and the revival of life in the natural world. Egg decoration, the planting of seeds, and paying homage to the interdependence of all living things are common activities associated with the Ostara holiday.

Holi, also known as the Festival of Colors:
Holi is a holiday that is celebrated by Hindus in India and other parts of South Asia, and it normally takes place around the time of the Spring Equinox. It is called as the "Festival of Colors," and it is distinguished by the joyful throwing of colored powders and water. This activity is meant to symbolize the triumph of good over evil as well as the approach of spring.

The festival of Holi is a time for bringing people together, forgiving one another, and celebrating new beginnings.

2. **The Summer Solstice: Embracing Light and Abundance in the Midsummer Season**

The Scandinavian and Baltic countries celebrate the midsummer holiday as follows:
The traditional celebration of Midsummer takes place at the same time as the Summer Solstice and is observed in countries located in Northern Europe and the Baltic region. It is a time for merriment, bonfires, and outdoor celebrations, which stand as a symbol of the peak of summer and the abundant harvest that is still to come. Traditional folk dances, the adornment of maypoles, and the meeting of communities for communal feasting and merrymaking are typically part of the activities that take place during midsummer celebrations.

The Inca Festival of the Sun is known as Inti Raymi.
The ancient Incan holiday of Inti Raymi, which is still observed in some regions of South America, is a commemoration of the sun god Inti and takes place at the same time as the Winter Solstice in the Southern Hemisphere. It is a time for requesting blessings for a successful harvest season and expressing gratitude for the life-giving energy provided by the sun. The festival of Inti Raymi is characterized by ornate rituals, vibrant processions, and the presentation of offerings to the sun deity. These activities highlight the interdependence of humankind and the natural world.

The Wiccan holiday known as Litha is:
The modern Wiccan festival known as Litha is a celebration of the Summer Solstice as a time of plenty, vigor, and the full blossoming of nature. Litha takes place on the longest day of the year. This festival is a cheerful celebration

of the sun's strength and the life-giving energy that it provides. The lighting of bonfires, the harvesting of medicinal herbs, and the staging of ceremonies to commemorate the fertility of the soil and the interrelated web of life are common components of the liturgical practices that take place during Litha.

3. **The Autumn Equinox: Paying Respect to the Harvest and Achieving Balance**

    (The Mabon Festival Celebrates):

    Mabon is a contemporary Pagan celebration that takes place around the time of the Autumn Equinox and is meant to be an expression of gratitude for the many gifts that the earth and the crop have bestowed upon humanity. It is a time for giving thanks for the blessings bestowed upon us by nature and for making preparations for the colder months that are to follow.

    The creation of harvest-themed altars is a common component of Mabon rituals, as is the exchange of seasonal delicacies and the performance of rites that commemorate the cyclical essence of life as well as the interconnectivity of all living things.

    Chuseok, also known as the Korean Harvest Festival:

    An important Korean harvest festival known as Chuseok is held around the time of the equinox in autumn. It is a time for offering thanks for the harvest of the previous year, honoring the spirits of the land, and paying homage to the ancestors who formerly lived on it. Chuseok is distinguished by the performance of ancestor rites, the cooking of traditional dishes such as songpyeon (rice cakes), and the gathering of the community to participate in folk games and traditional dances.

    The Traditional Western Festival known as "Harvest Home":

    A traditional celebration in the Western tradition, "Harvest Home" is celebrated in a variety of different ways all over Europe and North America. Communities join together at this time of year to celebrate the end of a fruitful harvest season and to express gratitude for the many blessings bestowed upon them by the earth. Home harvest festivals typically entail the decorating of houses and churches with seasonal food, the sharing of meals among participants, and the singing of harvest songs that represent the themes of thankfulness and the sense of community.

4. **The Winter Solstice: Embracing Darkness and the Coming of the New Year**

    Yule is a festival celebrated by Germanic and Norse peoples:

    Traditional Germanic and Norse peoples observe the Winter Solstice as a time to celebrate rebirth, the return of the sun, and the triumph of light. Yule is a holiday that honors the Winter Solstice. It is distinguished by the adornment of Yule trees, the lighting of Yule logs, and the exchanging of gifts in order to signify the spirit of giving and the sense of community that is associated with the holiday. The winter holiday of Yule places an emphasis on topics such as hope, renewal, and the interconnection of all living species.

The Dongzhi Festival, also known as the Chinese Winter Solstice, is when:
The Dongzhi Festival, which is celebrated in China as well as in other East Asian countries, takes place around the same time as the Winter Solstice. It places an emphasis on the balance between yin and yang, and it represents the turning point from the darkest days of the year to the slow return of light. Traditional delicacies, such as tangyuan (glutinous rice balls), which symbolize unity and family togetherness, are prepared in groups by families and then enjoyed by members of those families.

The Ancient Roman Festival Known as Saturnalia
The ancient Roman celebration known as Saturnalia took place around the time of the Winter Solstice and featured festivities such as feasting, drinking, and the reversal of traditional gender roles. During Saturnalia, people temporarily disregarded the conventions of social interaction in order to participate in communal celebrations, the exchange of gifts, and gestures of kindness toward one another. The festival emphasized the importance of joy, freedom, and the acknowledgement of the repetitive patterns that are inherent in life.

5. **Contemporary Expressions and Their Influence on the World**

Intercultural Communication and Compatibility:
Seasonal celebrations have evolved into occasions for intercultural dialogue and interaction as a result of today's rapid pace of globalization. Communities all around the world are increasingly embracing the customs and holidays of other ethnic groups, which has resulted in an increase in the number of multicultural festivities that aim to promote intercultural understanding.

Consciousness of the Environment and Long-Term Sustainability:
Many modern celebrations of the changing seasons place a significant amount of focus on being environmentally conscious and sustainable. Efforts are taken to lessen the amount of waste produced, lessen the influence that celebrations have on the surrounding environment, and educate participants on the need of ecological preservation and responsible behavior.

Celebrations that are Digital and Virtual:
The advancement of technology has led to the creation of digital and virtual versions of traditional celebrations during holiday seasons. Live-streamed events, virtual tours of cultural exhibits, and online community gatherings are all becoming more prevalent, enabling participants to attend from all over the world.

Celebrations that Include People of Different Religions and Faiths:
There is a growing movement toward interfaith and interdenominational celebrations of seasonal festivals in communities that are culturally and religiously diverse. These gatherings encourage religious tolerance and cooperation by bringing together people of all religions with the purpose of celebrating shared ideals.

Accessibility and inclusiveness both:
The community as a whole is invited to participate in the seasonal festivities that are held, and every effort is made to make sure that everyone may participate.

These efforts might include making accommodations for people who have physical or mental impairments, making translated information available, and cultivating welcoming environments for people who come from a variety of backgrounds.

The perpetual celebration by humankind of life, nature, and the order of the cosmos can be seen in the form of seasonal festivals that are related to the changing of the seasons. These celebrations offer chances for cultural growth, spiritual nutrition, and the strengthening of community bonds. They serve as ever-present reminders of the interdependence of all living things, the cyclical cycles of existence, and the necessity of living in harmony with the environment.

Seasonal celebrations continue to be important in terms of both cultural identity and spiritual importance, despite the ongoing transformation and development of the world. They are a demonstration of our common humanity as well as our collective responsibility to take care of the planet that we have chosen to call home. These festivals, whether they are honored in their more ancient or more modern versions, serve as celebrations of life, light, and the natural order that persists through the ages.

4.2 Agricultural festivals and the celebration of nature

Agricultural festivals are a celebration of the bountiful earth, an acknowledgment of the important role that farming plays in maintaining human life, and a testimony to the fundamental link that exists between humans and the natural world. These celebrations celebrate major milestones in the agricultural calendar, such as planting, harvesting, and the change of the seasons. These celebrations have their roots in ancient agricultural techniques and cultural traditions. They serve as a manner of expressing thanks for the products of the land, of cultivating community relationships, and of restoring one's spiritual connection to the natural environment. This investigation dives deeper into the diverse fabric of agricultural celebrations, shedding insight on their historical origins, cultural import, and modern manifestations.

1. **The Importance of Fairs and Festivals Dedicated to Agriculture**
   Voici Some Ways to Say Thank You:
   Celebrations of agriculture are occasions for expressing appreciation for the bountiful nature of the land and the results of agricultural labor. These ceremonies recognize the significant contribution that agriculture makes to the maintenance of life and the provision of nourishment.
   Integration into the Community:
   Participation in group activities, communal feasts, and exchange of experiences are common features of these celebrations. They generate a sense of belonging, cooperation, and a common purpose within communities, bringing such communities together.

FESTIVALS AND CELEBRATIONS

Taking Care of Our Cultural Heritage:
Agricultural celebrations are known for being rich in customs, rites, and practices that have been handed down from generation to generation. They contribute to the maintenance of a connection with the past and the preservation of cultural heritage.

Connection to the Spiritual World:
A great number of agricultural celebrations contain some sort of religious or spiritual meaning. They provide an opportunity for religious introspection and purification, as well as acts of devotion, strengthening the connection that exists between humankind and the divine.

The Natural World's Rhythms:
These celebrations are significant in the agricultural calendar because they coincide with important events such as planting, harvesting, and the change of seasons. They serve as a reminder of the cyclical patterns that occur in the natural world and the significance of maintaining a lifestyle that is in harmony with nature.

2. **Notable Agricultural Celebrations from Around the World**
Pongal (the Indian holiday)
Pongal is a harvest festival that is observed in Tamil Nadu, which is located in the southern region of India. It is a celebration of the successful harvest of rice and is distinguished by the production of a unique dish known as Pongal, which is comprised of newly harvested rice, lentils, and jaggery. The event features a number of different rites and activities, including the adornment of cattle, and places an emphasis on expressing appreciation to the sun god, Surya.

Thanksgiving is a holiday celebrated in the United States and Canada:
Thanksgiving is a harvest holiday that is observed in North America on the fourth Thursday of November in the United States while Canada celebrates Thanksgiving on the second Monday of October. It celebrates the prosperous harvest that the early immigrants shared with the Native American nations and honors their cooperation with those people. Turkey, stuffing, cranberry sauce, and pumpkin pie are traditional components of the Thanksgiving feast, which is traditionally cooked and served by family and friends.

(Songkran) in Thailand:
The Thai New Year event is called Songkran, and it is celebrated with the ritual of spraying water in order to signify purification and the washing away of the problems that were experienced in the previous year. The celebration includes activities such as water fights, trips to temples, and the ritual of pouring scented water over Buddha images and the hands of elderly people in order to seek blessings and show respect for them.

Festival of the Cherry Blossoms in Japan:
Hanami is the Japanese word for the Cherry Blossom Festival, which is held

annually in Japan to commemorate the coming of spring and the blossoming of cherry trees, also known as sakura. People congregate in parks and gardens to observe the blossoms, and while they are there they frequently enjoy picnics and traditional Japanese performances. The fleeting beauty of life is a theme that is highlighted throughout the event.

The Gawai Dayak people are native to both Malaysia and Indonesia:
The Dayak people of Malaysia and Indonesia get together to celebrate the harvest with a holiday known as Gawai Dayak. This event celebrates the harvesting of rice as well as the planting of new padi, or rice, seeds. Traditional songs and dances, as well as feasts and rites, are performed at this festival to show appreciation for the bountiful harvest and to invoke favors for the years to come.

3. **Cultural Customs and Ceremonies Participated In Agricultural Celebrations**

   Traditions Regarding Food Preparation and Consumption:
   Agricultural celebrations frequently include feasts that highlight traditional recipes that are prepared using the most recently gathered crops. These culinary customs emphasize the use of regional ingredients and family recipes as a means of expressing gratitude for the bounties bestowed by the earth.

   Performing Arts Including Dance and Music:
   Festivals are brought to life with performances of traditional dance and musical recitals that reflect the artistic expressions and cultural heritage of the town. During these performances, narratives about planting, harvesting, and the shifting of the seasons are frequently conveyed.

   Offerings and Expressions of Gratitude in Rituals:
   Many celebrations of agriculture include rites of thankfulness, in which participants make offerings and pray to express their appreciation for the goods bestowed by the land and to request blessings for a prosperous growing season. During these ceremonies, the participants would present the gods or spirits with gifts like as fruits, grains, flowers, or incense.

   Arts and Crafts: Decorative Arts and Crafts:
   Celebrations serve as a source of motivation for the production of works of ornamental art and craft, which are then used to embellish private residences, public areas, and ceremonial sites. The community's cultural aesthetics and artistic sensibilities are often reflected in these artistic manifestations through the use of seasonal motifs, brilliant colors, and traditional designs.

   Processions and Parades for Ceremonial Occasions:
   Participation by local people, farmers, and cultural groups is required for many of the ceremonial processions, parades, and community gatherings that are a part of agricultural festivals. The public display of agricultural goods, the donning of traditional garb, and the making of symbolic images of deities or historical people are all possible components of these processions.

4. **The Meaning of Agricultural Celebrations from a Religious and Symbolic Perspective**

The Fruits of Your Labor and Abundance:
The harvesting of crops is a symbolic act that represents plenty, provision, and the satiation of human requirements. Agricultural festivals bring attention to the significance of acknowledging and enjoying the richness that the earth provides.

Rejuvenation and expansion:
Planting and sowing are acts of ritualization that are related with the regeneration and expansion of plant life. They represent the repetitive patterns that are inherent to existence as well as the opportunity for fresh starts.

Harmony with the Natural World:
Many agricultural celebrations place an emphasis on the interdependence of humans and their natural environments. They highlight the role of humans as stewards of the Earth, whose responsibility it is to care for and preserve the natural world around them.

Cycles of the Seasons:
The passage of time through the seasons is typically a major focus of agricultural celebrations.
These celebrations serve as important reminders of the recurring patterns found in nature and the significance of attempting to live in concordance with the natural cycles of the Earth.

The principles of Gratitude and Reciprocity:
Gratitude and giving back to those who have helped are typically at the heart of agricultural celebrations. They consist of expressing gratitude for the bountiful harvest and recognizing the importance of maintaining the health of the land in order to ensure continued prosperity.

5. **Modern Expressions of Agricultural Celebrations and Their Historical Developments**

Responsible management of the environment:
Many of today's agricultural celebrations include an emphasis on responsible land care and environmentally conscious agriculture methods. They educate people on the significance of environmentally responsible farming practices and the protection of natural resources.

A Merging of Cuisines:
Fusion cuisine is frequently included during agricultural festivals. This style of cooking infuses traditional meals with flavors from around the world and contemporary touches. These advancements are a reflection of the multiethnic makeup of today's cultures.

Celebrations that are Digital and Virtual:

The advancement of technology has led to the creation of digital and virtual versions of the celebrations that are traditionally held during agricultural festivals. Live-streamed events, online forums, and digital storytelling have become more prevalent, making it possible for anyone from all over the world to participate.

Movements From the Farm to the Table:

The farm-to-table movement, which encourages the consumption of food that is obtained locally and produced in an environmentally responsible manner, is closely associated with a number of agricultural festivals. The relationship that exists between consumers and farmers is honored during these events, which also highlight the significance of sustaining local agricultural practices.

Education and Community Engagement:

The educational components that are frequently included in modern agricultural festivals are intended to heighten attendees' awareness of farming techniques, sustainability, and the difficulties that are currently affecting the agricultural business. They provide opportunity for visitors to learn about the production of food and the improvements in agricultural practices.

The enduring connection that exists between humans and the natural world is celebrated through the practice of holding agricultural festivals. They serve as a celebration of the bountiful nature, a reminder of the cyclical cycles of life, and a manner of expressing thanks for the blessings that the earth has bestowed upon humanity. These celebrations help to maintain cultural traditions, strengthen communal ties, and revitalize people's spiritual connection to the land.

Agricultural festivals continue to be a source of cultural enrichment, agricultural education, and community bonding in spite of the ongoing change and development that is occurring in the world. They are a timeless celebration of life, the natural world, and the unbreakable bond that exists between humanity and the planet they call home. The significance of agricultural festivals is that they serve as a reminder of our interconnectedness with the land and our shared obligation to take care of the world in an era in which environmental issues are mounting and agricultural innovations are being developed at a faster rate.

4.3 How seasonal festivals vary by region and climate

The profound link that exists between human civilizations and the natural environment is reflected in the seasonal celebrations that take place throughout the year. They mark key transitions in the natural world, agricultural cycles, and the order of the cosmos, and they are honored all throughout the world. On the other hand, the manner in which these celebrations are carried out can change drastically from one geographic location and environment to another. This variety is a reflection of the distinctive cultural and environmental circumstances present in various locations. During this investigation, we will look into the ways in which seasonal celebrations can vary from area to region and climate to climate, with a focus on the influences that geography, climate, and local customs have.

1. **The Effects of Geography and Climate on the Occurrence of Seasonal Festivals**
   Position on the Earth's Surface:
   A region's physical location, notably its latitude and proximity to the equator, plays a vital part in determining the kinds of seasonal celebrations that can be held there. For instance, there is not much of a change in the amount of daylight available throughout the year in areas that are closer to the equator.
   In contrast, regions that are located at higher latitudes, such as northern Europe, have more significant seasonal shifts. As a consequence of this, festivals that take place during the Winter Solstice place great emphasis on the return of light.
   Patterns of the Climate:
   The way in which people celebrate the changing of the seasons is profoundly influenced by climate, regardless of whether it is tropical, temperate, dry, or arctic. In tropical areas, where the seasons are not as clearly distinguished from one another, festivals may center on agricultural cycles and rainfall. Celebrations in dry areas frequently center on the remembrance of past droughts and the offering of prayers for favorable weather. Festivals may be held to commemorate the dramatic changes in light and darkness that occur in polar locations.
   Methods Employed in Agriculture:
   A region's seasonal celebrations are often heavily influenced by the kinds of crops that are cultivated there as well as the agricultural methods that are used. For instance, localities that are home to a large number of vineyards could celebrate the grape harvest with a festival, but districts that are known for their rice production might hold celebrations to honor both the planting and harvesting of rice. Agricultural celebrations are frequently connected to the particular requirements and cycles of the region's farming operations.
   Considerations Based on Past Events and Cultures:
   The manner in which a place celebrates the changing of the seasons is influenced not just by its history but also by its culture. For instance, celebrations that are thought to have originated in indigenous cultures may center on the customs and beliefs of the communities to which they are native. In contrast, areas that are influenced by a wide variety of cultures are more likely to include aspects of a variety of traditions into their festivities.
2. **Holidays Celebrated Throughout the Year in Various Climate Zones**
   Regions of the Tropics:
   There is less of a distinction between the seasons in tropical locations that are located close to the equator, such as certain portions of Africa, Southeast Asia, and Central America. The climate in these places is marked by high temperatures and substantial rainfall. Seasonal celebrations are frequently centered on the rainy and dry seasons. These festivals may commemorate the beginning of the rainy season with rituals intended to bring about rain, or they may celebrate

the end of the rainy season when crops become mature. The Great Migration in East Africa is one example of a festival that is celebrated as a natural spectacle, and in some instances, the timing of festivals might coincide with the movement of wildlife.

Regions of a Temperate Climate:
Festivals frequently serve as a reflection of the shifts in weather and the natural cycles that occur in locations that are characterized by distinct seasons. Midsummer festivals, for instance, are held in northern Europe to commemorate the extended daylight hours of summer. These festivals include customs such as maypole dance and the burning of bonfires. The autumnal equinox is celebrated with a variety of celebrations around the world, one of the most well-known of which is Oktoberfest, held annually in Munich, Germany, and centered on the enjoyment of beer and the nation's abundant agricultural produce.

Dry and Desert Areas:
In areas of the world that receive little rainfall, celebrations are frequently centered on prayers for water and the protection of this valuable resource. One such event is the Pushkar Camel Fair, which takes place in Rajasthan, India, and combines the buying and selling of livestock with religious rites near a holy lake. It is a time for people to join together in their communities, engage in some commerce, and pray for some much-needed rain.

Arctic and Antarctica:
The dramatic shifts in daylight and darkness that occur throughout the year in polar locations have a tremendous impact on the celebrations that take place during each season. For instance, the Winter Solstice, which occurs in areas such as the Arctic Circle, is characterized by the year's longest night. Celebrations such as the Sami National Day honor indigenous peoples and their ability to thrive despite living in tough environments. On the other hand, the Midnight Sun rituals that take place in the same places mark the beginning of the season of continual daylight following several months of nighttime.

3. **Adaptations to the Local Environment and Cultural Traditions**
The Day of the Dead is celebrated in Mexico:
The Day of the Dead, also known as Dia de los Muertos, is a holiday that is celebrated in Mexico as well as other Latin American countries. The event takes place during the end of October and the beginning of November, which coincides with the transition from fall to winter. The celebration depicts a cultural perspective on death and the afterlife, combining elements of Catholicism with indigenous practices and customs. Families will construct ornate memorial altars in order to pay respects to departed loved ones, and lively parades will be held in order to celebrate both life and death.

Known as Loi Krathong in Thailand:
The month of November sees the celebration of the Thai holiday known as Loi

Krathong.

It occurs at the same time as the conclusion of the rainy season, during which the rivers are swollen and moving quickly. People pay tribute to the goddess of the water by casting little adorned floats called krathongs into the water as a symbol of letting go of their problems. The climate of Thailand, its changing seasons, and the country's veneration for water are all reflected in the celebration.

Festival of the Moon in the Autumn (China):

The festival of the mid-autumn, which is observed not only in China but also in other East Asian nations, takes place in either September or October. It falls during the time of year when the moon is at its most full and coincides with the harvest season. People get together with their families to gaze at the moon, set off lanterns, and eat mooncakes. This celebration celebrates China's rich agricultural history and places an emphasis on getting together with extended family.

Karneval is celebrated in Germany:

Before the beginning of Lent, the joyful season known as Karneval is observed in countries such as Germany and other areas of Europe. This time of year falls in either the late winter or the early spring. It features colorful processions, ornate costumes, and social merriment among participants. Traditions associated with Karneval vary from region to region and might be affected by the local climate. For example, coastal areas frequently incorporate maritime motifs, whilst alpine areas may celebrate by participating in winter sports.

Pahiyas Festival is celebrated in the Philippines:

The Philippines, more especially the town of Lucban in the province of Quezon, is the location where the Pahiyas Festival is held. May is the month when it takes place, and it marks the beginning of the rainy season, which is when crops are planted. Rice, fruits, and vegetables are just some of the items that are displayed in brightly colored arrangements inside and outside of homes. The weather patterns and agricultural rhythms of the area are reflected in the festival.

4. **Present-Day Expressions and the Influence of Globalization**

Exchange of Cultures: Seasonal festivals are frequently used as meeting places for people of different cultures. Communities are increasingly embracing the customs and holidays of other regions, which has led to the rise of multicultural and intercultural festivities that aim to foster better understanding between people of diverse backgrounds.

Environmental Consciousness A large number of today's festivals integrate components relating to environmental consciousness and sustainable living. They bring attention to the critical importance of environmentally responsible activities, conservation, and the protection of natural resources.

Celebrations in the Digital Age Innovations in information technology have made it possible to hold celebrations of various holidays in the digital realm. People are able to participate from any location on the planet thanks to live-streamed events, virtual cultural displays, and online community gatherings, which eliminates the need for restrictions based on geography or climate.

Interfaith and Interdenominational Celebrations: There is a growing trend of interfaith and interdenominational celebrations of seasonal festivals in many countries. These festivities are becoming more common. These gatherings encourage religious tolerance and cooperation by bringing together people of all religions with the purpose of celebrating shared ideals.

The rich cultural tapestry of humanity and its symbiotic interaction with the natural world are brought to life through the celebration of the changing seasons. They are a reflection of the regional geography, climate, and local customs, which results in the creation of one-of-a-kind festivities that bring people together in the spirit of appreciation, renewal, and interconnectedness. Seasonal celebrations continue to be a way for people all around the world to honor the enduring connection that exists between humans and the natural world, despite the ongoing transformations in both the world and its cultures. They serve as a reminder of our collective obligation to take care of the Earth and to recognize the beauty that can be found in our many different cultures around the world.

Chapter 5

Cultural Festivals

Festivals of culture are undeniably lively representations of a society's core ideals, long-standing customs, and inherited traditions. They are extremely important in the maintenance of cultural identity, the promotion of community cohesion, and the transmission of traditions and rituals from one generation to the next. Festivals of culture, which are often celebrated with intensity and excitement, are an essential component of human civilization and contribute to the rich tapestry that is worldwide cultural diversity. This investigation will dig into the many facets of cultural celebrations, shedding light on their historical beginnings, symbolic meanings, societal implications, and contemporary expressions.

1. **The Historical Roots of Different Cultural Celebrations**
   Ancient Rituals and Their Meanings:
   Ancient peoples all across the world participated in a vast variety of ceremonial ceremonies and rituals, many of which have now developed into modern cultural celebrations. The spiritual and community features of early human cultures were reflected in the rituals that were typically related with agricultural fertility, astronomical events, and rites of passage.
   Observances Related to Religion:
   Easter, Diwali, Eid al-Fitr, and Hanukkah are some examples of religious holidays that have historical beginnings that are firmly rooted in the religious texts, traditions, and practices of different faiths. Other examples include Hanukkah. These celebrations frequently pay homage to pivotal moments in the annals of religious history and serve as an opportunity to recommit oneself to one's religious beliefs, to cultivate spiritual development, and to forge stronger ties with one's community.
   Celebrations Throughout the Year:
   Cultural celebrations that coincide with the changing of the seasons, such as

the Spring Equinox, Harvest Festivals, and Winter Solstice, can trace their roots back to the early agricultural communities of the world. These celebrations were characterized by rituals, feasts, and community get-togethers that praised the riches of nature and recognized the reoccurring patterns that can be found in the natural world.

The Commemoration of Historical Events:
Historical commemorations of key events, such as triumphs in battles, the building of cities, and the establishment of governmental institutions, were the roots of many cultural celebrations. These celebrations were distinguished by the presence of processions, reenactments, and symbolic gestures, all of which served to bolster a feeling of national identity as well as a common collective memory.

2. **The Symbolic Significance of the Rituals Involved in Cultural Celebrations**
   Processions for Ceremonial Purposes:
   At cultural celebrations, there are frequently ornate ceremonial processions that feature people dressed in traditional garb, displaying cultural objects, and making symbolic representations of gods, historical individuals, or mythical occurrences. The purpose of these processions is to provide a visual spectacle that brings attention to the community's shared identity and the pride it has in its culture.

   Performances in the Traditional Style:
   Traditional performances at festivals, such as dance, music, theater, and storytelling, which encapsulate the cultural history and artistic expressions of a community, contribute significantly to the overall quality of the event. These performances frequently impart narratives of historical events, mythological tales, and moral lessons; they maintain a feeling of cultural continuity while also providing opportunities for artistic innovation.

   Prayers and Gifts of Symbolic Significance:
   Offerings of flowers, incense, and food are common components of many different types of cultural celebrations. These offerings may be made to deities, ancestors, or spirits. These sacrifices represent thankfulness, devotion, and the community's spiritual connection with the divine or other realms that are beyond our understanding.

   Arts and Crafts: Decorative Arts and Crafts
   Celebrations serve as a source of motivation for the production of works of ornamental art and craft, which are then used to embellish private residences, public areas, and ceremonial sites. Oftentimes, these artistic expressions will integrate traditional themes, colors, and designs in order to reflect the community's cultural aesthetics as well as the craftsmanship that exists within it.

   Traditions in the Kitchen:
   Festivals are celebrated with foods and culinary pleasures that have been passed

down through generations and that reflect the gastronomic heritage and flavors of the region. These culinary customs represent communal feasting, hospitality, and the celebration of shared cultural values as well as the culinary talent that goes along with them.

3. **The Effects That Cultural Festivals Have On Society**

   Preservation of Culture and Cultural Revitalization:
   Festivals of different cultures play an essential part in the process of rescuing and reviving behaviors, languages, and creative customs that are in risk of extinction. They act as catalysts for cultural revival, urging new generations to embrace their cultural history and participate in old rites and rituals. In this way, they contribute to the revitalization of culture.

   Development of the Economy in Relation to Tourism:
   Festivals of culture frequently pull in visitors from all over the world, which is beneficial to the expansion of both the local economy and the travel and tourism sector. Festivals provide opportunity for local artisans, small business owners, and local vendors to display and sell their wares, which in turn stimulates economic growth and the creation of new job possibilities.

   Participation in the Community and Maintaining Social Cohesion:
   Festivals encourage participation from the community, a sense of social cohesion, and a sense of belonging among the many different groups that make up a society. People are able to come together, celebrate their cultural values in common, and develop long-lasting friendships on the basis of mutual respect and understanding thanks to the platform that these events give.

   Exchange of cultures and an understanding of the world:
   Festivals of culture serve as a platform for communities to disseminate their customs, artistic
   expressions, and gastronomic delights to people from a variety of various origins, thereby fostering intercultural understanding and fostering cultural exchange. They develop a sense of mutual appreciation for the richness and variety of human civilizations, as well as facilitate conversations between different cultures.

   Education and Promotion of Cultural Activities:
   Festivals are educational platforms that promote cultural awareness, diversity, and cross-cultural understanding, and they do it in a way that brings people together.
   They provide chances for participatory learning, cultural workshops, and cultural demonstrations, all of which contribute to an increase in public knowledge of and respect for a variety of cultural customs and practices.

4. **Modern-Day Reinterpretations of Traditional Cultural Celebrations**

Artistic Exhibits and Installations that Push the Boundaries:

Innovative art installations, interactive exhibitions, and multimedia performances that combine technology, visual arts, and immersive experiences are frequently featured at contemporary cultural festivals. These artistic works invite engagement from the audience and reflect the junction of conventional and contemporary modes of artistic expression.

Festivals in the Digital and Virtual Realms:

The development of digital and virtual cultural festivals that are open to participation from people all over the world as well as accessibility has been made possible by recent advances in technology. People from all around the world may participate in cultural festivals in real time thanks to innovations such as virtual exhibitions, online performances, and interactive forums. These innovations are breaking down geographical borders and boosting global connectivity.

Respect for the Environment and Long-Term Sustainability:

Quite a few of today's cultural celebrations place a high level of importance on preserving the environment and raising people's awareness of environmental issues by fostering eco-friendly practices, campaigning for waste reduction, and encouraging responsible consumption. Workshops, seminars, and other community outreach programs that teach attendees about the significance of protecting natural resources and the environment are frequently incorporated into festival programming.

Collaborations across Disciplinary Boundaries:

Festivals of contemporary culture actively foster interdisciplinary cooperation across various creative fields, including the sciences, performing arts, and academia. These collaborations help to develop creative innovation, multidisciplinary research, and the examination of contemporary social issues, which in turn promotes a comprehensive awareness of cultural diversity and the challenges faced by society.

Engagement with the World's Cultures and Cultural Diplomacy:

Festivals of culture act as stages for cultural diplomacy and global involvement, making it easier for people from different cultures to communicate with one another and share their traditions.

They contribute to worldwide efforts to address common concerns and develop bridges of collaboration by fostering peace, mutual understanding, and the celebration of shared cultural values.

Festivals of culture are the vivid threads that are used to weave together the variegated fabric that human civilization is made of. They represent the historical beginnings, symbolic meanings, societal impacts, and modern manifestations of artistic expression and cultural legacy. Cultural festivals are held to celebrate diversity, to encourage unity, and to remind us of the richness of human cultures that continue to develop and evolve despite the fact that we live in a world that is always changing. In this day and age of increased globalization and internet connectivity, these celebrations continue to serve as a living tribute to the common history we all share as human beings, as well as to our collective obligation to protect and honor the splendor of cultural diversity.

5.1 An in-depth look at culturally specific celebrations (e.g., Chinese New Year, Carnaval, Holi)

Festivities that are distinctive to a culture are almost always firmly ingrained in the norms, beliefs, and practices of the society in which they are observed. This is true no matter where you go in the globe. These joyous gatherings serve as vivid expressions of cultural identity, historical legacies, and community bonds in their respective communities. The rituals, symbolism, and celebratory behaviors that make up a particular culture are woven together in a one-of-a-kind pattern throughout each and every festival. This investigation takes a comprehensive look at three festivals that are deeply ingrained in their respective cultures: the Chinese New Year, Carnaval, and Holi. The rich cultural heritage and diversity of the Chinese, Latin American, and Indian cultures are each represented by these celebrations, which offer a complete grasp of the historical significance, symbolic meanings, and contemporary expressions of that communities' respective traditions.

1. **The Celebration of Reunification and Rebirth That Is the Chinese New Year**

   Origins that are Steeped in History and Mythology:

   The traditions that make up the Chinese New Year can be traced back to long-forgotten agricultural rites and mythological beliefs. Legend has it that this celebration honors the myth of the Nian, a legendary beast who terrorized the people until they learned that it shied away from the color red and from loud noises. Because of this, it became customary to decorate the holiday with red decorations and to let off firecrackers during the celebration.

   Customs and practices that have been around for a long time:

   Traditional customs that are observed during the celebration of the Chinese New Year include getting together with one's family, paying respect to one's ancestors, exchanging red envelopes (hongbao) that contain money as an act of good fortune, and decorating one's home with red lanterns and other decorations that stand for wealth and contentment. In addition, there will be traditional lion and dragon dances performed at the celebration. These dances are meant to bring good fortune and fight off evil spirits.

   Symbolism and the Pleasures of Gastronomy:

   The Chinese New Year is celebrated with a wide range of delectable dishes as well as symbolic

   delicacies that are believed to convey positive connotations. Fish, dumplings, spring rolls, and sweet rice cakes are some of the special foods that are cooked to represent prosperity, happiness, and the fulfillment of desires for the next year.

   Expressions of the Present and Their Influence on the World:

The New Year of the Chinese calendar is celebrated not only in China but also in a number of other countries and regions throughout the world that have sizeable Chinese communities. The festival has evolved into a global cultural celebration that is characterized by parades, cultural performances, and festive marketplaces that highlight the arts, crafts, and culinary customs that are traditional to China. This helps to promote cross-cultural respect and understanding.

2. **The Festive Extravaganza That Is Latin American Culture During Carnaval Historical Origins and the Merging of Cultures:**

The European pre-Lenten traditions that were transferred to Latin America by Spanish and Portuguese invaders are the historical origins of the celebration known as Carnaval. Over the course of its history, it has developed into a dynamic event that is marked by brilliant costumes, masquerade balls, and exciting street performances. This celebration got its start as a vibrant combination of European, African, and indigenous cultural elements.

Parades, which feature dancing and music, also take place:

Carnaval is linked with rhythmic music, captivating dance rhythms, and spirit-filled street parades that highlight the rich cultural history of Latin American music and dance traditions, such as samba, salsa, and calypso. The event is known for its ornate floats, dancers in costume, and lively musical acts, all of which light up the streets and captivate crowds.

Traditions Regarding Dress Up and the Masquerade:

The lavish costumes and masquerade customs of Carnaval are one of the defining characteristics of the celebration, as they allow individuals to take on the persona of legendary figures, real-life historical figures, and cultural icons. The elaborate patterns, vivid colors, and symbolic motifs of the garments are reflective of the cultural diversity and artistic manifestations of the communities of Latin America.

Variations Across Regions and Joyous Occasions to Celebrate:

In each country of Latin America, the celebration of Carnaval takes on a shape that is distinctive to that country's culture and incorporates local elements such as folklore, music, and the performing arts. The festival brings together a variety of communities to celebrate the richness of their cultural backgrounds and to express their collective joy via the exchange of artistic expressions and joint celebrations.

3. **Holi, also known as the Festival of Colors, is Celebrated in India**

Legends and their Corresponding Mythological Significance:

The festival of Holi may be traced back to Hindu mythology, more specifically to the story of Prahlada and Holika. This story is significant because it illustrates the triumph of devotion and goodness over tyranny and evil. The festival also commemorates the heavenly love that existed between Lord Krishna and Radha, which lends a more sensual air to the overall mood of the celebration.

Practices Regarding Rituals and Festivities:
Bonfires are lit on the eve of the festival to represent the triumph of good over evil. This is one of the many rituals and festive practices that are performed during the Holi holiday. The next day is highlighted by the jubilant throwing of colored powders and water, singing, dancing, and the sharing of traditional sweets and delicacies with one another.

Unity of culture and harmony throughout society:
Holi is a traditional celebration that is meant to bring people together, as it transcends social barriers, promotes social harmony, and is open to everyone. People get together to celebrate the festival, to meet one another, and to create community links through the spirit of joy, forgiveness, and the sharing of festive treats. These activities take place in the context of the celebration of the festival.

Celebrations in the modern era and their influence on the world:
The festival of Holi has garnered attention from people all over the world and is now celebrated in a number of different countries, fostering cross-cultural communication and understanding. Holi festivals are held all over the world, and many of them contain the participation of individuals from a wide variety of cultural traditions. This serves to promote the principles of unity and diversity as well as the celebration of our shared humanity.

Celebrations that are distinctive to a culture, such as the Chinese New Year, Carnaval, and Holi, are excellent examples of the wealth, diversity, and vitality that characterize the cultural legacy of the world. These celebrations serve as windows into the beliefs, customs, and artistic expressions of other cultures, so promoting unity in variety and developing cross-cultural understanding. They transcend regional boundaries and cultivate a common appreciation for the exquisiteness of human culture. They exemplify the spirit of joy, unity, and communal peace. These events serve as timeless reminders of the lasting power of cultural traditions to unify people and celebrate the richness of the human experience at a time when the globe continues to embrace cultural variety and global interconnectedness.

5.2 Cultural festivals as windows into the customs, values, and art of a community

Festivals of a community's culture act as vivid windows into the heart and soul of that community, providing a one-of-a-kind and immersive look into the traditions, values, and artistry of that town. These festivals, which have been enriched by centuries of traditions, symbols, and customs, are powerful manifestations of the cultural identity of their participants. Whether it's the intricate designs of rangoli during Diwali or the vibrant dances of Brazil's Carnaval, cultural holidays offer a multi-sensory experience that enriches our awareness of diverse communities around the world. In Japan, tea ceremonies are known for their complexities, while Carnaval in Brazil is known for its lively dancing. In the course of this investigation, we will dig into the ways in which cultural festivals offer a profound prism through which to evaluate customs, values, and art, so improving our overall awareness of the global fabric.

1. **Traditions that Are Still Active in Daily Life**
   Rituals of Ceremonial Importance:
   Ceremonial rites that have been practiced in a certain way for many generations are frequently presented at cultural festivals. It's possible that historical traditions, religious tenets, or even agricultural customs are where these rituals got their start. For instance, during the Jewish holiday of Yom Kippur, participants are expected to abstain from food and pray in order to demonstrate their commitment to the practices of atonement and penitence.
   Rituals of Coming of Age:
   Rites of passage are an integral part of many different types of celebrations and represent significant life events such as birth, marriage, and death. The cultural values and beliefs linked with these key life events are brought to light via the performance of these rituals. The Indian holiday known as Raksha Bandhan, for instance, is a celebration of the link that exists between brothers and sisters and places an emphasis on the significance of love and protection.
   Dress in accordance with custom:
   Festivals frequently afford local communities the opportunity to display their traditional garb, an aspect of appearance that is imbued with profound cultural connotations. It's possible that these garments have elaborate stitching, colors, and patterns that convey a sense of individuality and belonging to the wearer. A prime example is the Hanbok, which originates in Korea and is known for its vivid colors and unique patterns.
   Decorations Carrying Symbolic Meaning:
   The decorations that are used at cultural festivities typically have significant meanings behind them. For instance, during the Mid-Autumn Festival in China, lanterns are used as a sign of unity and family reunion. On the other hand, during the Day of the Dead celebration in Mexico, ofrendas (altars) are decorated with marigold flowers to help lead souls back to their homes.
2. **Beliefs that are Bodily Expressed as Values**
   The importance of community and fellowship:
   Because of this conviction in the transformative potential of having a common experience, numerous cultural celebrations lay a significant amount of stress on the importance of community and coming together. This principle is exemplified by the Brazilian tradition of "saudade" during the celebration of Carnaval. Saudade refers to a yearning for the happiness and closeness that comes from shared experiences.
   Regard for the Natural World:

FESTIVALS AND CELEBRATIONS

Festivals frequently display values that are connected to the natural world and the environment. Participants in the Native American Sun Dance, for example, display their reverence for the natural world by abstaining from food and drink, dancing, and offering sacrifices to the sun as part of the rite.

Resistance to stress and fatigue:
At certain ethnic celebrations, values such as resiliency and perseverance are honored. The Hindu festival of Navaratri, which is characterized by nine nights of dance and prayer, is a celebration of the triumph of good over evil as well as the resilience to persevere through difficult times.

Aspects of Spirituality and Faith:
A significant number of celebrations incorporate a profoundly spiritual element, with the purpose of paying homage to deities or petitioning for divine favor. The Hindu holiday of Diwali, which is also known as the Festival of Lights, is a celebration of the triumph of light over darkness and knowledge over ignorance, and it is aligned with the principles of spirituality and enlightenment.

3. **Art as an Outlet for Creative Expression**

The arts of Music and Dance:
Festivals honoring a culture's heritage typically include performances of its distinctive music and dance, both of which are essential components. Expressions of creative innovation include the samba and bossa nova music of Brazil's Carnaval, the mesmerizing rhythms of African drumming during Mardi Gras in New Orleans, and the traditional kathak dance of India's Diwali.

Performing Arts:
The intricate patterns, paintings, and sculptures that are displayed at festivals frequently play a vital role in the festivities. Festivals serve as a canvas for the visual arts. The elaborate sand mandalas of Tibetan New Year, the hypnotic kolam patterns of Pongal in Tamil Nadu, and the bright murals of Mexico's Day of the Dead are all examples of the breadth of artistic expression.

Skill in handiwork:
Traditional arts and crafts are frequently displayed and demonstrated by highly trained artisans at festivals. For instance, the painstaking artistry of Japanese origami during Tanabata, the elaborate beadwork of Native American powwows, and the delicate embroidery of Hungarian folk costumes are all examples of the artistic skill that exists within these cultures.

Traditions in the Literary Arts:
Storytelling, poetry, and other forms of written rites frequently play an important role in the celebration of literary traditions. For instance, during the Persian New Year celebration known as Nowruz, the poetry of Hafez is read aloud in order to gain insight into the coming year.

4. **An Immersive Experience That Will Bring All Five Senses to Life**

Vision :

The most memorable aspects of cultural festivals are frequently the ones that can be seen. The eye is drawn in by the intricate costumes, vibrant decorations, and artistic displays, which together provide a kaleidoscope of different visual sensations. For instance, the parades of Thailand's Loy Krathong, which are illuminated by lanterns, and the parades of New Orleans' Mardi Gras, which feature colorful floats, are both a visual feast.

To be heard:
The guests are immersed in a specific auditory tapestry that is created by the traditional music, chants, and celebratory revelry that surround them. This sensory dimension is exemplified by events such as the pulsating beats of African drums during Ghana's Homowo celebration and the jubilant hymns sung by carolers in Europe during the Christmas season.

Flavor :
During festivals, culinary customs frequently take center stage, giving attendees the opportunity to sample traditional cuisines and flavors. The sumptuous and varied meals given at the celebrations of Eid al-Fitr in India, as well as the mouthwatering beignets and king cake that are served during Mardi Gras in New Orleans, provide a stimulating experience for the taste buds.

Feel it:
During the celebration of Holi in India, participants engage their sense of touch by engaging in activities such as dancing, donning costumes, and the fun spreading of colors. These activities help establish a physical connection with the event's traditions.

Inhale :
The olfactory senses are engaged by aromatic components, such as the incense that is burned during a Chinese New Year temple ceremony or the fragrant foods that are placed on an ofrenda for Dia de los Muertos in Mexico. This evokes the smells that have cultural importance.

5. **The Importance of the Present and Interactions Around the World**

Festivals of culture do not remain unchanged over time; rather, they develop and change in response to new circumstances. They act as bridges across civilizations in our interconnected globe, which promotes mutual understanding and trade among all parties involved. Festivals are known for embracing technology and engaging with global influences, all the while keeping their traditional practices and beliefs intact.

For instance, the celebrations of Dia de los Muertos in Mexico have not only kept their ancestral customs but also incorporated contemporary elements, which has led to the creation of sugar skull art and other iconic symbols that have acquired notoriety all over the world.

Festivals of a culture serve as everlasting narratives that encapsulate the traditions, values, and artistry of the community in which they take place. People are able to engage with the very center and essence of a variety of cultures through these living traditions, which provide fully encompassing and multisensory experiences. These festivals deepen our comprehension of the wide variety of human cultures and the shared ideals that unite us as members of a worldwide society. They illustrate that the universal human experience is one of common expression, connection, and a celebration of our individual identities, despite the fact that the particulars of traditions, values, and works of art may vary from one culture to another. Festivals of culture bestow onto the globe the enduring gift of unity in variety and shed light on the limitless creativity and brilliance of the human spirit.

5.3 The globalization of cultural festivals

Festivals of culture are lively windows that provide a glimpse into the very essence of a community. They offer a look into the very core of a people's identity by providing distinctive insights into the traditions, values, and art of a particular community. These festivals are more than just colorful displays; they serve as live manifestations of culture, reflecting the historical legacy, communal ethos, and artistic traditions that characterize a community. They bring people together to celebrate their heritage and share their artistic traditions. This investigation goes deeper into the function of cultural celebrations as potent conduits that shed light on the traditions, beliefs, and artistic expressions of the communities that they stand for.

1. **The Preserving of Traditions and Rituals Through the Practice of Customs Recollections of the Past:**

   Festivals serve as living museums of cultural memory because they are the settings for the reenactment and remembering of customs and traditions. These rituals facilitate a reconnection between communities and their histories, thereby instilling a sense of continuity and identity in the group.

   Rituals of Coming of Age:

   Rites of passage are a common component of many different types of cultural celebrations. These ceremonies are meant to honor key life milestones such as birth, coming of age, marriage, and death. These rites serve not just to guide individuals through the various stages of life but also to strengthen the links that unite the community.

   Observances of the Sacred and the Profane:

   Traditions associated with festivals might be either religious or secular. Both religious and secular activities, such as feasting, dancing, and sharing stories of the past may be a part of them. Examples of religious rites include prayer and offering. The paradoxical essence of the human condition is mirrored in these practices.

   Protection of Cultural Properties:

   Festivals of culture are an essential component in the continued maintenance of a community's intangible cultural heritage. This encompasses folklore, myths, stories, oral traditions, and other forms of cultural expressions that, in today's fast-paced modern society, stand a good chance of being lost to time.

2. **Values, or the transmission of cultural beliefs and guiding principles**

    The Meaning of Community and Unity:
    There are a lot of celebrations that revolve around ideas of community and coming together. They stress the significance of getting together as a group and reiterating the necessity of trusting one another, supporting one another, and working together. These beliefs and ideals shine through most clearly in the rites and customs that call for participation from the community.

    Reverence and respect for the sacred:
    During cultural celebrations, values like as respect and reverence for environment, ancestors, and deities are frequently encouraged. During numerous celebrations, it is typical to participate in rituals that involve the worship of natural elements, the honoring of the wisdom of elderly people, and the acknowledgment of divine powers.

    Identifying One's Culture
    The celebration of a culture's unique identity is what festivals are all about. They validate the singular qualities that define a community and generate a sense of pride in its individuals. Celebrations like these help to foster admiration and appreciation for heritage while also fostering cultural preservation, authenticity, and originality.

    The Communication of Social Values:
    During cultural celebrations, ideas of social justice, equality, and inclusiveness are often discussed and modeled for attendees. Some festivals, for instance, may place an emphasis on philanthropy and sharing with those who are less fortunate in order to encourage a spirit of generosity and concern for the community.

3. **The Arts: A Forum for Creative Expression and Exploration**

    Craftsmanship and the Decorative Arts:
    The visual arts and handicrafts of painters, sculptors, textile artists, and other artists who create elaborate designs are frequently showcased at festivals. These artistic manifestations, which incorporate traditional themes and methods, represent the aesthetics and craftsmanship of the culture of the community in which they are created.

    The arts of Music and Dance:
    The rhythms, melodies, and patterns of movement that are distinctive to a culture are reflected in the music and dance that are performed at cultural celebrations. They express feelings, narrate events, and encapsulate the gist of a community's core values and important moments throughout its history.

    Craftsmanship in the Kitchen:
    Traditions in the art of cooking are a fundamental component of cultural artistry. The regional flavors and culinary history are celebrated through the

presentation of traditional dishes and methods of cooking at various festivals. The fine art of gastronomic preparation and presentation is an essential component of many different types of parties.

Writing and the Art of Storytelling:
A significant number of cultural celebrations center on literary works and oral storytelling. Myths, legends, and folktales are passed down through generations either verbally or in recorded form. These stories are used to teach important life lessons, recount historical events, and communicate a culture's accumulated knowledge.

4. **The Maintenance of Culture while Fostering Intergenerational Understanding**

   Sharing Knowledge Across Generations:
   Elders can use the platform provided by cultural festivals to talk to younger people about their life experiences and the wisdom they've gained over the years. Younger people gain a better understanding of their culture's norms and principles when they take an active role in the preparations for festivals and the rituals that take place during them.

   The Education of Cultures:
   Workshops, demonstrations, and exhibitions are some of the kind of cultural education activities that can be found at festivals.
   Younger members of the community have the opportunity to participate in conversations about their background with more seasoned community members and cultural specialists.

   History Confronted Daily:
   At cultural celebrations, traditions and values are not just discussed but are put into reality, making these events a form of living history. The younger generation is able to better understand the value of these traditions with the support of this experiential learning approach.

   Instilling a Sense of Cultural Pride:
   The younger generation gains a sense of cultural pride and identity through the participation in festivals. They become stakeholders in the preservation and continuation of their cultural inheritance when they take an active role in these events and contribute to the activities that take place during them.

5. **In a Global Context, Cultural Festivals Serve to Connect Communities Around the World**

The Exchange of Cultures:
Festivals of culture serve as forums for the exchange of culture, providing communities with opportunities to share their traditions, values, and artistic expression with people from a variety of various backgrounds. Through interactions like these,

a greater awareness and mutual understanding of the richness and variety of human cultures can be fostered.

Dialogue Between People of Different Faiths and Cultures:

Festivals of different cultures often act as a spur for discussion between different faiths and cultures in societies that are diverse. People of varying religious persuasions and cultural traditions are brought together at these gatherings, which helps to encourage cooperation, tolerance, and the celebration of shared ideals.

Diplomacy in the World's Cultures:

Festivals of different cultures are a sort of cultural diplomacy that can help to strengthen international relationships and collaboration. They act as tools for soft power, fostering peace, mutual understanding, and global solidarity by bringing people together from different backgrounds.

Travel within a Culture:

There are several cultural festivals that draw tourists and travelers; these festivals help to drive cultural tourism and promote economic development. These events attract visitors from all over the world, thereby boosting the regional economy and cultivating a greater appreciation for the region's cultural traditions.

Festivals of culture are lively windows into the traditions, principles, and artistic expressions of a society. They provide light on the ageless traditions that bind generations together, the principles that are responsible for the formation of identities, and the artistic forms that give culture its vitality. These festivities act as bridges that connect different communities and cultures, which helps to build mutual understanding, appreciation, and unity in our diverse and interrelated world. Cultural festivals are a living witness to the enduring power of culture to bring people together, educate new generations, and celebrate what it is to be human, despite their ongoing evolution and adaptation to the changing times.

Chapter 6

Music and Dance Festivals

People from all walks of life can be brought together through a shared appreciation of rhythm, melody, and physical expression through the global languages of music and dance. Festivals of music and dance are lively celebrations of these art forms. They provide a venue for artists, dance fans, and communities to join together in the spirit of cultural expression and harmony. These festivals provide a fascinating excursion into the world of music and dance by displaying a wide variety of musical and dance genres, styles, and customs from throughout the world. During this in-depth investigation, we will delve into the core of Music and Dance Festivals, examining its historical beginnings, cultural value, impact on society, and contemporary manifestations. This will allow us to gain a better understanding of these events.

1. **An Introduction to the Influence That Music and Dance Can Have**
   Both music and dance are fundamental ways in which humans express themselves, and they are intricately woven into the fabric of our cultural history. They serve as vehicles for conveying feeling, for telling stories, and for making connections. Dance, with its movements and rhythms, has the ability to transmit tales and bring communities together, whereas music, with its melodies and harmonies, has the potential to provoke profound emotions in its audience. Festivals of music and dance are large venues where these art forms are celebrated, showing the diversity of human ingenuity and the richness of cultural traditions.
2. **The Historical Beginnings and the Development of**
   Ancient Practices and Occasions for Festivities:
   Ancient rituals and festivities are where music and dance festivals got their start, and they can be traced all the way back to their beginnings. The agricultural cycles, solstices, equinoxes, and other key natural phenomena were often celebrated in conjunction with these festivals in many different cultures.
   Importance from a Religious Perspective:

The celebration of religion was at the heart of many music and dance events. They were presented to deities, performed during rituals in which divine favor was sought, or celebrated on important religious occasions as offerings. As expressions of devotion, these festivals frequently featured lavish displays of musical performance and dance.

The Exchange of Cultures:
As nations began to contact with one another and trade goods, music and dance evolved as a medium for the sharing of cultural ideas. This resulted in the hybridization of musical and dancing styles as different styles and traditions influenced and were influenced by one another.

Transformation of the Secular:
The origins of many music and dance festivals may be traced back to religious or ceremonial gatherings, but throughout the years, these gatherings have morphed into more general celebrations. They started putting more of an emphasis on entertainment, artistic expression, and the enjoyment of their culture.

The Convergence of Modernity and Globalization:
Festivals of music and dance have evolved into widespread cultural occurrences in the modern period. They are influenced by modern fashion, technology, and pop culture, and they unite people from a variety of different origins through shared musical experiences.

3. **The Importance of Music and Dance Festivals to Cultural Identity**

Protecting Our Cultural Heritage:
Festivals of Music and Dance are extremely important to the continuation of traditional forms of musical expression and dance. These celebrations serve an important role as stewards of cultural history by insuring the continuation of time-honored customs into the foreseeable future.

Narratives and the Art of Storytelling:
Stories and narratives are frequently communicated through the mediums of music and dance. They may relate historical occurrences, myths, or stories, or they may impart culturally significant lessons. These stories are essential to the formation of a community's unique cultural identity.

Promoting a Sense of Cultural Pride:
Communities gain a sense of cultural pride and belonging via the participation in music and dance festivals. They instill a community with its distinct identity and tradition, and they give individuals the opportunity to feel pride in their own cultural origins.

The Merging of Cultures:
Festivals of music and dance frequently act as meeting places for people of different cultural backgrounds.
They do this by combining aspects of a number of different cultures in order to produce novel, hybrid forms of artistic expression, which in turn promotes

communication and understanding amongst people of different cultures.

Expression of One's Culture:
These events offer artists and performers a stage on which they can freely express their cultural
identities as well as their creative impulses. They provide artists with a blank canvas on which they can express the myriad hues of their culture through music and dance.

4. **Repercussions for the Society**

   Boost to the Economy:
   Festivals of music and dance make major contributions to the economies of their host communities. They entice tourists, which in turn generates employment opportunities and stimulates businesses associated to hospitality, cuisine, and retail sales.

   Travel within a Culture:
   Festivals frequently evolve into prominent tourism destinations, bringing in guests from all over the world. These events attract tourists who want to immerse themselves in the culture of the host community. As a result, the community benefits from increased cultural tourism and global exposure.

   Maintaining Social Cohesion:
   These celebrations strengthen communal ties and contribute to greater social cohesion. People are given the chance to get together, celebrate their common interests, and form connections that will last a lifetime because of these events.

   Diplomacy through the Arts:
   Festivals of music and dance play an important part in the promotion of cultural diplomacy, which in turn helps to foster international connections and collaboration. Participation from musicians and performers from a variety of nations frequently contributes to increased international understanding and goodwill.

   Education and Promotion of Cultural Activities:
   The audience is exposed to new artistic practices and cultural traditions through the medium of festivals, which function as teaching venues. They do this via hosting workshops, seminars, and demonstrations, all of which serve to increase public understanding and appreciation.

   A Stage for Social Transformation:
   Festivals of music and dance can also serve as stages for social activism and transformation. They push for change, increase awareness about urgent social issues, and create a platform for activism and advocacy.

5. **Highlights from the International Music and Dance Festival: Cultural Expressions from All Over the World**

   Carnival in Rio de Janeiro (Brazil):
   The Rio Carnival is one of the most well-known celebrations in the world, and it is celebrated with lavish parades, lively samba dance performances, and colorful

costumes. It symbolizes Brazil's vibrant culture, which is a fusion of influences from Africa, Europe, and Brazil's indigenous people.

The Festival of Lights (in India):
Traditional music, dancing, and performances are performed during the celebration of Diwali, also known as the Festival of Lights. It is the day that commemorates the triumph of light over darkness, and it is commemorated with zeal and devotion on a spiritual level.

Festival de Woodstock (États-Unis):
The Woodstock Music and Art Fair in 1969 was a pivotal time in the annals of music history. It was a festival honoring nonviolence, love, and music, and it reflected the counterculture of the 1960s as well as the anti-war feelings of that era.

The Oktoberfest is held in Germany.
The Oktoberfest is a beer and folk festival that is celebrated all over the world. It is known for its traditional Bavarian music and dance. It provides a look of the diverse cultural history that Germany possesses.

Known as hanami in Japan:
The festival of Hanami, which honors cherry blossoms, is celebrated with performances of music and dance, as well as picnics held beneath cherry trees in full bloom. It is a manifestation of the Japanese people's profound respect for the splendor of nature.

Carnaval de Barranquilla is a festival held in Colombia:
This carnival is well-known for the lively folk music and dancing that it features, both of which are representative of the numerous cultural traditions and Afro-Caribbean influences that exist in Colombia.

Sunburn Festival is celebrated in India:
The Sunburn Festival is recognized as one of the most important gatherings for electronic dance music in all of Asia. It is a celebration of modern music culture, specifically electronic dance music.

6. **The Influence of Globalization and Contemporary Expressions**

Combining Musical Styles and Genres:
Fusion music and collaborations between musicians of different genres are common features at modern festivals. They combine current and old musical approaches, which ultimately results in original and forward-thinking musical forms.

The Integration of Technology:
Festivals make considerable use of technology to improve the whole experience and interact with audiences all around the world. This technology includes sophisticated sound systems, light shows, and live broadcasting of the event.

Promotion via Social Media and Digital Platforms:

The advertising of the festival and the engagement with attendees is made significantly easier by social media. It gives festivalgoers and fans the opportunity to interact with one another, discuss their observations, and broaden the festival's scope.

Sustainability in Relation to the Environment:
A growing number of events are making eco-friendly changes and emphasizing the importance of sustainability. They put an emphasis on recycling, trash reduction, and energy saving, all of which contribute to an increased understanding of environmental issues.

The International Festival Scene:
A sense of global community and interconnectedness has been fostered as a result of the proliferation of music and dance festivals, which have resulted in the creation of a global festival circuit. Festival aficionados now travel to different nations to take part in various events.

Festivals of Music and Dance are more than just a source of entertainment; rather, they are a worldwide celebration of culture. They act as windows into the hearts and souls of other communities, showing the traditions, values, and artistic accomplishments that constitute our common humanity. These festivals are a living witness to the continuing ability of music and dance to bring people together, share stories, and celebrate the splendor of cultural diversity, even as they continue to change and adapt to the shifting times in which they are held. They remind us of the transforming and unifying potential of the arts by representing a global celebration of rhythm, harmony, and culture.

6.1 The power of music and dance to transcend language and borders

Both music and dance can be considered universal languages because of their exceptional capacity to communicate over a wide range of linguistic and geographical boundaries. They build a sense of togetherness, understanding, and shared experience among individuals on a profound and emotional level, connecting people in the process. It is a credit to the widespread appeal of music and dance that they are able to overcome divisions in a world that frequently struggles with them. This investigation explores at the exceptional power of music and dance to cross linguistic and geographical boundaries, illuminating the roles that music and dance play as unifying factors in human culture.

1. **The All-Pervasive Nature of Music**
   Expressions of Feeling and Emotion:
   There is no medium more powerful than music when it comes to communicating sentiments and moods. Joy, grief, wrath, or love are all feelings that can be elicited by a song, and it's not just one culture that experiences these responses.
   Appeal Across Multiple Cultures:
   There may be vast differences in the musical forms and genres performed in different parts of the world, but there is a universal respect for the aesthetic value

of music, the skill of its performers, and the feelings it evokes in its audience.

Communication That Is Not Verbal:
Music, on the other hand, is a form of nonverbal communication. It does so via conveying information through tempo, pitch, dynamics, and timbre. Because of this, it is able to get across language boundaries and transmit its message directly to the person's emotions and spirit.

The Exchange of Cultures:
The sharing of cultures can be facilitated through the medium of music. There is a rich tapestry of global musical influences because musical styles and instruments from one culture are frequently incorporated into the music of other cultures.

Narrative expression:
The art of telling stories via song has a long and storied history. Even if the words are in a language that the audience is not familiar with, the feelings that are communicated by the music allow them to understand the gist of the story.

2. **Dance as a Form of International Communication**

    Expression through the body:
    The physical expression of thoughts, feelings, and stories is what dance is all about. Individuals are able to communicate their happiness, sadness, celebration, or protest by the movements of their bodies.

    Significance Across Multiple Cultures:
    The significance of dance as a means of community and artistic expression is something that is shared by cultures all over the world, despite the fact that the styles and types of dance might differ widely from one another.

    Traditions of the Culture:
    The cultural practices and rituals of many societies include dance as an essential component. It is a means of commemorating key life events, rites of passage, and religious observances in a particular tradition.

    Cohesion of the Group:
    People tend to come closer together after a good dance. It encourages a feeling of community and belonging, whether it is performed in the form of traditional folk dances or contemporary dance genres.

    The language of the body:
    Feelings and emotions can be communicated through dance, which is a sort of body language. It is accessible to people of a variety of cultural backgrounds, allowing them to comprehend and appreciate its meaning.

3. **The Linking Together of Different Cultures**

    Integration of Different Cultures:
    Fusion of different cultures occurs frequently in the context of music and dance. Artists coming from a variety of cultural traditions work together, fusing aspects of their own artistic canons with those of other traditions in order to produce

novel, hybrid modes of expression.

Language Required for Cooperation:
It is possible for musicians and dancers from different countries to work together even if they do not speak the same language. They communicate with one another through the universal languages of music and dance in order to create.

Exchanges Across Cultures:
Festivals of international music and dance serve as forums for the sharing of cultural traditions. They encourage cooperation and communication amongst people of diverse cultural backgrounds by bringing together artists and fans from all over the world.

Understanding on a Global Scale:
Building a worldwide awareness and appreciation for the diversity of human civilizations is facilitated by the arts of music and dance. They impart a sense of our common humanity and serve as a jumping off point for education regarding the practices of various cultures.

The Advancement of Peace:
The sharing of musical and dance traditions can contribute to the promotion of peace and diplomacy. Performers and artists are frequently invited to take part in activities that aim to strengthen international relationships and collaboration.

4. **Narratives of Culture and the Art of Storytelling**

   Legends and Myths: Folklore and Mythology
   A great number of civilizations have handed down to us musical and dance traditions that tell stories about their mythology and folklore. These tales are handed down from generation to generation, which helps to keep cultural history alive.

   Narratives of Historical Events:
   The narrative of historical activities and occurrences is often told through the medium of music and dance. These creative forms are how civilizations commemorate and honor their ancestors and their history.

   Commentary on Social and Political Issues:
   Performers in the performing arts, such as musicians and dancers, frequently utilize their craft to remark on social issues and political events. The audience's emotional state can be expressed even when they do not understand the language being used.

   Celebration and Observance of Custom:
   Celebrations and rituals that highlight significant life events, such as weddings, funerals, and religious ceremonies, often include music and dancing as fundamental parts of the experience. These activities frequently include narrative components that communicate cultural values and ideas to the audience.

   Symbols Used Around the World:
   There are certain patterns and symbols in music and dance that are known all

across the world. They are universal and may be comprehended by persons of many different linguistic and cultural backgrounds.

5. **The Role of Music and Dance as Diplomatic Instruments**
   Diplomacy through the Arts:
   On the global stage, nations will frequently exhibit their cultural history through the music and dance traditions that are unique to their nation. Initiatives in diplomatic relations can take the shape of cultural performances and exchange programs, as well as collaborations.
   Festivals held all over the world
   Festivals of international music and dance serve as important forums for the exchange of cultural norms and values. They invite artists and performers from all around the world, thereby fostering cross-cultural understanding and encouraging international collaboration.
   Programs for Intercultural Understanding of Young People:
   Programs for youth and cultural exchange between nations are frequently carried out, and they frequently make use of music and dance as a means of creating goodwill and building ties between individuals.
   Dialogue Between People of Different Faiths and Cultures:
   Music and dance have the potential to act as catalysts for interfaith and intercultural discourse, so building cooperation and understanding in communities that are home to a wide variety of religious and cultural traditions.
   The Resolution of Conflict:
   Music and dance have been utilized as methods for conflict resolution and peacebuilding in areas that are currently experiencing armed conflict. They offer a shared foundation upon which discussion and reconciliation can take place.

6. **Current Instances That Illustrate the Global Connection**
   Festivals de musique du monde :
   At world music festivals, a wide variety of musical traditions from all around the world are presented. They facilitate cultural exchange by bringing together musicians from a variety of cultures and audiences from those backgrounds.
   The Merging of Dance and Music:
   Fusion styles and collaborations between artists of many genres are commonplace in contemporary dance and music. Artists from a variety of cultures combine aspects of their respective heritages to produce works that are both original and cross-cultural.
   Connectivity via Digital Means:
   The dawn of the digital age has broadened the audience for music and dance around the world. Through live streaming and social media, individuals are able to connect with musicians and performances taking place in a variety of nations.
   The World's Pop Culture:
   Pop music and dance styles frequently become phenomena that occur all across

the world. Hip-hop and Korean pop music are two examples of genres that have achieved widespread success and successfully crossed linguistic and cultural barriers.

The Effect of Dance on the World:
Hip-hop and breakdancing are two types of dance that have gained popularity all over the world. Dance competitions and events encourage unity and respect by bringing together dancers from a variety of cultural and socioeconomic backgrounds.

7. **The Meaning of Music and Dance in Difficult Times**

Indulge in Some Solace:
When people are going through tough circumstances, music and dance can be a source of comfort and solace, helping them cope with loss, stress, and uncertainty.

Encourage a resilient mindset:
Music and dance have the capacity to uplift spirits, encourage resiliency, and create a sense of optimism and unity when circumstances are difficult.

Help the Patient Heal:
As therapeutic instruments, they contribute to the physical as well as psychological healing of patients. In the realms of healthcare and rehabilitation, music therapy and dance movement therapy play important roles.

Bring to People's Attention:
Performers in the performing arts, such as musicians and dancers, frequently make use of their platforms to bring attention to important global topics such as social justice, environmental concerns, and humanitarian catastrophes.

Both music and dance are more than just means of entertainment; rather, they are profound expressions of the experience of being human. They are capable of transcending language and boundaries, connecting people across cultural differences, and encouraging togetherness, understanding, and appreciation for the richness of human diversity. They are the language of the heart, which is universal, and they are the language of the heart. The ability of music and dance to bring people together, share experiences, and form connections is a tribute to the continuing force of human culture in a world where divisions often appear to be insurmountable. They serve as a reminder that, in the end, we are all connected by the common language of feelings and expressions shared by all humans.

6.2 Iconic music festivals (e.g., Woodstock, Coachella, Samba Fest)

Festivals of music are more than just events; they are cultural phenomenon, gatherings that transcend time and location, and commemorate the universal force that music possesses. In particular, legendary music festivals occupy a unique and significant position in our cultural memory. They have had a significant impact on culture, culture has had a significant impact on them, and they have offered platforms for legendary performances. Within the scope of this investigation, we will delve into the world of illustrious music festivals, shining light on their rich history, significant cultural value, and ongoing influence on music and society.

1. **Woodstock: The Beginning of a Cultural Revolution**
   Contextual Information Regarding Culture and Politics:
   The events of Woodstock took place during a tumultuous era that was characterized by struggles for civil rights, protests against the Vietnam War, and a general sense of societal discontent. The event promoted togetherness and transformation, which were both goals of the time period in which it took place.
   The Greatest Musical Icons:
   Artists such as Jimi Hendrix, Janis Joplin, The Who, and Joe Cocker gave unforgettable performances at Woodstock. These legendary performances have left an indelible mark on the annals of music history and shaped a whole period.
   Connecting with Others and Sharing:
   The strong sense of community that existed at Woodstock is one of the festival's most enduring legacies. The attendees created a sense of unity and togetherness by sharing food, shelter, and a passion for music with one another.
   Influence on the Culture of Festivals:
   Woodstock established a standard for the culture of music festivals by highlighting the importance of music in the process of social transformation and laying the way for subsequent festivals that celebrated more than just the entertainment industry.

2. **Coachella, a Contemporary Example of a Cultural Phenomenon**
   The Integration of the Arts:
   In addition to being lauded for its musical performances, the Coachella Valley Music and Arts Festival is also renowned for its emphasis on visual arts, installations, and interactive experiences. It's a combination of music, art, and technology all rolled into one.
   A Mixed Bag of Performers:
   The event is known for putting together lineups that feature a wide variety of musical styles, ranging from rock and pop to electronic and hip hop. It has evolved into a stage for both up-and-coming musicians and established celebrities to perform on.
   Attendance by Famous People:
   The fact that Coachella draws a diverse crowd, including celebrities, musicians, and music enthusiasts further solidifies the festival's standing as a phenomenon in popular culture.
   The Latest in Fashion and Style:
   The fashion and style trends that people wear to music festivals all over the world were largely shaped by Coachella, which had a big impact on these trends.
   Influence on the Culture of Festivals:

Many other festivals have been encouraged to integrate more immersive and multi-dimensional experiences as a result of Coachella's approach to merging music and art. Coachella is the most well-known example of this type of festival.

3. **Celebrating Samba and Brazilian Culture during the Festa do Samba**
   Music and Dance of the Samba:
   The music style known as samba, which is considered to be one of the most recognizable types of Brazilian music, is the focus of the annual Samba Fest. It perfectly captures the spirt and vitality of the Brazilian cultural tradition.
   Spirit of the Carnival:
   The celebration frequently embodies the joyous spirit of the Brazilian Carnival, complete with elaborate costumes, parades filled with vibrant colors, and performances of samba dance.
   The Diversity of Cultures:
   The Samba Fest is a chance to showcase the cultural variety that exists throughout Brazil. It integrates elements of Afro-Brazilian culture as well as indigenous Brazilian customs, and it features regional variations of the Samba.
   Community Involvement:
   Because it encourages local engagement and interest in the community, the festival is an essential component of Brazil's schedule of cultural events.
   Recognizance on a Global Scale:
   The Samba Fest has earned a reputation on a global scale, helping to spread awareness of Brazilian culture while welcoming attendees from all over the world.

4. **Glastonbury, an English Tradition and Institution**
   Diverse styles of music:
   The music at Glastonbury encompasses a wide variety of genres, ranging from rock and pop to electronic, folk, and even world music. Its varied roster ensures that it will appeal to a large audience.
   The Importance of Being Active:
   The festival frequently encourages people to become involved in social and environmental activism, discussing topics including the environment, inequality, and human rights.
   Performance and the Visual Arts:
   In addition to musical performances, other forms of entertainment including as theater, art installations, and circus acts are presented during Glastonbury. It is a space where artistic expression and intellectual inquiry can take place.
   Community and Environmental Stewardship:
   The event places a strong emphasis on the community as well as sustainability, with a number of projects aimed at lowering the festival's negative impact on the environment and building a sense of togetherness.
   Importance in the Course of History:

There have been many iconic performances that have taken place at Glastonbury over the years, including ones by David Bowie, Beyoncé, and The Rolling Stones. It is an important moment in the evolution of music.

5. **Tomorrowland: The World's Largest Electronic Dance Music Festival**
   Spectacle to the Eyes:
   Tomorrowland is famous for its ornate and visually beautiful stage designs, which create an otherworldly experience for the attendees of the festival.
   Appeal to International Audiences:
   DJs performing at the festival represent a wide variety of electronic dance music subgenres, which brings together fans of electronic music from all over the world.
   Building Up the Community:
   With its "People of Tomorrow" philosophy, Tomorrowland helps to cultivate a feeling of community by placing an emphasis on unity, love, and respect for one another.
   Expansion Across the Globe:
   Tomorrowland now has locations all over the world, including the United States of America, Brazil, and other countries, significantly strengthening its presence on the worldwide stage.
   Engaging in Digital Activities:
   The festival takes advantage of digital technologies and live broadcasting in order to interact with an online audience that is larger than the one that attends the actual event.
6. **Influence on Musical Genres and Cultural Aspects**

   Discoveries and Developments in the Music Industry:
   Iconic festivals frequently serve as launching pads for the careers of up-and-coming musicians and musical movements, so having an effect not just on the local music industry but also on the global music business.
   The Exchange of Cultures:
   These festivals serve as a forum for the exchange of cultural traditions by bringing together performers and attendees from a wide variety of cultural and ethnic backgrounds, so fostering an increased awareness of and appreciation for the world's myriad traditions.
   The Latest in Fashion and Style:
   The clothing that individuals choose to wear to events and even in their everyday life is often influenced by the fashion and style trends that are established at various festivals.
   Community and the Shifting Social Order:
   The value of community, social action, and environmental sustainability is highlighted during festivals, and thus highlights the need for constructive societal change.

FESTIVALS AND CELEBRATIONS

Importance in the Course of History:
Festivals that are considered iconic often find a place in history books because they mark significant turning points in music, culture, and social movements.

Not only are iconic music festivals about the music, but also about the experiences, feelings, and interactions that attendees have with one another. They are occasions for the celebration of culture, manifestations of unity, and stages for the development of innovative artistic practices. The significant influence that these festivals have had on music, culture, and society is evidenced by the fact that their legacy will go on for years to come. Iconic music festivals continue to shape our world by bringing people together in the name of music, art, and community. From the love and peace of Woodstock to the worldwide appeal of Coachella, the vibrant spirit of Samba Fest, the cultural institution that is Glastonbury, the electronic dance music phenomenon of Tomorrowland, and countless others, these festivals continue to bring people together in the name of music, art, and community.

6.3 How music and dance festivals have evolved over time

Festivals of music and dance have undergone a remarkable transformation throughout the course of time, allowing them to adapt to shifting cultural, technological, and social landscapes. These festivals have continuously shaped and been shaped by society, beginning with their roots in ancient rites and local festivities and continuing all the way up to their modern prominence on a global scale. In the course of this investigation, we will embark on a journey through the years, during which we will investigate how music and dance festivals have developed and adapted over the centuries, eventually becoming the rich and lively cultural phenomena that they are today.

1. **Ancient Roots and the Beginnings of Ritualistic Practices**
   Celebrations Throughout the Year:
   Numerous ancient celebrations had strong ties to the agricultural calendar, which served to mark the passing of the seasons as well as the planting and harvesting cycles. These festivals mixed various aspects of religion with dancing, music, and other forms of expression.
   Importance from a Religious Perspective:
   Festivals of music and dance have been known to hold significant religious or spiritual meaning in a number of different civilizations. They were either acts of worship, offerings to deities, or commemorations of holy occurrences and occasions.
   Integration into the Community:
   The first celebrations were meant to bring the community closer together. They brought people together so that they could express their cultural identities, establish social cohesion, and share the experiences they had had.
   The Exchange of Cultures:
   As new trade routes were established, festivals evolved into venues for the

interchange of cultural practices. The exchange of music, dance, and artistic forms between various locations led to the hybridization of previously distinct cultural practices.

2. **The Influence on the Renaissance and the Age of Enlightenment**

    A rise in the number of formal performances:
    The idea of putting on formal performances and courtly spectacles grew widespread during the time period known as the Renaissance. During festivals, there were frequently extravagant performances of music and dance that highlighted the talents of court musicians and entertainers.

    The period known as the Enlightenment:
    The age of enlightenment brought with it an emphasis on reason, science, and rationality, all of which influenced the topics that were discussed at festivals and the activities that were performed at them. The expression of ideas through music and dance eventually became more intellectual and secular.

    The impact of classical music:
    During this time period, classical music and dance forms rose to prominence, contributing to the refinement of festival performances. Classical music and dance styles are best exemplified by composers such as Mozart and Beethoven.

    Both the Opera and the Ballet:
    New opportunities for the performance of music and dance within the setting of festivals were made possible as a result of the development of opera and ballet in the 17th and 18th centuries.

3. **The Origin of Contemporary Music and Dance Festivals**

    Woodstock and the Emergence of the Counterculture
    Festivals were transformed into venues for social change and cultural revolution as a direct result of Woodstock Music and Art Fair in 1969, which came to be seen as a symbol of the counterculture movement that emerged in the 1960s.

    Integration of Different Cultures and Diversity:
    In the second half of the 20th century, there was a rise in the number of music festivals that celebrated the diversity of musical styles. Festivals such as the Montreux Jazz Festival and WOMAD were designed to highlight a diverse array of musical styles from a variety of ethnic backgrounds.

    The Revolution of Electronic Dance Music (EDM) :
    Festivals like Tomorrowland and Ultra Music Festival, which celebrate DJ performances and electronic music genres, emerged as a result of the proliferation of electronic dance music in the latter part of the 20th century.

    The Processes of Globalization and Commercialization:
    The evolution of music and dance festivals into global commercial organizations has resulted in huge events attracting crowds from all over the world and starring performances from a variety of countries.

FESTIVALS AND CELEBRATIONS

4. **The Current State of the Festival Scene**
   A Wide Range of Genres:
   Modern music festivals feature artists from a diverse range of musical genres and subgenres, including rock, pop, and hip-hop as well as electronic, world, and more specialized forms of music.
   The Integration of the Arts:
   Many contemporary festivals now include visual arts, installations, and interactive activities, so creating spaces that are immersive and engage multiple senses.
   The Exchange of Cultures:
   International festivals provide as forums for intercultural conversation by bringing together artists and audiences from a variety of nations and fostering the exchange of cultural ideas.
   Activism and Environmental Stewardship:
   As a reflection of the concerns that are currently prevalent in society, the modern festival
   landscape frequently places an emphasis on sustainability, social action, and environmental
   awareness.
   Engaging in Digital Activities:
   Live streaming and other forms of social media have made it possible for festivals to connect with audiences online, thereby expanding the scope of their reach beyond those who actually attend the events.
   Expansion Across the Globe:
   Iconic festivals have expanded their operations to include hosting editions in many countries, ensuring that they have a presence and appeal on a global scale.

5. **Opportunities and Obstacles to Overcome**

   Excessive reliance on the market:
   Concerns have been voiced over the increase in price of festival tickets, the narrowing of attendance, and the disappearance of the festivals' original sense of community as a result of commercialization.
   Security and Transportation:
   Safety and crowd management have become key difficulties for festival organizers as a direct result of greater audiences and more complicated logistical arrangements.
   Sustainability in Relation to the Environment:
   The control of waste, the reduction of carbon emissions, and the protection of natural areas ought to be important concerns of festivals with regard to environmental sustainability.
   Both diversity and inclusivity are important:
   It is important to continue working toward the objective of making festivals more welcoming and varied environments for artists, fans, and staff.

Influence on the Music Industry:

The music industry is significantly influenced by festivals, which have an effect on the ways in which music is produced, sold, and consumed.

Integration of Digital Technology:

The internet age presents opportunities for festival promotion, audience involvement, and money production, but it also raises problems about how artists should be compensated and what audience members should anticipate from the event.

Festivals of music and dance have developed into multidimensional cultural phenomena that reflect the alterations in society that have occurred in recent decades. They have a significant bearing on the music industry, the dissemination of culture, and the various ways in which individuals experience and engage with music and dance. The origins of these festivals lie in ancient rituals; nevertheless, in the global and digital world of the 21st century, they continue to evolve, adapt, and inspire. They are vivid celebrations of culture, community, and the enduring power of song and dance.

Chapter 7

Food and Culinary Festivals

Food is more than just a means of subsistence; it is an expression of culture, a journey for the senses, a source of community, and a cause for celebration. The collective affection that we have for flavors, customs, and the activity of eating is reflected in the popularity of food and culinary events. They commemorate the wide variety of cuisines, culinary arts, and regional specialties from all over the world. In this in-depth investigation, we will go on a mouthwatering journey through the intriguing world of food and culinary festivals, beginning with their historical roots and progressing through the myriad forms that these celebrations take in modern times.

1. **The Traditional Beginnings of Gastronomic Celebrations**
   Ancient Celebrations of the Harvest:
   The conclusion of the growing season was celebrated with feasting and thanksgiving during harvest festivals like the Roman Saturnalia and the Jewish Sukkot. These celebrations marked the transition from one agricultural season to the next.
   Importance to Different Cultures and Religions:
   A significant number of the earliest celebrations of food had religious or cultural roots. For example, the Chinese Mid-Autumn Festival celebrated the harvest of the moon, and the Christian feast of Thanksgiving expressed thanks for a prosperous harvest. Both festivals occurred in the fall.
   Feasts in the Middle Ages:
   The nobility and royal families of the Middle Ages were responsible for hosting an increase in the number of lavish feasts and banquets during this time. These parties were meant to be a showcase of one's wealth, kindness, and extraordinary culinary prowess.
   Commerce and the Exchange of Cultures:
   The proliferation of trade channels resulted in the dissemination of gastronomic

customs and ingredients from one region and culture to another, which ultimately led to the development of food festivals.

2. **Regional and International Variation in Gastronomic Celebrations**

    The Oktoberfest is held in Germany:
    The Oktoberfest in Munich, Germany, is one of the most well-known beer festivals in the world. It is a celebration of Bavarian culture that includes music, traditional Bavarian dishes, and beer.

    The Festival of Lights (in India):
    Diwali, also known as the Festival of Lights, is one of the most important festivals in Hinduism and is celebrated with a wide range of desserts, snacks, and specialized cuisines.

    (Chicago, United States of America):
    Taste of Chicago is an annual event that takes place in Chicago and features a wide variety of cuisines from the city's well-known dining scene.

    Spain's "La Tomatina":
    Festival of the Throwing of Tomatoes, also known as "La Tomatina," is a one-of-a-kind event that blends food, fun, and vivid culture.

    Pahiyas Festival is celebrated in the Philippines:
    The Pahiyas festival is a colorful celebration of the harvest during which homes are decked out with various agricultural products and delicacies.

    (In India) Holi:
    The Festival of Colors, also known as Holi, is celebrated with many different kinds of sweets, snacks, and drinks that are passed around between friends and family.

3. **The Importance of Food and Drink Events to the Maintenance of Cultural Authenticity**

    Regional gastronomy:
    Festivals of cuisine draw attention to the singular aromas, flavors, and meals that are characteristic of a given area. They make it possible for local chefs and vendors to demonstrate their mastery of the culinary arts at these events.

    Methods Used in Traditional Cooking:
    Numerous food and drink celebrations educate attendees on classic cooking skills, helping to ensure that these time-honored practices are not abandoned in favor of more contemporary approaches.

    Ingredients from the Area:
    These activities put an emphasis on using seasonal products that are produced locally, with the goal of supporting local farmers and promoting the responsible use of resources.

    Participation in the Community:
    The community is typically invited to participate in the production of the food at culinary festivals, which inspires engagement and fosters the transmission of

expertise between generations.
Education in the Culinary Arts:
They provide visitors with an educational opportunity to learn about the history of food, various cooking skills, and the cultural importance of the foods that they eat.

4. **The Culinary Arts on Display: Competitions and Shows in the World of Gastronomy**
Competitions known as MasterChef and Iron Chef include:
Competitions in the kitchen have become increasingly popular thanks to the success of shows like MasterChef and Iron Chef. They highlight the abilities of both professional chefs and home cooks, thereby motivating a new generation of people to get interested in the culinary arts.
Demonstrations of Real-Time Cooking:
Live cooking demonstrations given by prominent chefs are frequently featured at culinary festivals. These provide guests the opportunity to observe the chefs in action and learn from the very best.
Competitions of Taste and Rating:
Taste-offs and judging panels are common components of competitions, and they offer participants a glimpse into the evaluation criteria that are used to rank meals.
Emerging Tendings in the Kitchen:
As a result of the chefs' willingness to innovate and push the boundaries of classic cuisine, these events serve as a breeding ground for new culinary trends.
Education in the Culinary Arts:
Attendees can gain knowledge about materials, techniques, and the art of presentation by participating in culinary competitions and exhibitions, which provide an educational experience.

5. **Considerations of Ethical Standards and Environmental Impact**
Ingredients Obtained from the Nearby Community:
To lessen their impact on the environment, festivals are placing an increased emphasis on the utilization of sustainably sourced and locally sourced ingredients.
Efforts Made to Reduce Food Waste:
In order to reduce the amount of food that is thrown out at festivals, efforts are being made to promote portion control, recycling, and composting.
Alternatives for Vegans and Vegetarians:
More vegetarian and vegan options are being made available at culinary festivals in order to accommodate a wider variety of dietary preferences and to lessen the negative impact that the production of meat has on the environment.
Ethics in Procurement:
The use of ethical sourcing practices, such as fair trade by numerous festivals, helps to promote the production of food in a responsible and compassionate

manner.

Sensitivity to the Environment:
Attendees are being encouraged to make decisions that are better for the environment by festivals that are raising awareness about the impact of food production and consumption on the ecosystem.

6. **The Emergence of the Contemporary Food Truck Revolution**

Various Types of Food:
Food trucks provide a diverse selection of dishes, ranging from American classics like gourmet burgers and tacos to more exotic fare like Korean barbecue and Thai street food.

Enterprise on your own:
The market of food trucks has spawned a plethora of options for entrepreneurs, making it possible for chefs and home cooks to launch their own businesses with much reduced overhead expenses.

Facilitation of:
Food trucks provide festival-goers with convenience and flexibility by allowing them to enjoy a variety of foods without having to move from one site to another.

Creativity in the Kitchen:
In order to differentiate themselves from the other vendors in the competitive festival food scene, many food trucks provide dishes that are both original and innovative.

The Culture of Street Food:
The rise in popularity of food trucks has helped to spread an appreciation for the tradition of street food around the world; as a result, there are now festivals that are devoted only to this type of cuisine.

7. **Festivals of Food Based on a Specific Theme or Interest**

Festivals of the Truffle:
The highly coveted edible delicacy known as the truffle is the subject of celebration at truffle festivals. During the events, there are frequently tastings, truffle hunts, and cookery demonstrations.

Festivals devoted to Chocolate:
The world of cocoa and chocolate is celebrated in full at chocolate festivals, which also showcase artisanal chocolatiers and offer sampling of chocolate-inspired meals and beverages.

Festivals of Fish and Seafood:
Festivals celebrating seafood are frequently held in coastal areas. These festivals call attention to the region's rich seafood resources and feature delicacies like lobster, crab, and oysters.

Competitions of chili:
Cook-offs for chili provide cooks the opportunity to demonstrate their most

impressive chili recipes, and guests get to sample and vote on their favorites.

Festivals de Grilling:
The skill of grilling and smoking meats is honored during BBQ festivals, when participants from a variety of locations showcase their regionally distinctive approaches to the cooking method.

Festivals that bring local produce directly to the table:
The farm-to-table movement is promoted through the hosting of these festivals, which place an emphasis on the utilization of locally farmed and farm-fresh ingredients.

8. **The Role of Festivals as Destinations for Gastronomic Tourism**

    Investigating the Different Regional Cuisines:
    Travelers have the option to immerse themselves in the local food scene and try the delicacies that are unique to the area they are visiting.

    Encounters with other cultures:
    The cultural performances, demonstrations, and other events that are frequently included during culinary festivals are intended to broaden the scope of the cultural experience beyond that of the food.

    Lessons on How to Cook:
    Travelers will have the opportunity to learn how to produce traditional meals from the area at many of the festivals that are held throughout the year.

    Products of the Market and Handmade Items:
    A common feature of festivals is the presence of marketplaces in which visitors can buy regional goods, spices, and artisanal items to take back with them as mementos.

    Participation in the Community:
    Participating in culinary tourism at events like festivals often involves mingling with members of the surrounding community, giving financial support to locally owned and operated enterprises, and gaining knowledge about local traditions and practices.

9. **The Importance of Culinary Festivals to the Participation in Social and Cultural Activities**

    Create closer ties within the community:
    People gather for culinary festivals, which encourages social contact as well as the sharing of both food and experiences among attendees.

    Foster Intercultural Communication:
    They promote cultural exchange by giving attendees the opportunity to learn about the culinary customs and cultural histories of a variety of regions via the medium of food.

    Honor the Richness of Differences:
    Festivals highlight the richness of many global food cultures while celebrating the variety of cuisines that exist around the world.

Participate in a Dialogue:
Food and drink celebrations have the potential to become forums for discussions on topics such as the ethics of consuming food, food sustainability, and responsible consumption.

Exhibit Your Skills in the Kitchen:
These events showcase the talents and ingenuity of chefs, providing motivation to those who aspire to careers in the culinary arts.

10. **Opportunities and Obstacles in the Landscape of Culinary Festivals**

    Assurance of Quality:
    It might be difficult, especially with the proliferation of food festivals, to guarantee the quality and originality of the meals and ingredients that are being served.

    Long-term viability:
    It is a challenging endeavor to lessen the negative effects that large-scale festivals have on the surrounding environment while also cutting down on waste.

    Appropriation de la culture:
    When festivals incorporate aspects of other cultures without displaying appropriate respect and knowledge for those traditions, they run the risk of being accused of cultural appropriation.

    Ability to be reached:
    Festival organizers need to make an effort to make culinary events accessible and inclusive for attendees who may have dietary restrictions, food allergies, or other limitations.

    Influence on the Economy:
    Even though festivals have the potential to provide the local economy a boost, organizers nevertheless need to be prepared for the potential economic issues that may arise, particularly during times of economic slowdown or pandemics.

    Concerning Health and Safety
    It is of the utmost importance to look after the guests' and the food vendors' health and safety, particularly with regard to the proper handling and sanitation of the food.

11. **Upcoming Developments and Breakthroughs in the World of Gastronomic Festivals**

Experiences That Are Only Virtual:
The proliferation of technologies such as virtual reality and internet streaming is opening the door to the possibility of attending virtual food festivals without having to leave the comfort of one's own home.

Intelligence simulated by computers:
Attendees of a festival can have more individualized and enjoyable food and drink experiences thanks to the application of AI, which can also provide them with specialized recommendations and insights.

Technologies that Enable Interaction:
By giving information about food, ingredients, and the cultural setting of the festival, augmented reality and interactive technologies can make the experience of attending the festival more enjoyable.

Options that Are Based on Plants and Are Sustainable:
The culinary options that are provided at festivals are likely going to be influenced by the growing interest in sustainable practices and diets based on plants.

Fusion cuisine from throughout the world:
Culinary festivals may start featuring fusion cuisines in the future as international travel
becomes easier to reach. These cuisines combine the flavors and cooking methods of a variety of different areas.

Collaborations with Neighborhood Organizations and Businesses:
Festivals are likely to create more partnerships with local food-related businesses, including restaurants, food trucks, and food enterprises in general, which will help to foster a feeling of community.

Festivals of cuisine are more than just get-togethers for people to gorge themselves on food; rather, they are celebrations of culture, community, and the pleasure of appreciating the myriad cuisines from around the world. They are a reflection of our mutual affection for food as well as our interest regarding the culinary customs that distinguish us. These celebrations have developed into an essential component of our world's cultural landscape, and they range from straightforward harvest celebrations to opulent international food competitions. They are a tribute to our desire to connect with one another through the universal language of food, so building a relationship that transcends borders and brings people together in the spirit of shared delight. They serve as a reminder that we want to connect with one another via the language of food. Culinary festivals provide a rich and complete experience that satisfies not only the taste buds but also the other senses and the soul. This is true whether you are sampling street cuisine in Asia, local specialties in Europe, or regional dishes in the Americas.

7.1 Exploring the world of culinary celebrations (e.g., Oktoberfest, Thanksgiving, Diwali)

The culinary festivities are a delightful trip into the heart of the traditions and civilizations that are being celebrated. They center on the pleasure of consuming food, the coming together of loved ones, and the expressing of thanks and unity with one another. These festivals offer a one-of-a-kind chance to learn about the varied culinary traditions and cuisines that have contributed to the formation of our planet. In the course of this investigation, we will delve into the vibrant tapestry of gastronomic festivities from all over the world. We will focus on the cultural significance of these events, as well as the one-of-a-kind meals and the sense of community that characterize these gatherings.

1. Oktoberfest, held in Munich, Germany, is a celebration of Bavarian culture and beer.

   The Significance of Culture:

   The Oktoberfest is a festival held annually in Munich, Germany, that honors Bavarian culture by presenting its traditional attire, music, dance, and customs. It provides an opportunity for both natives and tourists to participate in Bavarian cultural activities.

   Delectables for Your Mouth:

   The festival features a mouthwatering selection of Bavarian cuisine, such as sausages, pretzels, sauerkraut, and roasted chicken, among other mouthwatering options. Schweinshaxe, which is roasted pig knuckle, and Weisswurst, which is white sausage and is traditionally served with sweet mustard, are two of the highlights of this meal.

   Beer:

   The beer is, without a doubt, the highlight of the Oktoberfest celebration. Traditionally a Marzen-style lager, Oktoberfest beer is brewed in accordance with the Reinheitsgebot, also known as the Bavarian Purity Law. The beer is served in big steins, and guests have the opportunity to sample a selection of brews produced by Munich's six most prominent brewers.

   Friendship and cooperation:

   The purpose of getting to know new people and making memories to last a lifetime is what Oktoberfest is all about. People from all over the world congregate here to enjoy each other's company, have some laughs, move their bodies to the local music, and take part in the festive spirit.

2. Thanksgiving, a Celebration of Gratitude in the United States of America

   The Significance of Culture:

   The Pilgrims and Native Americans in the early 17th century are credited with establishing the tradition of Thanksgiving in the United States. It is a time for contemplation and expressing appreciation for the harvest, blessings, and the cohesiveness that exists among all people.

   Traditional Foods and Dishes:

   The traditional Thanksgiving meal consists of roasted turkey, stuffing, cranberry sauce, mashed potatoes, sweet potatoes, green bean casserole, and a variety of pies like pumpkin and pecan pie. These delicacies are put together with tender loving care, and frequently use family recipes.

   Get-Togethers With the Family:

   Thanksgiving is a time for loved ones to join together for a celebratory feast, during which they may show their appreciation to one another and make memories that will be cherished forever.

   Marching bands and football games:

   In addition to the meal, Thanksgiving is notable for the Macy's Thanksgiving

FESTIVALS AND CELEBRATIONS

Day Parade, which takes place in New York City, and a series of football games, which are watched by many people around the country.

3. **Diwali, or the Festival of Lights and Sweets, is Celebrated in India**
   The Significance of Culture:
   Diwali is a festival that is highly significant in the religions of Hinduism, Jainism, and Sikhism. It is a festival that celebrates the victory of knowledge and goodness over ignorance and evil.
   Desserts and Temptations:
   The festivities surrounding Diwali place a significant emphasis on delectable desserts. Mithai is a sort of candy, and samosas are only two of the many types of sweets and snacks that are prepared by the people. The bright and fragrant ladoo is one of the most famous sweets associated with the festival of Diwali.
   Turning on of the Lamps:
   During the festival of Diwali, people will adorn their houses with rangoli patterns made of colored sand, oil lamps, and candles. The light shines as a metaphor for the dispelling of darkness and the enlightenment that comes from within.
   Explosions in the Sky and Crackers:
   Celebrations of Diwali are not complete without the spectacular fireworks that paint the night sky with a kaleidoscope of colors and illuminated patterns.
   Gift Giving and Receiving:
   The festival of light known as Diwali is a time for gathering with family and friends to celebrate and exchange gifts. This act is one of love and gratitude toward the recipient.
4. **Hanukkah, the Festival of Lights in the Jewish Calendar**

The Significance of Culture:
Hanukkah is a Jewish holiday that celebrates the rededication of the Holy Temple as well as the victory of the Maccabees over the Seleucid Empire. It is a festival that celebrates light and the miraculous.

Lighting of the Menorah:
During Hanukkah, one candle on the menorah is lit for each night of the holiday. The eight candles are each lit up on the final night of the ceremony. The miracle of the oil is represented by the menorah, which was able to burn for eight days even though there was only enough oil for one day.

Dishes such as Latkes and Sufganiyot:
Hanukkah dishes include latkes, which are similar to potato pancakes, and sufganiyot, which are similar to jelly-filled donuts. In honor of the miracle that occurred with oil, these foods are fried in oil.

The Game of Dreidel

During Hanukkah, kids enjoy the game of dreidel, which involves spinning a special top that has been decorated on all four sides with Hebrew letters. It's a game of chance with a lot of history behind it.

Time Spent With the Family :

During the holiday of Hanukkah, family get together to celebrate by gathering around the menorah, eating festive foods, and exchanging gifts.

V. Christmas, a Time for Rejoicing and Feasting Celebrated All Over the World

The Significance of Culture:

Christmas is a Christian festival that commemorates the birth of Jesus, but it has also evolved into a secular cultural celebration that is commemorated by people from a wide variety of cultural traditions.

Dinner on Christmas Day:

In many nations, the Christmas meal is considered to be the most important element of the celebration. Stuffing, veggies, and cranberry sauce are typically part of the spread, as well as a roasted turkey, ham, or another type of meat.

Holiday Sweets and Treats:

Traditional sweets associated with Christmas include cookies, gingerbread, fruitcake, and eggnog. Traditional holiday desserts include fruitcake and Christmas cookies, both of which are frequently baked and decorated by families.

The Yule Log is:

A chocolate or sponge cake curled to resemble a log is a common representation of the Yule log, which is a symbol of the winter solstice. The Yule log is a tradition that dates back to ancient times. In a good number of the nations of Europe, you can get it as a dessert.

Exchange of Gifts:

The tradition of exchanging presents at Christmastime represents the sharing of affection and happiness between members of a family and their circle of friends. Children all throughout the world believe that Santa Claus or another person of a similar nature brings them gifts.

VI. Eid al-Fitr, or the Festival of Breaking Fast, Comes at the End of Ramadan

Importance from a Religious Perspective:

After a month of fasting, introspection, and spiritual development, the holy month of Ramadan

comes to a close with the celebration of Eid al-Fitr. This is a time for expressing appreciation to Allah and for engaging in deeds of charity.

Prayer during Eid:

On the morning of Eid al-Fitr, Muslims gather at their mosques to participate in a special prayer. The act of worship and offering thanks as a community is represented by the prayer.

Celebration Dinner:

The holiday of Eid is commemorated with a large dinner that often includes a range of meals that may differ from region to region but may include biryani, kebabs, haleem, and a selection of desserts such as baklava and maamoul.

Deeds of Benevolence:

The holiday of Eid al-Fitr places an emphasis on acts of kindness and giving to those who are less fortunate. It is common practice for Muslims to give a percentage of their money to others who are less well off.

Presents for Eid:

During the festival of Eid al-Fitr, it is traditional to give presents to people, particularly

youngsters. As a sign of affection and participation in the festivities, family and friends traditionally give and receive gifts.

VII. The Lunar New Year, also known as the Chinese New Year, is a Gastronomic Extravaganza

The Significance of Culture:

The coming of spring and the beginning of a new cycle of life are commemorated during the Lunar New Year. It is a time for getting together with extended family, performing traditional rituals, and paying respect to ancestors.

Foods for the Lunar New Year:

Dishes served during the traditional celebration of the Lunar New Year each have a specific meaning. Dumplings and nian gao (sticky rice cakes), both of which reflect a higher income or status, are hallmarks of the celebration. Dumplings symbolize riches, and nian gao represent higher social position.

Dances of the Lion and the Dragon:

The streets are filled with colorful lion and dragon dances, which are practiced to bring good fortune and fight off evil spirits. These performances are a visual treat that will not disappoint.

Red Envelopes, also known as Hongbao:

Children and other younger members of the family often receive hongbao, which are red envelopes holding money and are known as gifts. These are presented as a symbol of good luck and blessings.

Gatherings of the Family:

The Lunar New Year is a time for getting together with friends and family to celebrate, and many people travel back to their hometowns during this time. A significant portion of the festivities will consist of the "Tuan Nian" supper, which in Chinese translates to "reunion dinner."

Festivals of cuisine are held all over the world, and they are more than just occasions to indulge in delectable dishes; rather, they are windows into the cultural customs, values, and spirit of the communities that host them. These festivals offer a venue in which family, friends, and communities may congregate, share their appreciation, and honor the distinctive flavors and culinary traditions that distinguish them.

Each holiday, from Oktoberfest with its Bavarian feasting and beer to Diwali with its sweets and

lights, carries its own cultural importance and offers its own unique gastronomic delights.

The celebrations that take place during Thanksgiving and Hanukkah are centered on expressions of thankfulness and light, whereas Christmas and Eid al-Fitr are occasions for rejoicing, praying, and feasting. A brilliant display of color, dance, and symbolism is presented during the Lunar New Year celebration.

The beauty of our world's diverse cultures and the universal human experience of joining together to celebrate life, culture, and community are brought to the forefront by these gastronomic events. These festivals link us to our past, our present, and our dreams for the future through the medium of food, demonstrating that the world becomes a more vibrant and savory place when we embrace the customs and culinary delights that form our lives.

7.2 The role of food in cultural identity and celebration

Food is not only necessary for survival; it is also a potent expression of a community's cultural identity, heritage, and shared history. The act of preparing and sharing meals has long been an essential component of cultural practices and customs in many different parts of the world. It acts as a means of maintaining cultural history, encouraging the development of a sense of belonging, and appreciating the richness of diversity that exists within communities. In this investigation, we dig into the significant role that food plays in the formation of cultural identity and the promotion of celebrations. We also stress the value of food in maintaining traditions and creating social cohesion.

The Safekeeping of Our Cultural Traditions

The transmission of cultural traditions through the medium of food is extremely important

because it provides a direct physical link to times gone by. It is a compilation of culinary customs, recipes, and methods of preparation that date back hundreds of years and have been handed down from generation to generation. Communities ensure the continuation of their cultural history by preserving traditional recipes and cooking methods. This helps communities maintain their customs and heritage alive while also preserving their cultural legacy. The passing down of these cooking techniques from one generation to the next helps to instill a sense of pride in one's cultural history and contributes to the preservation of cultural identity in a world that is constantly evolving.

Traditions and Practices Relating to Food

Celebrations of important life moments and cultural holidays are inextricably bound up with culinary practices, rituals, and traditions. Food plays a significant role in a wide variety of cultural rituals, including but not limited to religious observances, festivals, marriages, funerals, and seasonal celebrations. These delicacies typically serve as symbols of many cultural beliefs, values, and behaviors. It is possible for these rituals to have spiritual importance, to remember historical events, or to mark key transformations in one's life. As a result, communities are brought closer together through the experiences and traditions they share.

Maintaining Social Unity and Connections Within the Community

Communities are brought together via the act of preparing and sharing meals, which contributes to the development of social cohesiveness and strengthens interpersonal connections. Food acts as a catalyst for social interaction, enabling the exchange of tales, ideas, and experiences and facilitating the building of strong communal relationships. Food brings people together and brings out their best stories, ideas, and experiences. The act of sharing food, whether at neighborhood get-togethers, communal feasts, or potlucks, fosters a sense of connection and belonging, establishing a social fabric that is supportive and inclusive and crosses cultural barriers.

Intercultural Communication and Merging of Cultures

Food has the unique potential to bridge the gap between different cultures, making it an excellent medium for international communication and contributing to the formation of new cultural hybrids. When communities come together and share the culinary traditions of their own cultures, they frequently influence and inspire one another, which can lead to the development of novel fusion cuisines that combine the cooking methods, flavors, and ingredients of a variety of different cultures. This cross-pollination of culinary traditions not only enhances the culinary landscape but also promotes mutual understanding and appreciation of other cultures, so contributing to the development of a global community that is more inclusive and interdependent.

Symbolism and its Relative Importance

There are a lot of meals that have been around for a long time and have been passed down from generation to generation. Many of these dishes have symbolic meanings that represent values, beliefs, and aspirations. In many cases, the ingredients, colors, and techniques of preparation all hold significant symbolic meanings that are reflective of cultural narratives and historical events. Culinary traditions serve as a means of transmitting cultural values and ideas. This is true of the symbolism of particular foods in Chinese cuisine as well as the ritualistic significance of food offerings in Hindu ceremonies. This helps to reinforce a common cultural narrative that brings communities closer together.

Festivals & Feasts in Honor of a Special Occasion

The expression of delight, appreciation, and reverence can be achieved by participation in culinary celebrations and feasting, both of which are essential components of cultural celebrations and noteworthy events. During celebrations, large feasts consisting of traditional dishes and delicacies are frequently served. These meals are meticulously prepared and then distributed to members of the community, including family, friends, and neighbors. These feasts not only serve to memorialize important events, but they also serve to reinforce the cultural significance of food as a source of enjoyment and communal celebration. As a result, they help communities feel a greater feeling of collective joy and solidarity.

Heritage of Regional Cuisines and Regional Diversity

The unique cultural legacy and geographical factors that have shaped gastronomic traditions are reflected in the wide variety of cuisines found across the world's regions. Cooking techniques, regional ingredients, and flavor profiles can vary greatly from one part of the country to another, and these differences frequently reflect the environmental, historical, and cultural settings of the local people. The preservation of regional culinary heritage and the celebration of that legacy contribute to the richness of cultural variety by drawing attention to the distinct personalities and cuisines that identify local communities all over the world.

The Role of Food as an Ambassador of Culture

Food acts as a cultural ambassador in a society that is becoming more globalized, promoting cultural interchange as well as understanding and enjoyment of other cultures. Culinary tourism has emerged as a potent tool for presenting a region's rich cultural heritage, since an increasing number of tourists are looking for genuine dining experiences that provide insights into the region's traditions and practices. Restaurants and food festivals that are devoted to displaying a variety of cuisines have become forums for building a deeper sense of cultural appreciation and respect, as well as promoting cultural understanding.

Adaptability and robustness go hand in one

Reflecting the resiliency and adaptability of communities across time, culinary traditions frequently alter and transform in response to shifting environments and conditions. Traditional recipes have been adapted as a result of migration, globalization, and shifting nutritional tastes, which has led to the formation of new culinary practices that integrate cultural aspects from a variety of different places. The adaptability of culinary traditions and the capacity to accept new influences not only ensures the continuation of these traditions but also represents the vitality and resiliency of cultural identity in the face of changes in social norms, economic conditions, and the natural environment.

The encouragement of cultural pride as well as awareness

Communities may build a sense of cultural pride and awareness as well as instill a greater respect for their roots and customs through activities such as honoring and promoting their culinary heritage. Events in the culinary world, such as food festivals, cultural exhibitions, and other cultural events, can serve as platforms for increasing cultural awareness and fostering cultural education. Communities are able to affirm their cultural identity and share the rich heritage of their ancestors with others as a result of these initiatives.

The significance of food in cultural celebrations and in the formation of cultural identities is illustrative of the power of gastronomy to bring people together, to maintain traditions, and to foster cultural variety. Communities celebrate their common heritage, express their core beliefs, and create memories that will last a lifetime through the medium of food. Culinary traditions play an essential role in the formation of cultural identities; they operate not only as a link between the past and the present but also as a means of promoting social cohesion and intercultural communication. Food acts as a worldwide language in a world that is marked by diversity, bringing together individuals and groups, celebrating their unique identities, and presenting the rich tapestry of cultures that shape our global civilization. In a world that is marked by diversity, food stands as a universal language.

7.3 Food festivals as reflections of local agriculture and cuisine

The purpose of food festivals is to create vivid celebrations of local agriculture, culinary traditions, and the spirit of the community. They offer a stage upon which to exhibit the myriad flavors, components, and cooking methods that come together to constitute the cultural and gastronomic identity of a particular place. These festivals not only emphasize the distinct cultural legacy and culinary talents that contribute to the diversity of the local food scene, but they also encourage local agriculture and sustainable food practices. This is a win-win situation for the community. In this investigation, we dive into the significance of food festivals as reflections of local agriculture and cuisine. We place an emphasis on the role that food festivals play in building community participation, promoting regional gastronomy, and conserving culinary traditions.

Putting Forward Regionally Sourced Products and Components

The richness of locally sourced vegetables and ingredients that are the foundation of a region's cuisine is brought to the forefront at food festivals, which play an essential role in this process. Farmers' markets, at which regional farmers and producers can display their wares of freshly harvested fruits, vegetables, meats, and dairy products are frequently featured at these festivals. Food festivals encourage guests to gain a better appreciation for the quality and diversity of local produce by highlighting the significance of using locally sourced items and those that are in season. These festivals also promote environmentally responsible agriculture methods and benefit the local economy.

Observing and Honoring the Culture and History of Agriculture

A great number of food festivals have their origins deeply ingrained in the agricultural history and customs of their respective regions. They do so in recognition of the historical significance of farming traditions and the cultivation of native crops, which have provided communities with food and sustenance for many centuries.

These festivals encourage a sense of pride and appreciation for the agricultural heritage of the region by providing attendees with insights into traditional farming techniques, crop cultivation methods, and the cultural significance of various agricultural practices through the use of interactive demonstrations, workshops, and educational sessions.

Advancing Skill in the Kitchen While Fostering Innovation

The purpose of food festivals is to provide stages upon which local chefs, culinary experts, and food aficionados can demonstrate their gastronomic prowess and present novel ways in which local ingredients might be utilized in their dishes. Participants get the opportunity to learn about new cooking techniques, flavor combinations, and culinary trends that showcase the distinctive flavors and textures of local products through the participation in culinary competitions, cooking demos, and chef-led workshops. These events are guided by chefs. These festivals contribute to the development of regional cuisine and help to cultivate a culture of culinary excellence within the community. They do this by encouraging the advancement of gastronomic knowledge and techniques.

Promoting Participation in the Community and Working Together

Food festivals encourage community participation and collaboration by bringing together customers, farmers, chefs, and other craftspeople, as well as the consumers themselves. They create possibilities for individuals and businesses to engage with one another and work together by offering a communal area for conversation, networking, and the sharing of ideas, thereby making the space available. The cultivation of a mutually beneficial link between agriculture and the culinary arts, which is to the advantage of the entire community, frequently leads to the production of original dishes that are inspired by the changing of the seasons in the local area.

The Maintenance of Gastronomic Customs and the Conservation of Cultural Objects

There are a lot of festivals that celebrate food that are focused on conserving and promoting traditional ways of cooking as well as cultural heritage. They function as living museums of culinary traditions, showcasing time-honored recipes, cooking techniques, and cultural rituals that have been handed down from generation to generation. These festivals help to conserve the intangible cultural history of a community by displaying traditional meals, culinary skills, and cultural acts. This ensures that the rich culinary legacy of the region will continue to thrive and resonate with future generations.

Putting an emphasis on environmentally responsible food practices

Food festivals are playing an increasingly important part in the promotion of sustainable food practices and the development of awareness about the significance of responsible consumption in this day and age, which is distinguished by growing concerns about the sustainability of food and the conservation of the environment.

The concept of sustainability is included into a wide variety of celebrations, with the aim of drawing attention to the significance of organic farming, zero-waste efforts, and environmentally friendly ways of food production. These festivals encourage guests to make educated decisions about the food they consume and support projects that contribute to the long-term health of the environment and the local agricultural ecosystem by encouraging sustainable food practices. These techniques include growing food in a way that minimizes its negative impact on the environment.

Celebrating the Diversity of Flavors and the Merging of Cultures

Food festivals honor the gastronomic variety and cultural synthesis that arise from the collision of various culinary traditions and styles that exist within a particular region. They provide a platform for communities to celebrate their cultural variety, fostering inclusivity and mutual appreciation for the culinary legacy of many ethnic groups and communities all over the world. The ever-evolving nature of regional cuisine, as well as the cultural interactions that have shaped the culinary landscape of the region, are frequently reflected in the prevalence of fusion cuisines. These cuisines combine regional flavors with those from other parts of the world.

Increasing Tourism While Preserving Regional Character

Food festivals are key attractions for tourists and visitors, which helps to promote culinary
  tourism and contributes to the growth of the local economy as a whole. These festivals provide visitors with an immersive experience that enables them to investigate the distinctive tastes, scents, and cultural nuances that are a part of the culinary history of a particular location. These festivals not only increase the region's overall attractiveness as a cultural and gastronomic destination by attracting tourists via the promotion of regional identity through food, but they also contribute to the development of a distinct culinary identity that acts as a source of pride for the population that resides there and increases the region's overall appeal.

Efforts to Improve Education in Agriculture and the Culinary Arts

Food festivals offer guests important educational opportunities, promoting agriculture and culinary knowledge through workshops, tastings, and interactive sessions. These educational options are available to attendees. Participants are encouraged to learn about the importance of sustainable agricultural practices, the nutritional worth of local produce, and the cultural significance of a variety of ingredients and meals through the participation in these activities. These festivals allow individuals to make informed decisions about their food consumption and acquire a deeper understanding of the interconnectedness between agriculture, culinary arts, and cultural heritage by supporting education in agricultural and culinary fields.

A Feast Honoring the Customs and Flavors of Each Community

Festivals of food serve as dynamic celebrations of local agriculture, culinary talent, and cultural legacy. They give a one-of-a-kind opportunity for communities to join together and celebrate the rich tapestry of flavors, ingredients, and culinary traditions that define their regional character. These festivals encourage sustainable food practices, create community interaction, and display the distinctive cultural diversity that helps shape the culinary landscape of a region through a variety of activities that fall under a wide variety of categories. Communities can contribute to the growth of a flourishing, environmentally conscious, and culturally diverse culinary ecosystem by appreciating the gastronomic gems that their local agriculture and cuisine have to offer. This, in turn, helps communities to maintain their cultural traditions. Food festivals are a living reminder of the enduring connection that exists between people, the land, and the sustaining customs that have been passed down from generation to generation in communities all over the world.

Chapter 8

National and Independence Day Celebrations

Celebrations of National and Independence Days are among the most important and culturally rich events that are held to remember a nation's history, hardships, and successes. These days fall on July 4th. These recurring celebrations are important reminders of how far a country has come on its path to achieving freedom, sovereignty, and a sense of national identity. In many cases, they include a wide variety of ceremonial activities, parades, cultural performances, and patriotic displays, all of which aim to bring the local populace together in a sense of common pride and togetherness. In this in-depth investigation, we dive into the profound significance of the celebrations that take place on National Day and Independence Day. We investigate the historical origins of these holidays, as well as the cultural symbolism that is associated with them, and we investigate the many ways in which these events are commemorated all over the world.

1. **Acquiring an Understanding of the Significance of History**
   Celebrations of National Day and Independence Day are generally tied to significant historical events that represent a nation's fight for self-governance, independence, or the founding of a sovereign state. These celebrations have deep roots in the history of the nation they are held in. The journey of a nation toward self-determination, liberty, and the protection of its cultural heritage often includes these events, which typically indicate turning points in that journey. The passage of the Declaration of Independence in 1776, which marked the separation of the country from British colonial control and the establishment of a new nation founded on the ideas of democracy and freedom, is commemorated on the Fourth of July in the United States, for instance. This holiday is known as "Independence Day."
2. **The Feeling of Loyalty to One's Country and Sense of Community**
   Celebrations of National Day and Independence Day help to instill a sense of

patriotism and togetherness in the populace, which in turn helps to strengthen feelings of communal membership and civic pride. These events frequently bring together people from a wide variety of social, cultural, and ethnic backgrounds, urging them to embrace their nation's identity and ideals in the process. Citizens display their steadfast dedication to the nation and express their gratitude for the sacrifices made by previous generations in order to secure their independence and sovereignty by participating in community meetings, parades, and ceremonies in which the flag is waved. These events often involve waving the flag.

3. **Commemorative Activities and the Hoisting of the Flag**
The raising of the national flag in a solemn ceremony is one of the most important aspects of the ceremonies that take place on National and Independence Day. This act serves as a symbol of the nation's independence, resiliency, and unity. This ceremonial ritual is frequently performed at public squares, government buildings, and historical landmarks. Military personnel, government officials, and residents come together to respect the national flag and pay homage to the country's basic ideals and values during this ceremony ritual. The playing of the national song and the reciting of patriotic speeches are common components of the solemnity that surrounds the raising of the flag during a ceremony. These elements serve to highlight the importance of the event.

4. **Traditional Celebrations and Other Forms of Artistic Expression**
National and Independence Day celebrations are marked by a spectacular display of cultural performances, traditional festivities, and artistic manifestations that reflect the rich cultural legacy and diversity of a nation. These celebrations often take place on or around July 4th. In the course of these celebrations, you will frequently encounter the presentation of traditional music, dance performances, theater productions, and art exhibitions that highlight the distinctive artistic customs and cultural heritage of many regions around the country. Citizens celebrate the cultural identity that they share with one another and express their pride in the diverse fabric that makes up their national heritage through the use of various cultural manifestations.

5. **Veterans Day Ceremonies and Military Parades to Honor National Heroes**
The bravery, valor, and sacrifices of national heroes and veterans who have fought the country's freedom and sovereignty are honored during a number of ceremonies that take place on National Day and Independence Day. These celebrations feature huge military parades and processions. These parades frequently feature demonstrations of military might, precision exercises, and flyovers by the air force. Their purpose is to highlight the nation's defensive capabilities and pay honor to the selfless service of its armed forces. Citizens congregate along parade routes to cheer on members of the armed forces, express their gratitude to them,

FESTIVALS AND CELEBRATIONS

and acknowledge the significant contributions they have made to maintaining national security and peace.

6. **Addresses to the Public and the President's Speeches**
Celebrations of National Day and Independence Day frequently involve public addresses and speeches given by the President of the United States. These speeches typically highlight the historical significance of the event and place an emphasis on the nation's accomplishments, difficulties, and goals. These addresses provide political leaders with a forum from which they can foster feelings of solidarity, advance the cause of national ideals, and bolster the community's shared vision for the future. They bring attention to the achievements of the nation, acknowledge the efforts of its citizens, and reaffirm the commitment to upholding the democratic, just, and equitable ideals of the country.

7. **Contributions to the Community and Voluntary Work**
In addition to the parties and formal activities that take place, celebrations of National and Independence Day emphasize community service and participation as a way to foster civic engagement and social responsibility. Many localities host volunteer events, charitable causes, and community outreach programs with the goals of addressing social concerns, promoting community development, and elevating underserved demographics. Citizens express their attention to the welfare of their fellow citizens and their commitment to create a society that is more inclusive and equitable when they take an active role in community service programs.

8. **Contemplation as well as Recollection**
Celebrations of National Day and Independence Day provide opportunities for residents to reflect on the history, progress, and enduring ideals of the nation, while also recognizing the sacrifices and efforts of those who have fought for the independence and sovereignty of the country. National and Independence Day celebrations take place on July 4th. Visits to national monuments and war memorials, as well as rituals of commemoration, the laying of wreaths at memorials, and other such activities, serve as powerful reminders of the resiliency and bravery of previous generations and emphasize the significance of preserving the collective memory of the nation's historical journey.

9. **Educational Programs and Museum Displays of Artifacts**
Many festivities of National Day and Independence Day include educational activities, historical displays, and interactive programs with the goal of educating residents, particularly the younger generation, about the history, cultural legacy, and democratic values of the nation. The purpose of organizing special exhibitions, workshops, and seminars that delve into the key events and personalities that have shaped the nation's identity is to encourage citizens to develop a deeper understanding of their shared history as well as the values that underpin

their national identity. These types of activities take place in historical museums, cultural centers, and educational institutions.

10. **Importance on a Global Scale and Its Effects on Diplomatic Relations**
National and Independence Day celebrations possess considerable diplomatic and cultural significance on a worldwide scale because they provide a chance for countries to establish diplomatic ties, encourage international cooperation, and expose their cultural legacy to the global community. As a result, these events hold a substantial cultural and diplomatic value on a global scale. During these festivities, events like as diplomatic receptions, cultural exchanges, and international festivals serve as venues for encouraging mutual understanding, building bridges between nations, and promoting peace, stability, and collaboration on the global arena.

11. **Acceptance of All Cultures and Diversity of Cultures**
National and Independence Day celebrations frequently stress the cultural diversity and inclusivity of a nation. This acknowledges the contributions that many ethnic groups, religious communities, and disenfranchised populations have made to the social, cultural, and economic growth of the nation. Citizens celebrate the richness of their cultural tapestry and affirm their commitment to establishing a society that accepts diversity, promotes social cohesion, and respects the values of equality and social justice through the participation in cultural festivals, interfaith dialogues, and multicultural events. These activities take place in a variety of settings.

12. **The Importance of Technology and the Dedication of Digital Memorials**
National and Independence Day celebrations are increasingly utilizing digital platforms, social media campaigns, and virtual events to engage citizens, promote national pride, and encourage active involvement in the festivities. This trend is occurring in an era that has been distinguished by technological developments and increased digital connectivity. Citizens are given the opportunity to explore the nation's history and cultural heritage without having to leave the comfort of their homes thanks to digital initiatives such as online historical archives, virtual museum tours, and interactive educational resources. This helps citizens feel a deeper sense of connection and engagement with their national identity.

13. **Communal feasting and culinary customs are next on the agenda.**
National and Independence Day festivities frequently include community eating, culinary traditions, and spectacular feasts that bring people together to share in the experience of savoring national cuisine, regional specialties, and traditional dishes from their home communities. Street fairs, food festivals, and other culinary events are great ways to highlight the variety of a country's gastronomic traditions. These events also give citizens the opportunity to sample regional flavors and cuisines that are representative of the cultural and gastronomic legacy of different sections of the country. These gatherings of the

community foster a feeling of solidarity and give everyone the opportunity to partake in the cuisine of their country of origin.

14. **Sustainable Celebrations and Practices That Reduce Their Impact On The Environment**

    In recent years, themes of environmental conservation, sustainability, and eco-friendly practices have increasingly been included into festivities of National Day and Independence Day. The significance of commemorating historical events in a manner that is respectful of the local ecosystem has been acknowledged by a great number of nations. To develop a sense of responsibility for the environment and to emphasize the significance of maintaining the nation's natural resources for the benefit of future generations, many initiatives have been undertaken, such as the planting of trees, the organization of clean-up efforts, and the reduction of garbage produced during celebrations.

15. **The Importance of Art and Creativity in Today's World**

    Celebrations of National Day and Independence Day feature prominently prominent roles for

    artistic expressions and creative endeavors. Citizens frequently take part in events such as art contests, craft exhibitions, and creative initiatives that provide them the opportunity to display their creativity as well as their national pride. A nation's cultural vitality, artistic traditions, and the artistic prowess of its population can be displayed for the world to see through the mediums of the arts, which include the visual arts, literature, music, and dance. Individuals enrich the value of the celebrations in terms of its cultural significance by virtue of the creative works that they give to the party environment.

16. **Difficulties and Disagreements**

    Celebrations of both Independence Day and National Day are not without their share of difficulties and debates. Disputes and tensions surrounding celebrations commemorating a nation's war for independence can, in certain instances, be traced back to political differences, social unrest, or disagreements over the historical narratives of the nation's fight for independence. Celebrations like these should be a unifying force that transcends political or social divides and reinforces the nation's commitment to democracy, freedom, and justice. It is essential for countries to address such challenges by fostering open dialogue, inclusivity, and respect for diverse perspectives.

17. **A Consideration of the World at Large**

    Celebrations of both Independence Day and National Day are not confined to a particular geographical area or cultural tradition. These events are celebrated by nations all over the world, each of which does so in a way that is distinctive with regard to its historical context, cultural traditions, and demonstrations of national pride. Even while the particulars of these festivities can differ from country to country, the core purpose of remembering a nation's journey towards sovereignty, liberty, and cultural identity stays the same and serves as a unifying factor among all nations. These celebrations, which range from those held in France to honor Bastille Day to those held in India to honor Independence Day, are a testimony to the global yearning for freedom and the right to self-determination.

18. The importance of embracing national identity and unity

The commemorations of a country's national and Independence Days serve as a living representation of the collective memory, values, and cultural identity of that country. They serve as a yearly reminder of the sacrifices made by previous generations as well as the unwavering devotion to the ideals of freedom, democracy, and justice. These festivities emphasize the significance of preserving a nation's heritage, creating togetherness, and encouraging inclusivity through activities such as raising the flag, participating in parades, viewing cultural performances, and participating in educational projects.

Even though they have their origins in past events, celebrations of National Day and Independence Day endure the test of time because they symbolize an unwavering dedication to a nation's enduring commitment to its common ideals, cultural diversity, and the quest of a better future for all of its residents. These festivities continue to be a source of motivation because they symbolize the everlasting spirit of patriotism and solidarity, as well as the collective journey towards a brighter and more inclusive future. This is true even as nations continue to change and face new difficulties.

8.1 The importance of national identity and independence

The cultural, social, and political fabric of a nation are all shaped to some degree by a nation's level of independence as well as its sense of national identity. They are symbolic of the awareness, ideals, and aspirations of a people as a whole, and they reflect the distinctive history, legacy, and cultural narratives that are shared by that group. National identity acts as a unifying force that develops a sense of belonging and solidarity among citizens, whereas independence reflects the fundamental right of a nation to govern itself and determine its own future. National identity also serves as a unifying force that fosters a sense of belonging and solidarity among citizens. In this investigation, we dive into the relevance of national identity and independence, demonstrating the tremendous impact that these concepts have on the evolution of nations, the protection of cultural legacy, and the advancement of world peace and stability.

1. **Creating a Stronger Sense of Unity and Belonging to the Group**
   The cultivation of a sense of belonging and solidarity among citizens is significantly aided by the development of a national identity. It provides a sense of community and common purpose that is independent of geographical, language, and cultural boundaries, serving as a unifying force in the process.

Instilling a sense of pride and belonging that links individuals together, regardless of their different backgrounds, national symbols, anthems, and cultural traditions help to strengthen the nation's collective identity and serve to further solidify the nation as a whole. Citizens have a shared sense of responsibility for the well-being of their nation when they embrace a common national identity. This fosters social cohesiveness and reinforces the values that constitute their collective identity.

2. **Protecting the Traditions and Cultural Heritage of Societies**
National identity is closely connected with the preservation of cultural heritage and traditions. It serves as a vehicle for conserving the rich tapestry of a nation's history, language, art, and customs, and this is because national identity is intricately intertwined with the preservation of cultural heritage and traditions. Sites of cultural heritage, historical monuments, and creative manifestations capture the core of a nation's identity by reflecting the nation's distinctive cultural legacy as well as the contributions of previous generations to the nation's social and intellectual growth. Nations are able to maintain their unique cultural identities while also contributing to the expansion of cultural diversity on a global scale when they take measures to protect and promote their cultural heritage.

3. **Upholding the Principles and Values of Democratic Governance**
There is a strong connection between the fundamental ideals of democracy, human rights, and social justice with the concept of national identity and independence. They are symbolic of the concerted effort made by a nation as a whole to defend the values of liberty, equality, and the rule of law in order to guarantee the defense of the rights and liberties of its citizens. Independence is a necessary component of democratic government because it gives individuals the ability to take part in the decision-making process and to contribute to the growth of a society that is equitable and welcoming to all. The cultivation of a sense of civic participation and responsible citizenship is made possible by the strengthening of a nation's commitment to the democratic values that underpin the nation.

4. **Encouraging Peace and Stability Across the World**
National identity and independence are important factors in the maintenance of international peace and stability because they encourage nations to respect one another, gain a common understanding of one another, and work together. They serve as a basis for the development of robust bilateral and multilateral partnerships by fostering the cultivation of peaceful ties, diplomatic conversation, and international engagement. Nations that respect each other's sovereignty and independence contribute to the establishment of a peaceful global community that values cultural diversity, respects human rights, and works collectively to address global difficulties such as climate change, poverty, and conflicts. This community loves cultural diversity, respects human rights, and

works collectively to address global challenges like as climate change, poverty, and conflicts.
5. **Cultivating an Attitude of Perseverance and Unity in the Face of Adversity**
In times of tragedy and crisis, a sense of resilience and solidarity can be fostered by cultivating a sense of national identity and independence. They serve as a source of inspiration and motivation for citizens to overcome problems, confront hardships, and work together to repair and enhance their communities. They also serve as a source of inspiration and motivation for government officials. National identity strengthens the spirit of solidarity and resiliency, encouraging individuals to contribute to the collective efforts of rebuilding their nation and assuring the well-being of their fellow citizens during times of natural disasters, economic downturns, or political unrest. This is because national identity is rooted in history and traditions that have been passed down from generation to generation.
6. **Facilitating Intercultural Communication and Comprehending One Another**
When it comes to the promotion of cultural interchange, mutual understanding, and intercultural conversation between nations, national identity and independence play an extremely important role. They provide a forum in which cultural experiences, values, and traditions can be discussed, so promoting a greater understanding for the variety and wealth of the world's cultural history. Nations promote cross-cultural understanding and respect through cultural exchanges, festivals, and educational activities. This helps develop a global community that accepts cultural diversity, promotes tolerance, and celebrates the shared human experience.
7. **Stimulating Creative Activity and Intellectual Progression**
The pursuit of greatness in a variety of sectors, such as science, technology, and the arts, is bolstered when there is a strong sense of national identity as well as independence from outside influences. They cultivate an atmosphere that encourages innovative thinking, critical analysis, and intellectual prowess; as a result, they motivate individuals to make significant contributions to the growth and improvement of their nation. By making investments in education, research, and the development of new technologies, nations improve their ability to compete on the global stage and contribute to the expansion of humankind's collective knowledge and technological capabilities.
8. **Providing Opportunities and Strength to Underrepresented Communities and Groups**
It is vital to strengthen underprivileged populations and minority groups in order to ensure their representation, inclusion, and participation in the sociopolitical life of the nation. This can be accomplished through maintaining a strong national identity and independence. They advocate for the rights and

well-being of all citizens, regardless of their socioeconomic background, ethnicity, or religion affiliation, and they promote the ideals of equality, social justice, and inclusivity. In addition, they work to eliminate discrimination. Nations may establish a society that is more equal and just, one that recognizes and appreciates the contributions and points of view of all of its residents, by actively fostering diversity and inclusivity.

9. **Enhancing the Resilience and Security of the National Infrastructure**
Having a strong sense of national identity and independence is essential to bolstering the country's resiliency and security, ensuring the protection of the territory's integrity, and looking out for the welfare of the people living there. They establish a spirit of patriotism and a dedication to the protection of the nation, which contributes to the development of a sense of national pride. When nations make investments in measures of national security, disaster preparedness, and crisis management, they increase their resilience to both foreign threats and internal obstacles, which protects their independence and sovereignty for future generations.

10. **A Stimulant for the Growth of the Economy and the Promotion of Prosperity**

Having a strong sense of national identity and independence may be a powerful driver of economic growth and success by pushing nations to make investments in environmentally responsible development, physical infrastructure, and economic diversity. They encourage entrepreneurship, innovation, and the development of new job opportunities, which in turn inspires residents to make a positive contribution to the expansion of their country's economy.

Nations may boost economic growth, alleviate poverty, and improve the standard of life for their residents, all of which contribute to the overall well-being and prosperity of society, provided that they foster an environment that is conducive to the creation of businesses, to the exchange of goods, and to investment.

National identity and independence are the embodiment of the spirit of collective desire and growth. They are a reflection of the common values, cultural heritage, and democratic ideals that are what constitute a nation. They encourage citizens to contribute to the growth of both their nation and the global world, serving as a light of hope, unity, and resiliency in the process. Citizens demonstrate their dedication to the values of freedom, equality, and justice when they embrace their national identity and maintain their independence. This paves the path for a more inclusive, prosperous, and peaceful future for future generations.

8.2 The blending of historical remembrance and contemporary celebration

An honoring of the past, an acknowledgment of the present, and the creation of a vision for the future are all accomplished through the dynamic process represented by the interplay between historical remembering and modern celebration. This merging of historical narratives with contemporary celebrations serves as a bridge between tradition and innovation, helping societies to preserve their legacy while also embracing the spirit of development and change. The combination of historical recollection and contemporary celebration, as seen in memorial days, anniversaries, cultural festivals, and modern commemorations, highlights the continuing significance of collective memory, cultural identity, and the progression of societal values. In this extensive investigation, we dive into the complicated relationship between historical remembering and contemporary celebration, showing how this interplay shapes cultural continuity, social resilience, and the transformational power of collective memory. Throughout this investigation, we focus on how this relationship shapes cultural continuity, societal resilience, and the transformative force of collective memory.

1. **Acquiring a Fundamental Comprehension of What It Means to Remember the Past**
   Remembering our past is essential to both the maintenance of our culture and the development of our identity. It is the collective memory of key events, struggles, and successes that have molded the identity and values of a society. It is what gives a society its sense of purpose and direction. In order to maintain the cultural legacy and ensure that the stories of the past are passed down to subsequent generations, commemorative activities, memorial rituals, and historical exhibitions serve as vehicles. A sense of reverence for one's cultural heritage and the lifelong lessons that history teaches can be fostered in a society by the practice of remembering prior generations in order to pay honor to the efforts, achievements, and sacrifices made by those generations.

2. **The Development of Different Forms of Commemorative Practices**
   The ever-changing character of cultural practices and the norms that govern society is reflected in the development of commemorative rituals. Commemorative activities in different civilizations have evolved over time to better represent modern sensibilities and meet the shifting requirements of an ever-shifting global scene. These practices have taken the form of traditional rites and religious celebrations, as well as more contemporary memorials and public commemorations. The method in which cultures interact with their historical narratives has been revolutionized as a result of the integration of technology, artistic expressions, and interactive platforms. This has resulted in the development of a more profound understanding of the past and the facilitation of significant linkages between historical recollection and modern experiences.

3. **The Importance of Recalling the Past Collectively**
   The collective memory of a community is a strong instrument that may be used to promote social cohesiveness, create cultural resilience, and cultivate a feeling of shared identity among the members of that community. It makes it possible for societies to develop a narrative that represents the distinctive historical

experiences, cultural beliefs, and social goals of their members. Communities demonstrate their dedication to maintaining their cultural legacy and passing on the knowledge and lessons of their ancestors to subsequent generations by committing to the preservation of their collective memory through the use of historical archives, oral traditions, and cultural institutions. This helps to ensure the long-term viability of their cultural identity as well as their historical heritage.

4. **Commemorative Traditions and the Construction of Cultural Identities**
Practices of commemoration are inextricably tied to cultural identity because they represent the norms, ideas, and customs that constitute a society's shared consciousness. Festivals of culture, national holidays, and historical recreations are all important aspects of the cultural identity of a country since they embody its historical narratives, artistic expressions, and social ideals. By taking part in these commemoration practices, individuals are able to reinforce their cultural identity and strengthen their sense of belonging to a common cultural heritage. This, in turn, fosters the development of a deeper understanding for the cultural values and traditions that create their society perspective.

5. **The Passing Down of Traditions and Memories from Generation to Generation**
For the purpose of maintaining cultural continuity and promoting a sense of cultural belonging among groups, the passing down of historical remembrance from one generation to the next is of the utmost importance. Oral histories, family traditions, and educational programs all play an important part in the transmission of the tales, values, and experiences of previous generations to newer members of society. This enables younger members of society to connect with their cultural history and develop a profound awareness of the historical legacy they have inherited.

Conversations between people of different generations and the passing down of oral histories both contribute to the development of a sense of cultural pride and identity, as well as an understanding for the complex web of cultural traditions and historical events that make up a society's collective memory.

6. **The Importance of Art and Literature in the Process of Remembering the Past**
Art and literature are two powerful tools that can be used to capture the essence of historical memories and translate it into artistic expressions that are meaningful to modern audiences. The maintenance of communal memory is aided by the visual arts, literary works, and performing arts since these art forms provide complex interpretations of historical events, cultural traditions, and societal ideals. Artistic expressions are one way for civilizations to honor their historical history, elicit a sense of empathy and understanding, and foster a shared respect

for the varied cultural narratives that shape their cultural identity and societal values. These goals can be accomplished in a number of ways.

7. **The Modern Festival as an Expression of Cultural Identity**
A vibrant manifestation of cultural originality, social dynamism, and the ever-changing character of society ideals, contemporary celebration serves as a vehicle for this expression. The present spirit of cultural diversity, artistic innovation, and societal advancement is reflected in public gatherings, contemporary commemorations, and cultural festivals. They develop a sense of communal pride and identity that is independent of historical boundaries and cultural divisions by providing forums for communities to demonstrate their cultural history, artistic abilities, and societal achievements.

8. **The Potentially Changing Effects of Commemorative Activities**
Inspiring social change, fostering reconciliation, and promoting cultural understanding are all things that can be accomplished through the power of commemorative events. They work as catalysts for societal reflection, dialogue, and collective action, addressing historical injustices, developing intercultural interaction, and promoting a shared vision for a society that is more inclusive and equitable. Communities acknowledge their collective journey, face their shared difficulties, and renew their commitment to cultivating a more just, peaceful, and inclusive society for present and future generations through the practice of remembering historical milestones.

9. **Memorial Buildings and Places in Public Spaces**
It is important for a society to have memorial architecture and public spaces because they serve as physical embodiments of historical recollection and modern celebration. These spaces also provide visible representations of a society's collective memory and cultural ambitions.

   The purpose of public monuments, memorials, and sculptures is to pay homage to the resiliency of communities during times of difficulty; to memorialize historical events; to celebrate the efforts of former leaders; and to pay tribute to the contributions of past leaders. These architectural icons function as social spaces for thought, contemplation, and collective recollection, thereby contributing to the development of a sense of civic pride and cultural legacy that is unaffected by the passage of time or distance.

10. **Considerations of Right and Wrong in the Act of Remembering the Past**
The interpretation of historical events in a responsible manner, the promotion of historical accuracy, and the fostering of empathy and understanding among various cultures are all examples of ethical factors that should be taken into account when commemorating the past. For the purpose of promoting an inclusive and thorough understanding of historical events and the impact they had on society, it is vital to engage in truth-telling and reconciliation efforts, as well as to promote varied perspectives. Societies are able to resolve historical traumas and

create a more inclusive and equitable commemoration of their common history if they acknowledge past injustices, encourage historical empathy, and cultivate open conversation. These are all aspects of historical commemoration.

11. **Educational Initiatives and the Commemoration of Historical Events**

    Educational programs are extremely important in cultivating a more profound comprehension of a nation's cultural history in future generations, as well as in encouraging historical awareness and recall among younger people. Students can be provided with historical information, critical thinking abilities, and a feeling of historical empathy through the implementation of curricular changes, the implementation of interactive educational programs, and the establishment of historical museums as platforms for these educational goals. By incorporating historical remembering into educational curricula, societies nurture a new generation of informed and involved citizens, foster a feeling of civic responsibility, and encourage a thorough understanding of their cultural heritage.

12. **Movements Concerning the Commemoration of Past Events and the Promotion of Social Justice**

    Remembering the past frequently overlaps with social justice movements, which serves as a forum for addressing historical wrongdoing, advocating for human rights, and fostering societal change. Historical recollection acts as a catalyst for social change and collective action. It empowers communities to challenge systematic inequities, promote restorative justice, and develop a society that is more inclusive and equitable. This can take the form of truth and reconciliation commissions, grassroots activism and campaigning, or any combination of these. Healing, reconciliation, and the pursuit of a more just and equitable future for all can be promoted in society by remembering past injustices and pushing for social justice.

13. **Modern Obstacles to the Accurate Recollection of Historical Events**

    The preservation of cultural heritage, the promotion of historical correctness, and the preservation of historical relics in the face of globalization, urbanization, and technological breakthroughs are contemporary issues in the field of historical remembrance. The advent of the digital age has altered the manner in which civilizations interact with the historical narratives of their past. This has created both new challenges and opportunities for the preservation of cultural heritage, the transmission of historical knowledge, and the promotion of cultural continuity. In order for civilizations to effectively address the difficulties of the modern day, they need to strike a balance between embracing innovation and technology on the one hand, and maintaining the values of cultural preservation and historical remembering on the other.

14. **Commemorative Practices in the Context of the Global Community**

traditions of commemoration are not unique to any one culture or country; rather, they are traditions that are shared by communities all over the world, which reflects the global value of historical recollection and contemporary celebration. The blending of historical narratives with contemporary celebrations is a practice that can be seen in societies all over the world, and it occurs during worldwide commemorations as well as global cultural festivals. This practice is done to commemorate the past, acknowledge the present, and look ahead to the future. This global viewpoint highlights the importance of historical remembering in breaking down cultural barriers, creating mutual understanding, and celebrating the human experience we all have in common.

A profound journey of cultural continuity, societal evolution, and the everlasting relevance of communal memory is represented by the merging of historical remembrance and modern joy. By honoring their history, communities not only appreciate the accomplishments of previous generations but also pay tribute to the sacrifices made in the pursuit of cultural identity and sovereignty and embrace the spirit of cultural resilience and rebirth. It is possible to build a sense of shared identity, cultural pride, and an unwavering commitment to the preservation of the cultural legacy that defines a community through the interaction of historical narratives and contemporary festivities. Cultures, by means of this dynamic interplay, embrace the principles of continuity and change, which helps to develop a vibrant and inclusive cultural fabric that transcends historical bounds and resonates with the ever-evolving ambitions of the human spirit.

Chapter 9

Carnival and Mardi Gras

Celebrations such as Carnival and Mardi Gras are known for their exuberance and merriment, and they have won the favor of people from all over the world. These exuberant celebrations, which are well-known for their brilliant parades, lavish costumes, and loud music, have a deep history and are significant culturally. Even while Carnival and Mardi Gras are frequently connected with distinct local histories and customs, they both center on the same principles of joyous revelry, self-indulgence, and the commemoration of life. In this in-depth investigation, we will delve into the origins, customs, and global significance of Carnival and Mardi Gras, studying how they bring people together in the spirit of joy, unity, and cultural expression. We will also look at how these celebrations have evolved over time.

1. **Where Did Carnival and Mardi Gras Come From?**

It is vital to investigate the historical roots of both Carnival and Mardi Gras in order to have an understanding of both celebrations. Both of these events have profound roots that may be traced back to a variety of civilizations and customs.

1. **Carnival: A Joyous Celebration Held All Over the World**
   The word "Carnival" is thought to have been derived from the Latin phrase "carne vale," which translates to "farewell to meat." This phrase reflects the historical relationship of Carnival with the Christian observance of Lent, which is a season of fasting and abstinence leading up to Easter. However, it is possible to trace the origins of Carnival back to ancient pagan festivals that honored the coming of spring, fertility, and the regeneration of nature. These festivals occurred thousands of years before Carnival. These celebrations typically involved feasting, dressing up in masks, and breaking with conventional social mores.
   The spread of Carnival: European colonists are the ones responsible for

bringing Carnival traditions to the Americas. The event developed uniquely across the country, with each region including their own distinct cultural influences and customs. Today, people all over the world enjoy Carnival, including Brazil, Italy, Trinidad and Tobago, and many more countries.

2. **A Celebration of French Heritage in the United States**

Mardi Gras has deep roots in French culture, particularly that of the early French colonists who settled in the area that is now New Orleans, in the state of Louisiana.

The day before Ash Wednesday, which is considered to be the beginning of Lent, is known as "Fat Tuesday," which is where the phrase "Mardi Gras" originates from. In France, Mardi Gras was celebrated with elaborate feasts, masquerades, and parades.

Mardi Gras is a tradition that originated in France and was transferred to the United States by French colonists in the late 17th century. Since then, the festival has evolved into a defining characteristic of New Orleans' cultural heritage. It features unique aspects that distinguish it from other Carnival customs and traditions.

II. Traditions and Characteristics Central to Carnival

The festival known as Carnival is characterized by its wide range of distinctive customs and characteristics, which combine to make it an enthralling cultural phenomenon. These characteristics include vibrantly colored costumes, music, and dance, as well as regional differences.

1. **Masks and Costumes of Extreme Detail**

   The elaborate and brightly colored costumes that people wear during Carnival are one of the characteristics of the celebration that are most easily recognizable. Individuals are granted the ability to freely express themselves by donning different personalities, which is made possible by the use of masks and costumes. They frequently make use of feathers, sequins, and vivid textiles in their designs. For example, in Venice, which is well-known for the wonderful masks that are produced there, participants dress in garb that is reminiscent of Venice in the 18th century.

2. **Performers of Song and Dance**

   The celebrations around Carnival always include music and dance. The musical and dance styles of various places are uniquely their own and are strongly ingrained in the cultural traditions of those regions. Rio de Janeiro's Carnival is commonly associated with samba music and dancing, whilst Trinidad and Tobago's Carnival is known for its energetic soca music. The rhythms and motions of Carnival produce an infectious energy that captivates both the people who take part in the event and the people who watch it.

3. **Parades as well as Floats**

   The carnival parades are a spectacular event that takes on a monumental scale. The participants in these processions are typically attired in elaborate costumes, and they are joined by musicians and dancers who perform on gigantic floats that have been intricately adorned. The floats might be given a specific motif to tell a tale or to symbolize a certain facet of the culture.

The Krewe of Zulu and Rex parades are two of the most famous events that take place during Mardi Gras in New Orleans. In Rio de Janeiro, the Sambadrome plays host to samba school parades that are famous all over the world.

4. **Variations Across Geographies**

Carnival is celebrated in many different ways across the world, and each location has its own distinct set of traditions. For instance, during Carnival in Venice, Italy, the city is famous for its ornate masquerade balls as well as the "Flight of the Angel," a tradition in which a young woman descends from the Campanile of St. Mark's Basilica to the Piazza San Marco. "J'ouvert" is a pre-dawn street party held in Trinidad and Tobago, during which participants cover themselves in paint and mud.

III. Mardi Gras's Most Notable Characteristics and Customs

The celebration of Mardi Gras, which has clear roots in both French and American culture, is characterized by its own particular characteristics and customs.

1. **Beadwork and Knitted Throws**
   The custom of tossing items known as "throws" into the crowd is widely recognized as one of the most defining characteristics of Mardi Gras. Beads of various hues, trinkets, and other items of a similar size and shape are included. The participants on the parade floats hurl trinkets like this to the audience, which creates a thrilling and vibrant atmosphere.

2. **The King's Cake**
   Mardi Gras celebrations would not be complete without the indulgent sweet treat known as the King Cake. Typically, it takes the form of a spherical cake that is braided and decorated in the classic Mardi Gras colors of gold, purple, and green. A miniature plastic infant is hidden inside the cake, and whomever discovers it will be in charge of organizing the following Mardi Gras party.

3. **Organizations Related to the Krewe**
   Krewes are the organizations that are in charge of planning the festivities associated with Mardi Gras. These groups are responsible for the planning and execution of parades and events, each of which has its own distinctive look and subject. Mythological figures, significant events in history, or quirky ideas are sometimes used to inspire the naming of krewes. The floats and throws are collaborative efforts that need participation from all members of the krewe.

4. **Importance from a Historical and Cultural Perspective**

The history and culture of New Orleans are inextricably entwined with the Mardi Gras celebration. It is not merely a celebration, but also a reflection of the city's unique legacy, including the contributions of Native American communities in addition to the influences of French, Spanish, and African culture. The lively cultural tapestry of the city is highlighted during Mardi Gras, making it a source of pride for the people who live there.

IV. The Influence of Carnival Around the World

Carnival has transcended its regional roots and developed into a global phenomenon, which is

celebrated in a wide variety of countries and cultural contexts all over the world. Because of this, there is a diverse range of customs and festivities associated with Carnival because each region has given it its own distinctive spin.

1. **The city of Rio de Janeiro in Brazil**

   Each year, the Rio Carnival is one of the world's most well-known Carnival celebrations and draws in millions of tourists from all over the world. It is famous for its dazzling samba parades, in which different samba schools compete against one another to see who can give the best performance. These parades, which feature a brilliant display of lavish costumes, energizing samba music, and dance, are hosted at the Sambadrome, a site that is specifically designed for parades.

2. **City in Italy known as Venice**

   The extravagant and beautiful masquerade masks and costumes of the Venice Carnival are well-known around the world. The enchanting setting of the celebrations is provided by the one-of-a-kind atmosphere of the city, which is characterized by its historic buildings and canals. During the Carnival, there will be events like as the traditional procession known as the Flight of the Angel, which will take place throughout St. Mark's Square.

3. **The Commonwealth of Trinidad and Tobago**

   The Carnival celebration in Trinidad and Tobago is a colorful fusion of many different cultural influences, including those from Africa, India, and Europe. The festivities include the wearing of vibrant costumes, the playing of boisterous soca music, and the practice of J'ouvert, in which participants cover their bodies in mud and paint. The celebrations are characterized by an atmosphere that is inclusive and unified.

4. **Notting Hill is located in London.**

   The Notting Hill Carnival is among the most well-known and well-attended street celebrations in all of Europe.

   It is a celebration of the culture of the Caribbean and includes a large parade with colorful costumes, vibrant music, and food from the Caribbean. This event serves to highlight the multiethnic and diversified nature of both London and the United Kingdom as a whole.

5. **Barranquilla, Eastern Colombia Location**

   The colorful music and dance of the Barranquilla Carnival in Colombia are well-known around the world. During the celebration, one of the most prominent forms of music and dancing that is performed in Colombia is called cumbia. In addition, there will be a spectacular parade known as the Battle of the Flowers, which will feature ornate floats and costumes.

6. **Santa Cruz de Tenerife, which is located in Spain**
   The Carnival of Santa Cruz de Tenerife is one of the largest in Europe, and it is celebrated with parades full of flamboyance and costumes that are bright and colorful. The event includes the election of the Carnival Queen, who is in charge of the celebrations, as well as the burial of the sardine, which is a symbolic act that marks the end of the event.
7. **The city of Port of Spain, located in Trinidad and Tobago**
   The Carnival celebration in Trinidad and Tobago is a colorful fusion of many different cultural influences, including those from Africa, India, and Europe. The festivities include the wearing of vibrant costumes, the playing of boisterous soca music, and the practice of J'ouvert, in which participants cover their bodies in mud and paint. The celebrations are characterized by an atmosphere that is inclusive and unified.
8. **City in Australia: Sydney**

A celebration of diversity, inclusivity, and the rights of LGBTQ+ people, the Sydney Gay and Lesbian Mardi Gras takes place every year. It is one of the most important LGBTQ+ celebrations that takes place all over the world, and it is highlighted by a vibrant procession that includes brilliant costumes, music, and performances.

V. Mardi Gras is celebrated all around the world.

Celebrations in many different regions of the world have been impacted by the tradition of Mardi Gras, which has its roots in French culture but has found its permanent home in New Orleans.

1. **New Orleans, in the state of Louisiana**
   Mardi Gras celebrations in the United States are still centered in New Orleans as they have been for decades. The celebrations in the city are distinguished by their parades, ornate floats, masked balls, and boisterous street parties. Visitors numbering in the hundreds of thousands arrive in New Orleans each year in order to take part in the celebrations there.
2. **Mobile, located in Alabama**
   There is a claim that the Mardi Gras celebration in Mobile, Alabama, which has been going on since 1703, is the oldest one in the United States. Moon Pies and cracker jack goodies are thrown to the public during parades as part of the one-of-a-kind traditions that this community has. Mardi Gras in Mobile is characterized by a strong sense of community and events geared toward families.

3. **The city of Rio de Janeiro in Brazil**
   Despite the fact that Rio de Janeiro is most renowned for its celebration of Carnival, the city also hosts a lively Mardi Gras festival. Mardi Gras in Rio de Janeiro is known for its festive street gatherings, vibrant samba music, and colorful costumes. It is a celebration that is distinct and thrilling due to the fact that it is influenced both by Brazilian culture and by other cultures from across the world.
4. **The Canadian city of Quebec**
   Because of its French background, Quebec City celebrates a winter Mardi Gras known as "Carnaval de Québec." This celebration includes snow sculpture competitions, ice canoe races, and a masquerade gala. It demonstrates the tenacity required to celebrate Mardi Gras in a winter wonderland setting.
5. **City in Australia: Sydney**
   A celebration of diversity, inclusivity, and the rights of LGBTQ+ people, the Sydney Gay and Lesbian Mardi Gras takes place every year. It is one of the most important LGBTQ+ celebrations that takes place all over the world, and it is highlighted by a vibrant procession that includes brilliant costumes, music, and performances.
6. **The islands of Trinidad and Tobago**

In Trinidad and Tobago, the culture is inextricably linked to the Mardi Gras and Carnival traditions that have been practiced there for generations. The celebrations are well-known for the loud soca music, colorful costumes, and the J'ouvert custom that are all part of them. It is a celebration of the great cultural diversity that the nation possesses.

VI. Mardi Gras and Carnival: Their Meanings in Symbolism and Themes

Mardi Gras and Carnival share a wealth of themes and symbolism that speak to the cultural, historical, and social aspects of their respective festivals.

1. **A Feast in Honor of Life**
   The celebration of life plays an important role during both Carnival and Mardi Gras. The celebrations provide an escape from the daily grind, a chance to splurge, and a timely reminder to make room in one's life for merriment and festivity. The lively music, costumes, and dance all capture the idea of savoring every moment of life to the fullest.
2. **Independence and Emancipation**
   Both Carnival and Mardi Gras are well-known for their reputations as providing revelers with the opportunity to defy conventional social mores. Individuals are provided with a sense of anonymity as well as emancipation when they wear costumes and masks, which enables them to express themselves without fear of being judged. This concept of freedom has profound historical origins,

particularly in the carnival customs of Venice and the social disguising of New Orleans. Both of these cities have a long history of celebrating Carnival.

3. **Continuity and Openness to All**
Both ceremonies place an emphasis on togetherness and welcoming everyone. People of all walks of life come together to celebrate Carnival and Mardi Gras, helping to cultivate a sense of community and belonging in the process. The gatherings bring together people of different races, socioeconomic backgrounds, and countries, fostering an atmosphere of brotherhood and mutual happiness.

4. **Expression of One's Culture**
Both Carnival and Mardi Gras serve as significant forums for the expression of cultural identity. They shine a spotlight on the one-of-a-kind cultural traditions that have been preserved in the areas in which they are celebrated. These festivals are a monument to the diversity and ingenuity of human civilization. From the samba rhythms of Rio de Janeiro to the French-inspired parades of New Orleans, these celebrations can be found all over the world.

5. **The Observance of Traditions and Rites**

The celebrations of Mardi Gras and Carnival are rooted in a variety of customs and rites. These traditions, such as the crowning of a Carnival Queen or the tossing of beads and other trinkets during Mardi Gras parades, carry substantial cultural and symbolic weight. They introduce the attendees to the past and the customs that are associated with the celebrations.

VII. Influence on Both Society and the Economy

Both Carnival and Mardi Gras have huge effects, both socially and economically, on the areas of the world in which they are celebrated.

1. **Boosting the Economy Through Tourism**
Both Carnival and Mardi Gras are enormously popular events among tourists. They attract millions of tourists each year, which in turn provides a significant economic boost to the regions that play host to the events. The local economy benefits from the expenditures that tourists make on things like lodging, food and drink, entertainment, and trinkets.

2. **Protecting Our Cultural Heritage**
These ceremonies are an essential component in the process of maintaining cultural traditions and history. They serve as a foundation for the preservation of traditions, musical styles, and artistic practices that could otherwise become extinct. Both Carnival and Mardi Gras are examples of dynamic cultural celebrations that have adapted to the influences of contemporary society without losing their traditional meaning.

3. **Participation in the Community**
Both Carnival and Mardi Gras are not simply activities for spectators; rather,

they require substantial participation from the community. Residents in the area play a significant part in the planning and execution of the celebrations, which contributes to the development of a sense of communal pride and participation.

4. **Promotion on the International Stage**

Both Carnival and Mardi Gras have evolved into internationally recognized emblems of festivity
and ethnic diversity. They foster a favorable image of the host regions, which in turn attracts good attention and recognition on the global stage.

VIII. Disputes and Obstacles to Overcome

Even while Carnival and Mardi Gras are celebrated with a great deal of zeal, they are not exempt from the difficulties and debates that are associated with similar events.

1. **Influence on the Environment**

    The parades and festivities of Carnival and Mardi Gras can have effects for the environment, notably the littering and garbage accumulation that can result from them. Ongoing efforts are being made to address the environmental impact of these events, with an increased focus on ensuring that these efforts are sustainable.

2. **The appropriation of culture**

    In certain instances, cultural aspects of Mardi Gras and Carnival have been appropriated without an awareness of or respect for the significance of those aspects to the respective cultures. This topic brings to light the significance of maintaining cultural understanding and sensitivity when participating in the celebration of these customs.

3. **Disparities in the Economy**

There are significant socioeconomic differences in some areas due to Carnival and Mardi Gras celebrations. While the celebrations do bring in money, there may be obstacles to overcome in order to guarantee that the economic gains are shared fairly among the members of the community.

IX. The Unflappability of Joyous Occasions

The resilience of Carnival and Mardi Gras is one of the most impressive elements of each of these celebrations. Throughout the course of history, these festivals have persisted in spite of wars, difficult economic times, and shifting societal norms. They continue to adapt to changing circumstances and become more advanced over time, discovering new methods to celebrate and bring people together.

1. **Having a Party Despite Being in Unprecedented Times**

    Both Carnival and Mardi Gras have had to overcome obstacles in the past, including pandemics, social upheaval, and unstable economic conditions.

Particularly, the COVID-19 pandemic had a significant influence on these events, which resulted in cancellations and alterations. Despite this, there is still a robust celebration spirit, as evidenced by ongoing virtual events and imaginative solutions, as well as a collective commitment to maintain the traditions.

2. **Lessons in Being Able to Bounce Back**

Even in the midst of hardship, the yearning for joy and celebration is constant; Carnival and Mardi Gras are two celebrations that serve as potent reminders of this need and the resiliency of human culture. These festivities find new ways to bring people together and generate a sense of unity and cultural continuity as they adapt to changing conditions.

Both Carnival and Mardi Gras are exuberant and energetic festivities that have moved beyond their regional origins to become emblems of happiness, cultural diversity, and resiliency in the face of adversity. These celebrations, which honor life, freedom, and solidarity, offer a glimpse into the diverse patterns that make up the human cultural fabric. The celebration of life and culture is a common human urge that transcends boundaries and persists through the ages, as seen by the continued evolution, adaptation, and inspiration of the traditions of Carnival and Mardi Gras, which both continue to this day to honor and honor those who came before them.

9.1 The history and cultural significance of Carnival and Mardi Gras celebrations

Carnival and Mardi Gras are two of the most well-known and exciting festivals that take place all over the world. These events are well-known for their lively parades, lavish costumes, upbeat music, and celebratory atmosphere. These celebratory customs go back far into history and carry with them an enormous amount of cultural weight in the places where they are observed as a part of everyday life. By gaining an understanding of the history and cultural background of Carnival and Mardi Gras, one can gain insight into the diverse fabric that makes up human culture as well as the ongoing power of celebration.

The Beginnings of Carnival: A Joyous Celebration Held All Over the World

The history of Carnival stretches back to ancient civilizations, with its roots in pagan celebrations honoring the entrance of spring, fertility, and the rebirth of nature. In modern times, carnival is celebrated in many countries throughout the world. Feasts, masquerades, and a brief suspension of conventional standards were the hallmarks of these early celebrations. It is claimed that the word "Carnival" was derived from the Latin phrase "carne vale," which means "farewell to meat," indicating its relationship with the Christian observance of the season of Lent.

As the Christian religion spread over Europe, the traditions of Carnival melded with the ecclesiastical calendar and became a festival that took place before Lent began. Because the time leading up to Easter was characterized by fasting and abstinence, Carnival was an occasion for people to overindulge in food, drink, and celebrations before the gloomy period of Lent. The numerous Carnival customs that are practiced today are the product of a blending of religious and secular components.

The Carnival's Significance in Culture: Celebrating Diversity and Coming Together

Carnival is a festival that is observed in many different nations, each of which has its own distinct set of customs and traditions. This is a celebration of life, freedom, and the coming together of everyone. A departure from the everyday, the vibrant costumes, loud music, and dynamic movement signify a break from the norm, offering participants the freedom to openly express themselves. Individuals are encouraged to embrace joy and festivity because they are given the opportunity to feel liberated by the act of donning masks and costumes.

Carnival is celebrated all over the world, and each location brings its own unique cultural features to the celebration, reflecting the many traditions and histories of its people. Carnival is a tremendous platform for cultural expression and preservation all over the world, from the rhythms of samba in Rio de Janeiro to the parades in New Orleans that are inspired by French culture. It is able to transcend barriers of race, class, and nationality, so fostering an environment of inclusiveness and delight that is experienced by all.

Residents of the town take an important part in the planning and execution of the events that make up the carnival, which contributes to the development of a sense of civic involvement and pride. The economic impact of Carnival is substantial as well due to the fact that millions of tourists travel to the locations that host the event. These visitors inject money into the local economy and promote a favorable image of the host region.

The History of Mardi Gras: A Celebration of French Tradition in the United States

The celebration of Mardi Gras, whose name translates to "Fat Tuesday" in French, has strong ties to French culture as well as the French colonists who established New Orleans, Louisiana. Mardi Gras is a tradition that originated in France and was carried to the Americas by French colonists in the late 17th century. In France, it was celebrated with lavish feasts, masquerades, and parades, and it frequently took place on the day before the start of Lent.

The Cultural Significance of Mardi Gras: A Representation of Many Different Traditions and Cultures

The celebration of Mardi Gras in New Orleans is distinguished by its distinctive blending of influences from French, Spanish, African, and Native American cultures. During Mardi Gras, the city's diverse history and heritage are put on full exhibit, representing the city's rich cultural tapestry that is on full display. This festival is more than just a get-together; it is a representation of the lively cultural identity that can be found in New Orleans.

Traditions unique to Mardi Gras include the distribution of throws and beads into the audience, the consumption of King Cake, and the planning of parades by organizations known as krewes. Each krewe has its own signature look and concept, which are frequently derived from legendary characters or significant moments in the past. This event highlights the uniqueness and ingenuity of New Orleans's resident artists and musicians.

Impact of the Mardi Gras Holiday on Various Other Parts of the World

The celebration of Mardi Gras is no longer limited to just New Orleans. Different communities, such as Mobile, Alabama, and Rio de Janeiro, Brazil, each have their own unique take on the holiday celebration. The "Moon Pies" and "cracker jack" delicacies that are tossed to the masses in Mobile are unique to that region, and Rio de Janeiro puts its own touch on Mardi Gras by hosting street parties, playing samba music, and dressing up in colorful costumes.

Preserving Traditions and Getting Involved in the Community

The Mardi Gras celebration in New Orleans and its offshoots in other areas each play an important part in maintaining the city's rich cultural traditions and legacy. Residents of the area take an active role in the planning and execution of the celebrations, which contributes to the development of a sense of community involvement as well as civic pride.

Honoring Individuality and Perseverance in the Face of Adversity

The celebrations of Carnival and Mardi Gras are more than merely ostentatious gatherings; rather, they are a demonstration of the depth and variety of human civilization. These celebrations are continually reimagined and reimagined, resulting in the discovery of new ways to bring people together in the spirit of joy and harmony. The ability of Carnival and Mardi Gras to celebrate life, freedom, and cultural expression, while simultaneously transcending boundaries and creating a favorable image of the regions where they are celebrated, is the source of their ongoing power. These customs from throughout the world serve as a reminder of how important it is for people from different backgrounds to come together and celebrate, regardless of the obstacles they may encounter.

9.2 The role of masks, costumes, and parades

The use of masks, costumes, and processions in diverse cultural celebrations around the world adds depth to the overall experience of the festivities while also illuminating the deeply ingrained cultural practices and symbolism that are a part of local communities. In addition to their aesthetic value, these components frequently play an important role as potent instruments of cultural expression, the preservation of historical sites, and the consolidation of social ties.

Unveiling the Festive Atmosphere Through the Use of Masks

There is a long and illustrious history of masks being utilized in cultural events, extending back to ancient times when they were employed in rites, ceremonies, and theatrical performances. Masks are significant in more ways than just their aesthetic appeal, as they frequently have symbolic meanings and perform a variety of functions in a wide range of cultural contexts. Their relevance extends beyond only their aesthetic appeal.

Masks are used in many different cultural festivities as a means of changing the wearer into a different persona or spiritual entity. This gives people the opportunity to temporarily transcend their own identities and embody different personalities. This transformational potential of masks is apparent in rituals and celebrations all over the world, where they are used to call ancestral spirits, represent deities, or depict mythological characters. In some of these contexts, masks are also employed to protect the wearer from evil.

Additionally, masks are an essential component in the process of maintaining cultural history as well as traditional art forms. They function as physical objects that connect modern communities to the historical narratives of their ancestors. Furthermore, they offer a visual picture of the cultural ideas, values, and myths that underpin those societies.

In addition, masks enable a sense of anonymity and freedom of expression during celebrations, which encourages people to take part in the festivities without any inhibitions.

People of varying backgrounds join together under the pretext of their chosen mask, which fosters a spirit of unity and camaraderie, and this anonymity frequently leads to a sense of equality and inclusivity.

Expressions of cultural identity through clothing and accessories

In cultural festivities, costumes, much like masks, play a crucial role as visual symbols of cultural identity, historical tales, and artistic expression. Masks, on the other hand, are primarily used to conceal the face. They frequently feature traditional designs, colors, and textiles, which reflect the one-of-a-kind heritage of a community and convey a sense of collective pride and connection to that place.

Communities are able to demonstrate their artistic talent and cultural history through the elaborate designs and workmanship of their costumes, so helping to preserve the ancient practices that have been passed down through the decades. For instance, the magnificent feather headdresses, sequined clothes, and complex body art that are worn during Rio Carnival in Brazil depict the rich cultural fusion of African, European, and indigenous influences. These costumes, which showcase the history and richness of Brazilian culture, are worn during the festival.

Not only do costumes function as vehicles for current invention and innovation, but they also act as vehicles for celebrating the past. Numerous communities have begun incorporating current design aspects into their age-old garb, thereby fusing historical aesthetics with contemporary fashion trends and the usage of modern materials. This dynamic fusion illustrates the ever-changing character of culture as well as the tenacity with which traditional behaviors have persisted in the face of modernization.

FESTIVALS AND CELEBRATIONS

In addition, clothes frequently have social and ritualistic value, and they can be used to delineate particular roles and hierarchies within societies. In certain cultural events, such as religious processions or historical reenactments, participants wear costumes to differentiate between ceremonial leaders, spiritual figures, and regular participants. This helps to reinforce social structures and cultural norms within the setting of the celebrations itself.

Parades are joyful public displays of expression.

Parades are colorful and energetic spectacles that serve as the lifeblood of many cultural events. They help to develop a sense of social excitement, pride, and camaraderie among the participants. They frequently include elaborate floats, music, dancing, and theatrical presentations, generating experiences that are so immersive that they interest participants as well as onlookers.

The progression of parades acts as a collective narrative, recreating historical events, mythological tales, or religious allegories that are significant to the community's cultural identity. Communities are able to memorialize their history, pay tribute to their forebears, and pass down their heritage to subsequent generations through the use of parades, which become a live embodiment of the collective cultural memory of the community.

In addition, parades serve as forums for community participation and social cohesion, as they bring together people from a variety of backgrounds to celebrate shared norms and customs. They foster a sense of belonging and unity, promoting a shared cultural identity that transcends individual differences and fosters a spirit of inclusivity and mutual respect. Moreover, they encourage a sense of belonging and unity.

Parades also contribute to the economic and touristic vitality of communities by drawing visitors from across the world who come to watch and participate in the grandeur of cultural events. This attracts tourists who spend money in the local economy and boosts tourism. They act as cultural ambassadors, fostering intercultural communication and understanding while highlighting the diverse range of human creativity and expression. They achieve this by showcasing the rich tapestry of human creativity and expression.

Parades have evolved to incorporate current technology and multimedia features in contemporary situations, which has the effect of improving the entire spectacle and reaching wider audiences through live broadcasts and other social media platforms. The incorporation of technology has made it possible for cultural festivities to take place outside geographical bounds, which has contributed to a greater understanding of the world's different cultural traditions and appreciation for those traditions.

The use of masks, costumes, and parades are all fundamental elements of cultural festivities. These elements serve as dynamic manifestations of cultural heritage, creative expression, and communal spirit. They capture the core of what it means to be human and demonstrate the tenacity of cultural traditions, which helps communities develop a sense of belonging and a sense of pride in their heritage. These features not only represent the rich history and symbolism of a variety of cultures but also act as bridges that connect previous traditions with modern storylines. This highlights the ever-present significance of cultural celebration in the process of building global understanding and respect.

9.3 Global variations of these lively festivals

Festivals full of life are a phenomena that can be found all over the world; they transcend cultural and geographical barriers to bring people together in the spirit of celebration, togetherness, and joy. Every part of the world has its own distinctive approach to commemorating special milestones and satisfying the human desire for festivity. These can take the form of colorful carnivals, boisterous music festivals, and lively cultural celebrations. In the course of this investigation, we will delve into the myriad forms that vibrant celebrations take across the world and investigate the myriad ways in which other societies express their customs, values, and history via these extraordinary events.

Joyous Carnival Celebrations Can Be Found All Over the World

Carnival celebrations are among the most well-known and common types of colorful festivals. Variations of these celebrations may be seen in many different countries around the world. Despite the fact that the primary purpose of Carnival is to celebrate life, freedom, and togetherness, various regions of the world each bring their own distinctive cultural aspects to the party, resulting in a vibrantly diverse cultural mosaic.

1. **The city of Rio de Janeiro in Brazil**
   The Rio Carnival is recognized all over the world for its opulence and riotous spirit. It is inseparable from samba music and dance, with both performers and spectators getting into the celebratory spirit of the pulsating music. The Sambadrome is the location of samba school parades, which feature colossal floats, vibrant costumes, and high-energy performances. The Rio Carnival is a celebration of Brazil's rich cultural past and numerous influences, including aspects from the traditions of Africa, Europe, and the indigenous peoples of Brazil.

2. **City in Italy known as Venice**
   The enthralling show that is the Venice Carnival is distinguished by ornate and creative masquerade masks and costumes. The celebrations take place against a backdrop of enchantment provided by the city's picturesque canals and its historic buildings. During the Carnival, there are various activities that take place. One of these is called the "Flight of the Angel," and it consists of a young woman descending from the Campanile of St. Mark's to the Piazza San Marco. The history and cultural legacy of Venice are on full display during the city's famous Carnival celebration.

3. **The islands of Trinidad and Tobago**
   The Carnival celebration in Trinidad and Tobago is a colorful fusion of cultural elements, including those of European, African, and Indian origin. The festival

features raucous soca music, brightly colored costumes, and the time-honored ritual of J'ouvert, which is a pre-dawn street party during which participants cover themselves in paint and mud.

The celebrations exemplify the spirit of inclusiveness and unity, and they reflect the vast cultural diversity that the nation possesses.

4. **Notting Hill is located in London.**

   The Notting Hill Carnival is a celebration of Caribbean culture and is considered to be one of the largest street events in Europe. It includes a large parade with colorful costumes, vibrant music, and Caribbean cuisine as part of its festivities. The event highlights the value of diversity and inclusiveness while showcasing the multicultural nature of London and the United Kingdom as a whole.

5. **Barranquilla is located in Colombia.**

   Barranquilla Carnival in Colombia is famous for its upbeat music and dance, notably cumbia, which is a traditional form of music and dance in Colombia. The Carnival includes the colorful parade known as the Battle of the Flowers, which is characterized by ornate floats and costumes. It highlights the many different influences that have played a part in the formation of Colombian culture and displays the nation's rich cultural legacy.

6. **Santa Cruz de Tenerife, which is located in Spain**

   The Carnival of Santa Cruz de Tenerife is renowned for its extravagant parades and colorful costumes, and is considered to be one of the greatest celebrations in all of Europe. The event includes the election of the Carnival Queen, who is in charge of the celebrations, as well as the burial of the sardine, which is a symbolic act that marks the end of the event. The Canary Islands have a rich and distinct cultural heritage, and the Carnival is a celebration of that heritage.

7. **The city of Port of Spain, located in Trinidad and Tobago**

   The Carnival celebration in Trinidad and Tobago is a colorful fusion of many different cultural influences, including those from Africa, India, and Europe. The festivities include the wearing of vibrant costumes, the playing of boisterous soca music, and the practice of J'ouvert, in which participants cover their bodies in mud and paint. The celebrations are characterized by an inclusive and united spirit, which reflects the vast cultural diversity that exists throughout the nation.

8. **City in Australia: Sydney**

One of the most important events for the LGBTQ+ community that takes place all over the world is the Sydney Gay and Lesbian Mardi Gras. A vibrant procession filled with spectacular costumes, music, and performances marks the occasion as a celebration of diversity, inclusivity, and the rights of LGBTQ+ individuals. The event highlights the significance of celebrating individual identities while also putting an emphasis on acceptance and equality.

Carnival is celebrated in many different ways all across the world, which goes to show how appealing joy, cultural diversity, and the celebration of life are to people everywhere. Even while every region has its own distinctive customs, all of them revolve on a sense of togetherness and inclusiveness, which helps to cultivate a sense of pride and belonging within the local communities.

Celebrations of Mardi Gras serve as a reminder of the community's rich history

The celebrations of Mardi Gras, which have their roots in France, have also had an influence on a variety of regions all over the world, demonstrating the adaptability and persistence of cultural celebrations.

1. **New Orleans, in the state of Louisiana**
   Mardi Gras celebrations in the United States are still centered in New Orleans as they have been for decades. The celebrations in the city are distinguished by their parades, ornate floats, masked balls, and boisterous street parties. Visitors numbering in the hundreds of thousands rush to New Orleans every year to take part in the celebrations, so contributing to the city's distinct cultural identity and the vibrancy of its economy.

2. **Mobile, located in Alabama**
   There is a claim that the Mardi Gras celebration in Mobile, Alabama, which has been going on since 1703, is the oldest one in the United States. Moon Pies and cracker jack goodies are thrown to the public during parades as part of the one-of-a-kind traditions that this community has. Mardi Gras in Mobile is distinguished by a strong feeling of community and celebrations centered on the participation of families, both of which are reflective of the city's unique cultural background.

3. **The city of Rio de Janeiro in Brazil**
   In addition to the Rio Carnival, Rio de Janeiro also plays host to a lively Mardi Gras celebration, which is characterized by costumed street celebrations, lively samba music, and brightly colored musical instruments. The celebration is a fusion of Brazilian and foreign elements, which results in an experience that is both distinctive and exhilarating for Mardi Gras.

4. **The Canadian city of Quebec**
   Because of its French background, Quebec City celebrates a winter Mardi Gras known as "Carnaval de Québec." This celebration includes snow sculpture competitions, ice canoe races, and a masquerade gala. It demonstrates the tenacity required to celebrate Mardi Gras amid a winter wonderland while simultaneously celebrating the history and culture of the region.

5. **City in Australia: Sydney**
   A celebration of diversity, inclusivity, and the rights of LGBTQ+ people, the

Sydney Gay and Lesbian Mardi Gras takes place every year. It is one of the most important LGBTQ+ celebrations that takes place all over the world, and it is highlighted by a vibrant procession that includes brilliant costumes, music, and performances. The event highlights the significance of accepting others and ensuring that everyone has equal rights.

6. **The islands of Trinidad and Tobago**

In Trinidad and Tobago, the culture is inextricably linked to the Mardi Gras and Carnival traditions that have been practiced there for generations. The celebrations are well-known for the loud soca music, colorful costumes, and the J'ouvert custom that are all part of them. This event is a celebration of the nation's diverse cultural heritage as well as the significance of coming together as one.

Mardi Gras is celebrated in a variety of ways around the world, each of which demonstrates the adaptability of this custom by demonstrating how it can take on new forms and acquire new cultural meaning in different parts of the world. They highlight the evergreen allure of vibrant festivals as a means of bringing communities together and recognizing the distinctive cultural identities of their constituents.

Festivals of Music: A Shared Language That Brings Everyone Together

Festivals of music are a common and vibrant kind of celebration that may be found all over the world in a wide variety of cultural guises and geographical locations. Music is able to communicate feelings in a way that is independent of language, making it a potent instrument for the promotion of cultural harmony and expression.

1. **America's Woodstock**
   The legendary music festival that took place in 1969 and was known as Woodstock was a manifestation of the counterculture movement and a festival that celebrated love, peace, and music. It brought together thousands of individuals for the purpose of advocating for social change while also providing entertainment in the form of concerts by great performers.

2. **America, Coachella**
   One of the most well-known and prestigious music festivals in the United States is the Coachella Valley Music and Arts Festival, more generally referred to simply as Coachella. It features musicians and bands from a wide variety of musical genres, ranging from rock and pop to electronic and hip-hop. In addition to showcasing today's modern music scene, the festival helps to cultivate a sense of community and a celebratory spirit among music fans.

3. **Brazil's Samba Festival**
   The Samba Fest in Brazil is an annual event that honors the country's extensive musical history while putting an emphasis on samba music and dancing. It is an exuberant and energizing party that draws people together so that they can delight in the beats and melodies of Brazilian music.

4. **Tomorrowland is located in Belgium**
   Tomorrowland is an internationally known festival that features electronic dance music and attracts attendees from all over the world. It is well-known for its intricate stage designs, renowned DJs, and a sense of community and camaraderie among those who enjoy electronic music.
5. **The Glastonbury Festival, located in the UK**
   The Glastonbury Festival is one of the most well-known music events in the United Kingdom. It showcases a diverse array of musical styles and performances each year. It also places an emphasis on social activity and preserving the natural environment, turning it into a festival that celebrates both music and social responsibility.
6. **Melodies for Diwali in India**
   Diwali, also known as the Festival of Lights, is celebrated all over India with various forms of music and dance. The festivities are accompanied by traditional as well as contemporary tunes, which symbolically represent the triumph of light over darkness and good over evil. People get together to celebrate the cultural significance of the festival by singing, dancing, and generally having a good time.
7. **Hanukkah Melodies, in the Land of Israel**

Music and the lighting of the menorah are traditional ways to celebrate Hanukkah, also known as the Jewish Festival of Lights. Traditional melodies, such as "Ma'oz Tzur," are sung to honor both the celebration and the historical significance of the holiday's significance. During this joyous time of year, the Jewish communities are brought closer together by music.

The popularity of music as a medium for expression and celebration is demonstrated by the myriad forms it takes around the world in the shape of festivals. Music festivals are venues for solidarity, cultural expression, and the celebration of common passions. This is true whether the festival in question is Woodstock, with its counterculture message, or Tomorrowland, with its electronic sounds and rave atmosphere.

Festivals of Culture Serve as Windows onto the Diversity of the World

Festivals of culture offer a glimpse into the traditions, beliefs, and artistic expressions of a wide variety of societies, demonstrating the depth and variety that each culture possesses. People are given the chance to have an appreciation for, as well as participate in, the celebration of the traditions of others.

1. **Happy New Year in Chinese, China**
   The Chinese New Year, also known as the Spring Festival, is a significant holiday that commemorates the start of the lunar calendar used in China. The event is distinguished by the practice of traditional activities, such as the dragon and lion dances, fireworks, and the giving and receiving of red envelopes (hongbao) as a symbol of good fortune and the hope for a prosperous future.

2. **Brazil, and its Carnaval**
   Carnaval is a vibrant cultural celebration that takes place in Brazil and is noted for its raucous samba parades, bright costumes, and boisterous music. It is a celebration of Brazilian culture that draws on the varied historical and cultural influences that Brazil has experienced.
3. **India, Holi**
   Holi, also known as the Festival of Colors, is celebrated in India with battles fought with colored powder and water. It is a sign that spring has finally arrived, as well as the triumph of virtue over evil. People get together to engage in activities involving color and movement, such as dancing and eating traditional treats and snacks.
4. **Thailand, during Songkran**
   Songkran, also known as the Thai New Year, is commemorated with water celebrations that stand as a metaphor for the washing away of the sins of the previous year and the commencement of a new life. People show their respect for one another and for their elders by visiting temples and sprinkling water on each other.
5. **Day of the Dead celebrations in Mexico**
   The Day of the Dead, also known as Dia de los Muertos, is a traditional celebration in Mexico that pays tribute to departed family members and friends. Families put a lot of effort into constructing magnificent ofrendas, which are similar to altars, and fill them with food, candles, and marigold flowers. The celebration consists of parades, musical performances, and the traditional adornment of sugar skulls.
6. **Germany's Oktoberfest celebrations**
   The Oktoberfest is the most well-known event in Germany, and it is celebrated with a variety of
   musical performances, traditional Bavarian garb, and, of course, beer. It is a cultural event that highlights German customs as well as the country's cuisine and beverages.
7. **The Islamic World During Ramadan and Eid**

Muslims around the world observe the holy month of Ramadan by abstaining from food and drink from daybreak until sundown. Both Eid al-Fitr and Eid al-Adha are holidays that mark the completion of the month-long fasting period of Ramadan. These holidays are celebrated with special prayers, shared meals, and the giving and receiving of gifts. These events bring attention to the significance that the Islamic community places on faith, community, and charitable giving.

The traditions, beliefs, and artistic expressions of a wide variety of cultures can be better understood via participation in these varied cultural celebrations. They act as windows into the distinctive history and identities of many cultures, so promoting intercultural understanding and an appreciation for the stunning variety of the world's peoples and cultures.

Festivals of music and dance are a kind of celebration that is shared globally

Festivals of music and dance are global languages of celebration that bring people together to

share their happiness, creativity, and pride in their cultural traditions. These festivals encourage a sense of togetherness and connection among participants hailing from all regions of the world by transcending national boundaries and linguistic barriers.

1. **America's Woodstock**
   The renowned music event that took place in 1969 and was known as Woodstock was a celebration of love, peace, and music. It was successful in bringing together a varied group of attendees who all had a strong interest in music and a desire to see positive social change. Woodstock is and will continue to be an iconic emblem of the counterculture movement as well as the ability of music to bring people together.
2. **Rio de Janeiro, Brazil's Carnaval**
   The Rio Carnival is an annual festival that is known all over the world for its samba music and dance. Visitors from all over the world are drawn to the contagious rhythms and vibrant costumes worn by those participating in Carnival. This helps create an environment that is both energetic and welcoming. The potential of the festival to unite individuals through shared experiences of music and dancing is at the heart of its broad appeal.
3. **Tomorrowland is located in Belgium**
   One of the largest electronic dance music events in the world, Tomorrowland, is known for attracting attendees from a wide variety of cultural backgrounds. People from all over the world may come together at the event because they have a common appreciation for different kinds of beats and rhythms, which is a tribute to the widespread appeal of electronic music.
4. **Melodies for Diwali in India**
   Diwali, also known as the Festival of Lights, is celebrated all over India with various forms of music and dance. In addition to contemporary and traditional musical acts, the celebrations often feature dancers and choreographed dances. The festival of Diwali highlights the ability of music and dance to generate a celebratory mood that brings people from different groups together.
5. **Brazil's Samba Festival**
   The Samba Fest in Brazil is a festival that honors and celebrates samba music and dancing. People from all walks of life who have a common interest in this famous style of Brazilian art are brought together through this event. The ability

of samba to conjure up feelings of joy and festivity is a major contributor to the genre's widespread popularity.
6. **America, Coachella**
The Coachella Valley Music and Arts Festival brings together a diverse range of artistic styles and musical subgenres each year. It is successful in drawing visitors from all over the world, who congregate in order to watch a wide variety of performances. The festival is a shining example of how music and the arts can bridge the gap that exists between different cultures and foster a sense of harmony.
7. **The Glastonbury Festival, located in the UK**
The Glastonbury Festival is known for showcasing a diverse range of musical styles and acts, which in turn draws attendees from all over the world. It exemplifies the widespread attraction of music as a medium for the celebration of life's milestones and the expression of one's cultural heritage, and it brings people from all over the world together.
8. **Hanukkah Melodies, in the Land of Israel**
Traditional songs and music are performed during Hanukkah celebrations in Israel. These songs and tunes serve to emphasize the joyous nature of the holiday. The melodies and tunes are a reflection of the Jewish community's cultural pride and tradition, and they resonate with people from a variety of different backgrounds.
9. **Music of Mardi Gras, New Orleans, United States of America**
The exciting music that can be heard during Mardi Gras in New Orleans includes everything from jazz and brass bands to zydeco and blues. Mardi Gras is known for its lively environment, which is created by the music that is played throughout the festival. This music unites people from all different cultures and languages in the spirit of celebration.
10. **The carnivals of Trinidad and Tobago**

The beats of soca, calypso, and steelpan are the foundations upon which Trinidad and Tobago Carnival music is built. It is a demonstration of the widespread appeal of infectious beats and exuberant tunes that motivate people to dance together and celebrate.

These music and dance festivals serve as illustrative examples of the global languages of celebration that break down barriers of language and culture to bring people together. They place a strong emphasis on the ability of music and dance to foster a sense of togetherness, joy, and the expression of cultural identity.

Festivals of Food and Cooking: A Celebration of the World's Gastronomic Delights

Festivals dedicated to food and cuisine highlight the culinary arts, the unique flavors of specific regions, and the pleasure of eating together. These festivals highlight the variety of cuisines from throughout the world, the significance of food in cultural identity, and the ways in which local agriculture and cuisine are reflected in their offerings.

1. **Germany's Oktoberfest celebrations**
   The Oktoberfest is the most well-known beer festival in the world, and it is held annually in Munich, Germany, as well as in many other cities and countries. Beer is served alongside classic Bavarian dishes like pretzels, sausages, and sauerkraut, and there is a broad selection of beers to choose from. This event is a celebration of German culture, including its cuisine and brewing traditions.
2. **America's Thanksgiving**
   The traditional Thanksgiving meal in the United States includes roasted turkey, stuffing, cranberry sauce, and pumpkin pie. This holiday is considered to be one of the most important in the country. It represents thankfulness, solidarity, and the significance of family and community to one's life. The hearty meals eaten on Thanksgiving are a reflection of the United States' rich agricultural past.
3. **The Indian festival of Diwali**
   A variety of traditional sweets and snacks, together referred to as mithai, are enjoyed as part of the festivities surrounding Diwali, also known as the Festival of Lights. These mouthwatering confections, which are typically made at home, are symbolic of both the sweetness of life and the triumph of light over evil. Feasts are a significant component of the Diwali celebration, and their specific nature varies according to group and area.
4. **Italy's Annual Pizzafest**
   Pizzafest in Naples, Italy, is a celebration of the widespread affection for pizza around the world. The festival highlights the myriad of approaches to pizza making, both in terms of the ingredients used and the preparation methods. This is an homage to the rich culinary legacy of Italy as well as the widespread popularity of this renowned dish.
5. **Festival of the Cherry Blossoms, Japan**
   Hanami is the Japanese word for the Cherry Blossom Festival, which is held annually in Japan to celebrate the blooming of cherry blossoms and includes picnics held under cherry trees. While taking in the splendor of nature, participants indulge in traditional Japanese cuisine such as bento boxes, sushi, and tempura.
6. **Mexico's Day of the Dead celebrations**
   Traditional Mexican delicacies, such as pan de muerto (also known as "bread of the dead") and sugar skulls, are served during the celebration of Da de los Muertos, also known as "Day of the Dead." The traditional significance of the festival is reflected in these gastronomic offerings, which pay respect to ancestors and loved ones who have passed away.

FESTIVALS AND CELEBRATIONS

7. **Happy New Year in Chinese, China**
   Feasts held in honor of the Chinese New Year feature foods that carry particular connotations due to their association with the holiday. During the holiday, traditional dishes such dumplings, entire fish, and niangao (rice cakes) are cooked with the intention of bringing good fortune, wealth, and unity to the family.
8. **Canada, we give thanks to you**
   Thanksgiving in Canada, much like its cousin in the United States, is a time for families to get
   together and celebrate the harvest with a feast consisting of roasted turkey, stuffing, and vegetables in season. It reflects how important thankfulness and a bountiful harvest are in the agricultural traditions of Canada.
9. **Spain, La Tomatina (La Tomatina)**
   In Buol, Spain, there is a celebration known as La Tomatina, which is a tossing festival that celebrates the pleasures of food in an unusual way. Tomatoes that have passed their prime are collected from area fields and used in a fight between participants. The festival serves as a lighthearted celebration of the tomato's role as an emblem of Spanish cuisine.
10. **Italy's Annual White Truffle Festival**

The highly coveted white truffle is the subject of celebration at the White Truffle Festival in Alba, Italy. The restaurant provides a gastronomic experience with dishes based on truffles, drawing attention to the significance of regional agriculture and the culinary traditions of the area.

These food and culinary festivals bring attention to the widespread love of gastronomy as well as the central role that food plays in the formation of cultural identities and the commemoration of special occasions. They honor the wide variety of cuisines from throughout the world and highlight the distinctive tastes and customs that are connected with various ethnic foods.

Celebrations of Independence Day and Other National Holidays: Honoring Our Identities

Celebrations of a country's national and independence days serve as a window into the nation's past, present, and future, as well as a window into the ideals that its residents hold most dear. These events create a sense of solidarity and patriotism by combining historical commemoration with contemporary activities.

1. **America's Independence Day, July 4**
   The adoption of the Declaration of Independence on July 4, 1776, is being commemorated by the holiday known as Independence Day in the United States. The event is commemorated with the lighting of fireworks, the participation in parades, the cooking of barbecues, and the flying of the American flag.

It is a representation of the nation's history, as well as its freedom and cultural identity.

2. **France on the day of the Bastille**
The storming of the Bastille prison in 1789 is commemorated on Bastille Day, which is observed annually on July 14. Bastille Day is also the French national day. The celebration of the French spirit of liberty, equality, and fraternity is honored on this day with parades, fireworks, and communal feasts.

3. **Independence Day, Canada**
The first of July is celebrated as Canada Day, which honors the day in 1867 when the provinces of Canada came together to form a federation. The celebration features events such as parades, fireworks displays, and concerts that highlight the cultural diversity and solidarity of the nation.

4. **The Indian festival of Diwali**
Diwali, also known as the Festival of Lights, is a significant holiday in India since it also holds national significance. It is a sign that light has triumphed over darkness and that good has triumphed over evil. The necessity of maintaining both national unity and cultural diversity is symbolized by the illumination of lamps and the firing off of fireworks.

5. **The celebration of Mexican independence, Mexico**
The anniversary of Mexico's proclamation of independence from Spain in 1810 is commemorated annually on September 16, the Mexican Independence Day holiday. The festivities feature the Grito de Dolores, sometimes known as the "cry for independence," as well as parades and cuisine that are traditionally Mexican. It is a symbol of the history of the nation as well as the struggle for freedom.

6. **Australia, Australia on Australia Day, Australia**
The landing of the First Fleet of British ships in 1788 is commemorated on Australia Day, which is observed annually on January 26. Fireworks, barbecues, and citizenship ceremonies are all part of the celebration, which aims to highlight the nation's diverse history as well as the significance of coming together and welcoming everyone.

7. **India's Republic Day is today.**

On January 26, India celebrates Republic Day, which commemorates the day that the Indian Constitution was ratified in 1950. The day will feature a number of parades, cultural exhibits, and presentations that highlight the many customs and history of India. It is a manifestation of the democratic republic status that the nation holds.

These celebrations of national and independence days combine historical commemoration with contemporary festivities, fostering a sense of national solidarity and pride in a nation's identity and the principles it upholds. They place an emphasis on

FESTIVALS AND CELEBRATIONS

the significance of freedom, the richness of cultural diversity, and the resiliency of the people of a country.

Celebrations like Carnival and Mardi Gras have survived the test of time

Celebrations of Carnival and Mardi Gras are cultural phenomena that have crossed cultural boundaries and have continued to develop throughout the course of time. These celebrations are dynamic and diversified. They represent resiliency, unity, and the everlasting spirit of celebration in their roles as emblems.

1. **Rio de Janeiro, Brazil's Carnaval**
   The Rio Carnival is a living, breathing example of the transformative power of partying. In spite of the difficulties and shifts that have occurred over the course of the years, the Carnival has maintained its status as a spectacular event that highlights the culture and spirit of Brazil. It continues to develop under the impact of modern ideas despite the fact that it is a vital component of the nation's identity.
2. **Italy's Carnival, held in Venice**
   The Carnival of Venice has a long history that dates back to the 13th century and has experienced both phases of decline and renewal throughout its long history. It went through somewhat of a resurgence in the 20th century and eventually become an event that is known all over the world. It demonstrates the tenacity of cultural festivals as well as the evergreen allure of customs and rituals.
3. **Mardi Gras, New Orleans, United States of America**
   The celebration of Mardi Gras in New Orleans has persisted despite numerous obstacles, including conflicts, economic downturns, and natural catastrophes. The tenacity of celebration in the face of adversity is demonstrated by the city's commitment to preserving the spirit of Mardi Gras as well as the significance of the holiday to the community.
4. **The carnivals of Trinidad and Tobago**
   The Trinidad and Tobago Carnival has changed over the years, absorbing new ways of thinking and expression in the arts while still holding on to its more traditional components. It exemplifies the capacity of cultural festivals to adjust to new circumstances and maintain their significance in a dynamic environment.
5. **Notting Hill Carnival, which took place in London**
   The Notting Hill Carnival in London has become one of the largest street celebrations in Europe, highlighting the significance of togetherness and inclusivity in a city that is comprised of people from many different backgrounds. It demonstrates the strength that can be gained from celebrating cultural diversity and tradition.
6. **The Carnival of Santa Cruz de Tenerife, in Spain**

Because of political unrest, the Santa Cruz de Tenerife Carnival has been delayed or canceled on several occasions in the past. Despite this, it has continually made a comeback and continues to be an important cultural event that exemplifies the character and temperament of the Canary Islands.

These celebrations of Carnival and Mardi Gras serve as reminders of the strength of cultural traditions and the continuing power of celebration to bring people together in joy and harmony, as well as to unify communities and maintain cultural identities.

Lively festivals are a tribute to the universal human urge for celebration, unity, and cultural

expression. This can be seen in the form of Carnival, Mardi Gras, music and dance festivities, cuisine and culinary events, or national and independence day commemorations. These festivals are vibrant representations of the traditions, values, and histories of various groups. They bring to light the richness of human diversity as well as the potential of celebration to bridge divides and develop understanding.

Lively festivals are a reflection of the world's diversity and shared human experiences. From the exuberant samba parades of the Rio Carnival to the unity and inclusivity of the Notting Hill Carnival, from the iconic music of Woodstock to the traditional foods of Thanksgiving, and from the historical significance of Bastille Day to the resilience of Mardi Gras in New Orleans, these festivals span the globe and encompass a wide range of traditions.

People get together to celebrate these festivals so that they can express their own identities, make connections with one another, and take pleasure in the richness of the world's many cultural traditions. These festivities are not only portals through which one can gain insight into the traditions, principles, and artistic expressions of communities, but they are also bridges that connect people together, overcoming barriers of language and geography to weave a global tapestry of merriment and cohesion.

Chapter 10

Future Trends in Festivals

Celebrations, opportunities for self-expression, and opportunities for community building have long played a significant role in human civilization. Festivals have always been an essential component of human culture. Festivals have, over the course of their history, developed into events that better represent the shifting dynamics of society by incorporating technology advances, environmentally responsible methods, and cutting-edge experiences. When we look into the future, we can see that a variety of trends that are changing how we celebrate, interact with one another, and form connections with one another are likely to play a significant role in shaping the future of festivals. The future of festivals is expected to be dynamic, forward-thinking, and responsive to the changing needs and ambitions of varied groups all over the world. This will be accomplished through immersive digital experiences, initiatives for sustainability, and inclusive programming.

1. **Integration of Technology and Fully Submerging Oneself in Experiences**
   It is anticipated that in the future, festivals will make use of cutting-edge technologies in order to provide spectators with more immersive and engaging experiences. The technologies of virtual reality and augmented reality (VR/AR) are anticipated to play a big role in enhancing the entire festival experience. These technologies will make it possible for attendees to interact with art installations, performances, and cultural displays in novel and interesting ways.
   In addition, developments in holographic technology may make it possible to create projections of artists and performers that look and act just like the real thing, which will make it easier for live audiences to interact in real time with their virtual counterparts. This combination of technology will blur the barriers between physical and virtual experiences, giving attendees of the festival the opportunity to interact with their favorite performers and cultural icons in ways that have never been done before.

Additionally, the utilization of cutting-edge sound and lighting technologies, including as spatial audio and projection mapping, will elevate the sensory experience of festivals, thereby generating fascinating audio-visual spectacles that will resonate with spectators on a deeper emotional level. This will be accomplished by enhancing the sensory experience. Because of these technologies, the festival areas will be transformed into immersive and multisensory environments, which will generate a sense of connection and wonder among the attendees.

2. **Practices That Are Sustainable and Kind to the Environment**

   The growing global awareness of the need for responsible event management and the importance of preserving the environment will force a greater emphasis on sustainable and eco-friendly techniques in the future of festivals. This trend will be seen as a positive development. In order to reduce the amount of damage that festivals cause to the environment, event planners will give more priority to the implementation of sustainable initiatives. These initiatives will include zero-waste policies, renewable energy solutions, and eco-conscious infrastructure design.

   In addition, the implementation of sustainable food and beverage practices, such as the promotion of items obtained locally and organically, would contribute to the reduction of the negative effects that large-scale gatherings have on the surrounding environment. Efforts will be made to limit the use of plastics that are only used once, increase recycling and composting rates, and encourage more responsible actions for the management of garbage at festivals. These efforts will become normal practices.

   In addition, the incorporation of environmentally friendly technologies, including as solar-powered stages, water-efficient systems, and transportation alternatives that do not produce carbon emissions, will make it possible for festivals to run in a manner that is friendlier to the environment and more sustainable. Festivals may reduce their negative impact on the environment and serve as a model for the wider event industry by adopting environmentally friendly business practices and so fostering a culture of environmental care and responsibility. This can be accomplished by implementing sustainable practices into festival operations.

3. **Programming that is Both Inclusive and Diverse**

   The future of festivals will place a priority on inclusivity and diversity, with the intention of creating spaces that are friendly and accessible to people of all different kinds of communities and backgrounds. The organizers of the festival will place a strong emphasis on the curation of diverse programming that showcases a wide variety of cultural, artistic, and musical expressions in order to cultivate an atmosphere that promotes cultural understanding and exchange.

   Attendees will have the opportunity to interact with a wide variety of live performances, curated exhibitions, and hands-on activities thanks to the event's inclusive programming, which will cover a wide range of musical subgenres, aesthetic motifs, and artistic expressions. In addition, festivals will aggressively promote the involvement of marginalized populations, budding artists, and underrepresented voices by giving a platform for these groups to exhibit their abilities and communicate their distinctive points of view with an audience from all over the world.

In addition, the implementation of initiatives to promote accessibility for individuals with disabilities, such as the implementation of wheelchair-accessible facilities, sensory-friendly programming, and sign language interpretation services, will enhance the inclusiveness of festivals and ensure that all attendees can fully participate in the festivities. These initiatives include the implementation of wheelchair-accessible facilities, sensory-friendly programming, and sign language interpretation services.

4. **Engagement of the Community and Its Impact on Society**

   Festivals of the future will place a greater emphasis on community participation and social impact, highlighting the significance of cultivating meaningful connections and bringing about positive change within local and global communities. The festivals will work as catalysts for social initiatives by encouraging participants to actively participate in philanthropic events, community service projects, and charitable endeavors that address urgent social concerns and promote sustainable development.

   Festivals will be able to contribute to the growth and improvement of the areas in which they are hosted if they form partnerships with local nonprofit organizations, community groups, and social entrepreneurs. Festival attendees will be empowered to make a tangible and lasting influence on the lives of others through collaborative activities centered on education, healthcare, environmental conservation, and cultural preservation. This will develop a sense of social responsibility and civic participation among festival attendees.

   In addition, the incorporation of volunteer programs and chances for service-learning will encourage participants to actively participate in community-driven projects and engage in hands-on activities that build social cohesion, mutual understanding, and global citizenship. This will be accomplished through the integration of volunteer programs and service-learning opportunities. The organizers of a festival can start a chain reaction of good things to happen by harnessing the collective strength of the people who attend the event. This influence will continue well after the festival is over.

5. **Individualization as well as Tailoring of Experiences**

   The future of festivals will be characterized by an emphasis on individualized and bespoke experiences, which will be adapted to the preferences and interests of visitors on an individual level. The organizers of the festival will make use of data analytics and consumer insights to create personalized itineraries, recommendations, and material that caters to the individual preferences and goals of each attendee.

Smartphone apps and wearable technology will play a vital part in the delivery of tailored experiences, offering features such as real-time event schedules, personalized navigation, and interactive maps. These features will be made available to users.

Festival-goers will be able to design their own unique immersive experiences using the digital tools that will be available to them. They will be able to choose from a wide variety of performances, seminars, and attractions in order to create an event that speaks to their unique sensibility.

Additionally, the incorporation of artificial intelligence (AI) and machine learning algorithms will make it possible for festivals to study the behavior, preferences, and feedback of attendees, which will facilitate the ongoing development of subsequent events. Because of these technologies, festival organizers will be able to improve their offers and the quality of the event as a whole, making each iteration of the festival more personalized and interesting than the one that came before.

6. **Festivals that are Both Virtual and Hybrid**

The development of both virtual and hybrid festivals is expected to emerge as a significant trend in the festival business in the years to come. Virtual festivals, which are held and experienced entirely online, will make it possible for guests from all over the world to take part in the celebrations without the necessity of physically traveling to any specific location. These events will make use of cutting-edge virtual reality (VR) and augmented reality (AR) technologies in order to produce immersive digital settings that mimic the vibe of traditional festivals.

Attendees of virtual festivals will be able to enjoy a comprehensive and engaging experience without having to leave the convenience of their own homes thanks to the availability of live-streamed performances, interactive exhibitions, and virtual marketplaces. The attractiveness of virtual festivals will stretch beyond regional limits, which will make them accessible to an audience on a global scale and create new chances for artists and performers to connect with fans on a global scale.

On the other hand, hybrid festivals will integrate in-person and virtual components, making it possible for participants present at the event as well as those attending remotely to interact with festival material. These events will offer a seamless integration of digital and physical experiences, guaranteeing that the excitement and sense of community that is a hallmark of festivals can be experienced by a wide range of audiences regardless of their location or the specifics of their situation.

7. **Precautions Taken for One's Health and Safety**
   As the event business continues to be influenced by public health concerns, the future of festivals will prioritize the implementation of health and safety measures in order to protect the health and safety of festival goers.
   In order to provide participants with safe conditions, festivals will implement demanding health measures such as improved sanitary practices, fast testing facilities, and vaccine verification.
   In addition, the layout of festival areas will be modified to allow for social distancing and the management of crowds. These changes will make it easier for attendees to engage in risk-free interactions and will ensure that festivalgoers may enjoy acts and activities without putting their health at risk.
   Festival organizers may want to investigate the usage of digital health passports and contactless payment systems in response to the shifting environment of public health in order to minimize the amount of direct contact between attendees and reduce the likelihood of virus transmission. The comfort and security of festivalgoers will continue to be of the utmost importance, and the organizers will continue to prioritize the implementation of flexible and adaptable health and safety measures in order to address the ever-changing nature of the event.
8. **Festivals that are Good for the Environment and Circular Economies**
   In the design and organization of future festivals, there will be an increased emphasis placed on regenerative practices and circular economies. The term "regenerative festivals" refers to gatherings that go beyond the concept of "sustainable festivals" in order to actively restore and rejuvenate the natural and cultural resources that they engage with. These festivals aim to leave a beneficial impact on the communities and ecosystems that host them.
   The reduction, reuse, and recycling of resources and materials are the cornerstones of circular economies in the festival industry. These practices help to cut down on waste while also improving the long-term environmental health of the event location. Festival organizers will work in conjunction with the communities surrounding each event to ensure that sustainable development projects are supported, that environmental conservation is encouraged, and that festivals contribute to the regeneration of ecosystems.
   In addition, regenerative festivals will place an emphasis on the preservation of culture, the adoption of traditional customs, and the respect for the cultural legacy of the communities who host the events. Festivals have the potential to become agents of positive change if they engage in activities such as regenerative practices and circular economies. This will help to build harmony between humans, nature, and culture.
9. **Components Relating to Wellness and Mindfulness**
   In the future, festivals will recognize the significance of include wellness and mindfulness activities in their programming. This is because overall well-being

and mental health are becoming increasingly important. These components will include rooms for rest and rejuvenation, as well as wellness workshops, yoga and meditation classes, and other such activities.

In addition, festivals will make mental health resources a priority and provide participants with on-site counselors, support hotlines, and dedicated safe areas where they can seek emotional support and aid if they need it. The emotional and physical well-being of those who attend the festival will be given primary consideration during the planning process, and the organizers will strive to design environments that support these goals.

In addition, festivals will encourage people to engage with nature, engage in sustainable practices, and adopt conscious consumption habits by embracing the ideas of mindful living and incorporating them into their programming. These health and mindfulness components will encourage a feeling of balance and self-care, guaranteeing that festival guests will leave the event not only entertained but well nourished in mind, body, and soul.

10. **Collaboration as well as Partnerships Across Different Industries**

    The development of the festivals of the future will be significantly impacted by the importance of cross-industry collaboration and partnership. The organizers of the festival will attempt to produce one-of-a-kind and forward-thinking experiences by forming partnerships with various artists, brands, and technological and cultural organizations. Because of these relationships, there will be dynamic crossovers and synergies, which will provide attendees with a wide variety of immersive encounters to choose from.

    Additionally, cross-industry cooperation will expand into other fields, such as environmental development, cuisine, and the fashion and art industries. Festivals will play the role of platforms for artists, designers, chefs, and environmentalists to cooperate and co-create, infusing events with a diverse and welcoming personality.

    The future of festivals will also require tight coordination with local authorities, governmental agencies, and communities to guarantee that festivals are smoothly integrated into the infrastructure and development plans of the host city. This will be done to ensure that festivals have a sustainable future. Through the formation of partnerships of this kind, festivals will be able to make significant contributions to the economic, cultural, and social development of the areas in which they take place.

11. **Miniature and Specialty Festivals**

    We can anticipate a growth in the number of niche and micro festivals that will take place in the future. These festivals will appeal to highly specialized groups, subcultures, and interests. These gatherings on a more intimate scale will concentrate on particular topics, types of music, or activities, and will provide attendees with a more personal and specialized experience.

Festivals that cater to a specific type of music, art movement, culinary style, or cultural subculture might provide an opportunity for aficionados to network with other people who share their interests in the subject matter. Because of the low attendance at these events, there will be a strong sense of community and camaraderie among the people who do show up.

Micro festivals, which have a small number of attendees and provide only select individuals with access, will provide customized experiences that put an emphasis on quality rather than quantity. It is possible that these events will involve high-end culinary experiences, art exhibitions, or immersive performances, with the goal of providing participants with a premium and individualized experience.

12. **Architecture & Interior Design Inspired by the Future**

In the years to come, the architecture and design of festival spaces will take on a more cutting-edge and futuristic quality. Festival organizers will be able to build spaces that are both dynamic and adaptive if they make use of cutting-edge architectural concepts such as modular and environmentally friendly structures.

The aesthetics and functionality of festival venues will be shaped by the use of biomimetic design, which takes its cues from the patterns and systems found in nature. This will promote harmony with the natural world. Festival habitats can be created using temporary constructions that combine components such as living walls, green roofs, and renewable energy systems. This results in environments that are not only aesthetically stunning but also responsible for the environment.

Everyone will be able to take part in the celebrations and interact with their surroundings in a meaningful way since the festival spaces will be designed using universal design principles, which ensure that they are accessible to people of all different abilities.

The environment of future festivals is likely going to be one that is both dynamic and revolutionary, incorporating elements such as technology, sustainability, diversity, and creativity. Festivals will continue to function as cultural and social landmarks because they provide opportunity for people to congregate, celebrate their variety, and share the passions that drive them.

Festival organizers will be well-positioned to create events that resonate with the hopes and expectations of a global and interconnected audience if they embrace the future trends outlined here and incorporate them into their planning.

In this ever-changing world, festivals will continue to adapt, diversify, and innovate in order to reflect the shifting requirements and expectations of their attendees. Festivals will continue to be a source of inspiration, connection, and celebration for future generations as they continue to shape the cultural, artistic, and social fabric of our society.

10.1 How globalization and technology are reshaping festivals

Celebrations, opportunities for cultural expression, and opportunities for community building have been served by festivals since they have been a part of human culture for ages. Nevertheless, in the current period, festivals are going through a transition that is being driven by the forces of globalization and the rapid improvements in technology advancement. The organization of festivals, as well as how they are experienced and communicated, is undergoing significant change as a result of the convergence of global influences and cutting-edge technology. In this piece, we will investigate how globalization and technological advancements are contributing to the evolution of the festival industry.

Festivals and the Globalization of Culture

1. **The Merging of Cultures and the Diversity of**
   The coming together of people from different cultural backgrounds is one of the most obvious ways in which globalization is altering celebrations. The world is getting increasingly interconnected, which has resulted in an increase in the number of events that are becoming cultural melting pots. This is especially clear during music festivals, which bring together musicians from all over the world to create lineups that are both original and varied.
   For instance, music festivals such as Coachella and Glastonbury now feature performers from all over the world and showcase a wide variety of musical styles, ranging from hip-hop and electronic dance music to traditional folk music and world music. This cultural fusion adds to the depth of the festival experience by giving guests the opportunity to learn about and participate in the customs, music, and art of a variety of other countries.

2. **Cuisines & Foods from Around the World**
   The gastronomic traditions that are a part of celebrations have been dramatically altered as a result of globalization.
   Festivals today offer a wide variety of meals and cuisines from around the world for attendees to choose from, reflecting the different interests and preferences of the audience from around the world. Attendees at festivals are able to embark on gastronomic journeys without having to leave the festival grounds because food booths at festivals offer a wide variety of foods, ranging from classic cuisine to fusion concoctions.
   As a result of the globalization of food, the concept of food festivals that are dedicated to certain cuisines, such as taco festivals, sushi festivals, and barbecue festivals, has also come into existence. The cultural diversity of food is honored at these events, and participants are given the opportunity to sample dishes with flavors originating from all around the world.

3. **Collaborations Between Different Cultures**
   Collaborations between artists, performers, and innovators from other cultures have become easier as a result of globalization. These days, festivals frequently

incorporate collaborative performances and installations that mix aspects from a variety of cultural traditions. Not only does this offer a stage for artists on which they can investigate and experiment with a wide variety of artistic traditions, but it also gives attendees of the festival a one-of-a-kind and immersive experience.

For instance, performances of modern dance may integrate aspects of traditional dance from a variety of cultures. Installations of visual art can take their cues for inspiration from a wide variety of different cultural traditions. Within the context of festivals, such cooperation highlight the creative possibilities of globalization.

4. **The Encouragement of Intercultural Contact**

Festivals are becoming more and more common places for the exchange of cultural traditions. This is of the utmost significance in the context of international festivals and other events with a focus on the global community. Festivals such as the Edinburgh Festival Fringe and the Cannes Film Festival are well-known for their ability to draw artists, filmmakers, and performers from all over the world. As a result, these festivals encourage cultural exchange on a worldwide scale.

Workshops, talks, and panels at festivals often delve into global concerns and encourage people to engage in cross-cultural interaction by doing so. This not only encourages the sharing of ideas but also helps to increased global cooperation and understanding.

The Internet of Things and Public Festivals

1. **Purchasing of Admission and Monitoring of Entry**
   The introduction of new technologies has completely altered the process by which festivalgoers acquire tickets and obtain entry to events. Individuals now have an easier time securing their passes and organizing their festival experience in advance thanks to the proliferation of online ticketing platforms. The need for physical tickets has been minimized thanks to mobile ticketing and electronic ticketing systems, which has made access much more convenient and efficient. Additionally, festival grounds can be entered and exited without a hitch thanks to access control technology such as RFID wristbands and mobile apps. These technologies not only make the event more secure, but they also give the event organizers with vital data that they can use to improve the experience for the attendees.

2. **The terms "Virtual Reality" (VR) and "Augmented Reality" (AR) are both used.**
   The use of virtual reality and augmented reality has introduced wholly novel aspects to previously existing festival experiences. Festival-goers may now explore immersive virtual settings, engage with digital installations, and even attend festivals remotely thanks to the technologies that are now available.

For instance, music festivals have begun to experiment with virtual reality (VR) in order to establish possibilities for virtual attendance. This enables individuals from all over the world to take part in the event by way of live-streamed performances and VR environments that reproduce the mood of the festival. AR apps and experiences increase on-site interactions by providing festivalgoers with the opportunity to interact with augmented festival content using their smartphones or AR glasses.

3. **Marketing in the Digital Age and on Social Media**

It is impossible to stress how important the role of digital marketing and social media is in the promotion of festivals. The organizers of festivals make use of digital media in order to generate excitement about their events, market those events, and communicate with potential attendees. Platforms for social media such as Facebook, Instagram, and Twitter have emerged as indispensable resources for the development of communities, the dissemination of festival updates, and the connection with audiences.

Festivals' audiences are significantly expanded thanks, in large part, to the usage of hashtags and other forms of user-generated material.

The attendees of the event create a virtual word-of-mouth marketing campaign that extends well beyond the confines of the festival grounds by posting their festival experiences, images, and videos on social media platforms.

4. **Streaming live video and the distribution of content**

Technology that allows for live streaming has made it possible for festivals to broadcast their material in real time to an audience that spans the globe. Live streaming has become increasingly popular, particularly during music festivals. This has enabled fans from all over the world to see performances by their favorite musicians even when they are not physically present at the festival.

Festivals frequently produce high-quality video content that perfectly captures the spirit of the event, in addition to streaming the event live online. After that, the footage is disseminated over a variety of digital media, which further broadens the festival's reach and visibility.

5. **Mobile applications and electronic travel guides**

The creation of mobile applications that are unique to the event has significantly elevated the overall experience for attendees. These applications provide a variety of features, some of which include interactive maps, personalized timetables, artist profiles, and up-to-the-minute updates. These apps allow attendees to better traverse the festival grounds, better organize their day, and receive critical notifications, all of which contribute to an overall improvement in their experience.

The use of digital guides and festival applications helps reduce the need for printed materials like paper schedules and maps, which is another way these

technologies contribute to attempts to reduce the festival's impact on the environment.
6. **Payments made without the use of cash and smart wristbands**
At recent music events, cashless payment methods have become an increasingly common payment option. Transactions at the event can be completed rapidly and safely thanks to the use of smart wristbands or RFID cards that are linked to the participants' preferred methods of payment. The use of these systems eliminates the requirement for participants to bring cash, shortens the lines at food and merchandise stands, and makes it easier for attendees to keep track of their festival spending budgets.
7. **Analyses of the data and insights on the attendees**
The use of data analytics allows festival organizers to get useful insights into the behavior and preferences of festival attendees. They can use this information to make educated judgments about the lineups they choose, the event logistics, and the marketing techniques they employ. The perspectives of festivalgoers also help to the ongoing process of improving subsequent festivals.
8. **Works of Art in the Form of Light Installations**
The possibilities for art and light displays at festivals have been extended thanks to technological advancements. LEDs, projection mapping, and interactive sensors are just a few examples of the cutting-edge technology that artists and designers utilize these days to create installations that are both visually appealing and immersive. By providing festivalgoers with an opportunity for an immersive sensory experience, these installations contribute to the festivals' overall aesthetic and ambiance.
9. **Initiatives Concerning the Environment and Sustainability**
Festivals are becoming more environmentally responsible, thanks in part to the contributions that technology is making in this area. The utilization of technologies such as solar-powered stages, software for trash management, and infrastructure that is energy-efficient are just a few examples of how technology is being used to lessen the environmental impact of festivals.
10. **Methods of Communication and Precautions**

Technology is utilized at festivals in order to improve communication and safety precautions. The participants are able to keep up with vital changes, respond more rapidly to any problems that may occur, and stay informed thanks to mass notification systems, emergency alerts, and mobile applications.

The Complementarity of Technological Advancement and Globalization
The influence of globalization and technological advancement on the evolution of festivals can be seen in a number of different ways. The worldwide reach of technology makes it possible for festivals to attract attendees from all over the world and makes virtual attendance more convenient. On the other side, globalization provides a source of

energy for the varied and diversified programming of festivals, resulting in the creation of a vibrant cultural tapestry that is appealing to people from all over the world.

This synergy also has an effect on the marketing and promotion strategies used for festivals. The combination of globalization and technology is utilized by digital marketing and social media in order to generate buzz on a global scale and engage with people on a vast scale.

In addition, technology has evolved into a bridge between different cultures, making it easier for people from different backgrounds to interact with one another during festivals. Virtual reality (VR) and augmented reality (AR), for example, make it possible for guests to experience and interact with cultures from all over the world.

Concerns and Things to Take Into Account

1. **Authenticity with Respect to the Culture**
   Concerns have been raised over the maintenance of cultural authenticity in light of the increasing internationalization of festivals. It is absolutely necessary for festivals to find a middle ground between promoting variety and respecting the genuineness of cultural traditions. When incorporating aspects from a variety of cultures into their events, festival organizers should do so with cultural awareness and ethical considerations in mind.

2. **An Overload of Digital Content**
   There is a potential for experiencing a "digital overload" at festivals as a result of the growth of electronics. It is possible that attendees will spend an excessive amount of time on their smartphones or absorbed in virtual reality activities, which may detract from the live and community elements of the event. It is essential to find a happy medium and inspire festival-goers to make full use of the surroundings by actively participating in the festivities.

3. **Protection of Personal Information and Data**
   Concerns over data privacy and protection are raised by the use of cashless payment systems and festival applications. Attendees may be hesitant to share personal or financial information on these sites due to the potential for identity theft. The organizers of the festival have a responsibility to put an emphasis on data security and safeguard the information of the guests.

4. **Availability and Participation of All**
   Even though technology makes the festival experience better for a large number of attendees, it may be difficult for those attendees who do not have access to cellphones or the internet. The organizers of the festival have a responsibility to ensure that their digital products are accessible to all guests and to provide a variety of other ways for attendees to participate.

5. **The Effects of Technology on the Environment**

In spite of the fact that it has the potential to promote sustainability, technology also contributes to the production of electronic waste and the use of energy. The organizers of the festival need to investigate ways to reduce the negative effects that the technology they employ has on the surrounding environment.

The world of festivals is undergoing a fundamental transformation as a direct result of the interaction between globalization and technological advancement. These factors have contributed to an increase in the cultural diversity and inclusiveness of festivals, as well as enhanced opportunities for intercultural communication and an overall enhancement of the attendee experience. The future of festivals is expected to be even more thrilling, immersive, and internationally connected as a result of the further advancement of technology and the process of globalization, which unites people and cultures beyond international borders. Festival organizers need to maintain an awareness of the obstacles and factors that must be taken into consideration while simultaneously embracing the boundless opportunities that the convergence of globalization and technological advancement presents. Only then can they ensure that this evolution will be a success.

10.2 The sustainability and eco-consciousness of future festivals

The event industry's approach to environmental responsibility and conservation is likely to be significantly influenced by the eco-friendliness and sustainability of future festivals. This is an opportunity that should not be missed. As knowledge of climate change and the destruction of the environment grows on a worldwide scale, festival organizers are rethinking the techniques they use to reduce the negative impact their events have on the environment and to encourage the adoption of sustainable behaviors. The following trends and activities shed light on the expected trajectory that the eco-friendliness and sense of responsibility toward the environment at future festivals will take:

1. **Sustainable Energy and Infrastructure and Green Infrastructure**
   Future festivals will increasingly incorporate green infrastructure and renewable energy solutions to reduce their dependency on non-renewable resources and to minimize their carbon emissions. This will allow for the festivals to have a less overall impact on the environment. Festivals will soon be able to harness clean energy and lessen their impact on the environment thanks to the widespread use of features such as solar-powered stages, wind turbines, and lighting systems that are efficient in their use of energy. Festivals may demonstrate their commitment to sustainability and contribute to the worldwide shift to a future with lower carbon emissions by integrating technologies that use renewable sources of energy.

2. **Elimination or reduction of waste and recycling**
   In the not too distant future, environmentally aware festivals will place significant focus on recycling and reducing their overall amount of waste. The

organizers are going to put in place sophisticated waste management systems that put an emphasis on recycling, composting, and the utilization of materials that can biodegrade. Attendees will be encouraged to reduce the amount of waste they produce and to embrace environmentally friendly consumption behaviors if sustainable products such as reusable water bottles, compostable food containers, and sustainable goods are promoted at the event.

Festivals may dramatically reduce the amount of garbage they send to landfills and develop a circular economy within the event sector if they instill and encourage a culture of waste consciousness among their attendees.

3. **Alternatives to Polluting Transportation Methods**

   In the future, sustainable mobility choices will be prioritized at festivals in order to lessen the carbon footprint that is linked with the travel of attendees. When commuting to and from the festival grounds, attendees will be encouraged to select environmentally friendly modes of transportation through the implementation of initiatives such as shuttle services, incentives for carpooling, and bike-sharing programs. Festival organizers can lessen the environmental effect of large-scale events and encourage guests to engage in more environmentally responsible travel practices by encouraging the use of public transit and providing access to alternative mobility solutions.

4. **Food that is sourced locally and is organic**

   In the years to come, one of the most important aspects of environmentally conscious gatherings will be the prevalence of organic and locally sourced food options. The organizers will work in conjunction with regional farmers and food producers to create menus that highlight products that are in season and produced in a responsible manner. Festivals can help local economies and encourage participants to adopt environmentally conscious eating choices if they promote farm-to-table practices and reduce the carbon emissions connected with the transportation of food by lowering the amount of food that needs to be transported. In addition, the incorporation of plant-based and vegetarian options would facilitate catering to the rising demand for ethical and environmentally responsible dining experiences.

5. **Raising Awareness and Education Concerning the Environment**

   In the future, festivals will place a greater emphasis on environmental education and awareness programs in order to include festivalgoers in sustainability efforts and encourage environmentally responsible habits. Participants will gain knowledge about climate change, the preservation of biodiversity, and the significance of living a sustainable lifestyle through a series of workshops, panel discussions, and interactive exhibits. Festivals have the potential to inspire festivalgoers to become champions for environmentally sustainable practices in their areas and to help to the overall effort to safeguard the world. This is accomplished by cultivating a feeling of environmental stewardship and responsibility.

6. **Activities that promote the preservation and restoration of biodiversity**

In the not too distant future, eco-conscious festivals will place a significant emphasis on the maintenance and repair of biological diversity. In order to put into action activities that are beneficial to the ecosystems and habitats of local species, the organizers will work in conjunction with environmental organizations and conservation groups.

The festivals' dedication to maintaining the natural environment and minimizing the effect that human activities have on biodiversity will be demonstrated by initiatives like as reforestation projects, native plant restoration projects, and wildlife protection measures. Festivals have the potential to act as advocates for ecological resilience and environmental balance if they incorporate biodiversity conservation and restoration into their strategy for achieving sustainability.

Future festivals will be characterized by a comprehensive strategy that covers green infrastructure, waste reduction, sustainable transportation, locally produced food, environmental education, and biodiversity protection. This approach will characterize the sustainability and eco-consciousness of future festivals. Festival organizers can contribute to the global movement toward a more sustainable and resilient future by embracing these efforts, which will demonstrate their dedication to environmental stewardship, motivate guests to change their behavior in a positive direction, and inspire attendees to improve their own behavior. The growth of environmentally conscious festivals will not only establish new benchmarks for the management of events in a responsible manner, but it will also act as a catalyst for the development of a culture of sustainability within the larger event industry as well as throughout society as a whole.

10.3 Predictions for the future of global celebrations

Celebrations around the world have long been a reflection of the human experience, serving to mark significant milestones while also bringing people together and allowing them to showcase their cultures. As we look to the future, we can see that the landscape of global celebrations is getting ready for a huge transition that will be driven by changing societal trends, technology breakthroughs, and an increasing awareness of how interconnected the world is. The following are some forecasts regarding the development of future worldwide celebrations:

1. **Mixed-Genre Occasions to Celebrate**

   There will be an increase in the number of hybrid events in the future of global celebrations. These hybrid events will blend in-person and virtual experiences. People are now able to engage with one another across international boundaries thanks to technology, and in the years to come, this will become much more natural. Even if people are separated by physical distance, they will still be able to take part in celebrations by using technologies such as live streaming, augmented reality, and virtual reality. Because people from all over the world will be able to take part in the events that use this hybrid strategy, the previously existing geographical barriers to participation will be significantly diminished.

2. **An Increase in Cross-Cultural Contact**
Celebrations held all around the world will continue to act as conduits for cultural communication. Festivals and cultural events will showcase international collaborations, which is when artists, performers, and creators from different regions of the world come together to share their various cultural traditions. Participants will have the opportunity to witness a kaleidoscope of cultural facets, ranging from musical performances and dance to gastronomic delectables and artistic installations. This interaction will contribute to a deeper comprehension and appreciation of the unique tapestry of cultures found around the world.

3. **Environmental Consciousness and Long-Term Sustainability**
In the future, sustainability will be an essential component of worldwide festivities. Celebrations will increasingly involve environmentally sensitive activities, such as the use of renewable energy sources and measures to reduce trash as people become more aware of environmental issues. The attendees of an event will anticipate that efforts will be made to reduce the event's ecological imprint and to promote sustainable habits. Not only will festivals be occasions for celebrating culture, but they will also serve as forums for environmental education and awareness-raising.

4. **Inclusion and Availability of Services**
The principles of accessibility and inclusivity will play a significant role in the planning of future worldwide festivities. The events will promote gender and LGBTQ+ equality, as well as make accommodations for those with disabilities and give options that are pleasant to people with sensory issues. The objective will be to make sure that these events are enjoyable and accessible to everyone, irrespective of their history, physical ability, or gender identity, so that everyone may take part in them. Accessibility will extend to include both the real-world and the digital components of the events.

5. **The Incorporation of New Technologies**
Celebrations around the world will continue to evolve as a result of the incorporation of technology. The combination of artificial intelligence, augmented reality, and virtual reality will make it possible to create experiences that are so immersive that they go beyond the bounds of traditional reality. Interactivity will be enhanced thanks to technological advancements, giving attendees the opportunity to interact with performances, art installations, and cultural exhibitions in novel and interesting ways. In addition, data analytics will be of assistance to event organizers in understanding the preferences of festival-goers and in continually bettering the festival experience.

6. **Influence on Society and Donating to Charities**
   Celebrations on a global scale will place a greater emphasis on generosity and the positive impact they have on society. Festivals will operate as catalyzers for social initiatives, encouraging attendees to actively engage in philanthropic activities and community service projects and bringing together people from diverse backgrounds. Festivals will be able to address critical social issues through partnerships with nonprofit groups and social entrepreneurs. This will foster a sense of social responsibility and civic involvement among those who attend the festivals.
7. **Elements of Wellness and Personal Well-Being**
   Components of wellness and mindfulness will be incorporated into global celebrations in order to draw attention to the significance of achieving complete well-being. The participants will have the opportunity to participate in yoga and meditation classes, wellness workshops, and places designed for relaxation and regeneration. Participants will have access to a variety of mental health resources, such as on-site counselors and support hotlines, during the event. These aspects will contribute to the improvement of both physical and mental health, as well as a sense of equilibrium and care for oneself.
8. **A Wide Range of Programming Options**
   In the future, there will be global celebrations that feature a varied lineup of events that showcase a wide variety of artistic, musical, and cultural expressions. The participation of marginalized communities, budding artists, and underrepresented voices will be actively promoted at festivals, which will provide a stage for these individuals on which they may demonstrate their skills and discuss the distinctive points of view they hold. The attendees may look forward to a lively and varied assortment of concerts, exhibitions, and interactive activities that highlight the diverse cultural landscapes found around the world.
9. **The Protection of Cultural Assets and Heritage**
   As time goes on, more and more attention will be paid to the safeguarding of various cultural traditions during global celebrations. Traditional ways of doing things will be honored, endangered languages will be preserved, and indigenous traditions will be highlighted during the events. The organization of festivals will increasingly incorporate cultural preservation activities, which will serve to encourage a wider variety of cultural expressions from throughout the world.
10. **Collaborations Between Different Industries**

Future worldwide festivities will be distinguished by their emphasis on cooperative efforts. The organizers of the festival will form partnerships with various artists, brands, and technological and cultural institutions in order to produce one-of-a-kind and forward-thinking experiences.

The realms of fashion, art, gastronomy, and environmentally responsible development will all be open to collaboration. Festivals will evolve into collaborative platforms where creatives, designers, chefs, and environmentalists can work together to offer attendees an experience that is varied and welcoming to all.

Chapter 11

The Challenges and Controversies

1. **Misrepresentation of culture and appropriation of its symbols:**
   The problem of cultural appropriation and inaccurate depiction is one of the most contentious issues that arises in connection with festivals and other types of celebrations. Because cultural events are becoming increasingly globalized, there is a growing possibility that particular cultural practices will be sold or exploited without the appropriate level of comprehension or regard for the value of those practices. This frequently results in the traditional practices being distorted or oversimplified, which is offensive to the communities from which these traditions originate.
2. **The Effects of Human Activity on the Environment and Sustainability:**
   In recent years, there has been a growing level of worry regarding the effect that festivals and other large-scale events have on the surrounding environment. These occurrences frequently result in the production of significant trash, the consumption of significant quantities of energy, and the contribution of carbon emissions. The inflow of guests and the building of infrastructure can, in certain instances, be disruptive to the natural ecosystems and habitats that are located there. It is therefore absolutely necessary to ensure sustainability and put in place practices that are friendly to the environment in order to reduce these unfavorable effects and encourage responsible event management.
3. **Concerns Regarding Safety and Security:**
   For any event to be considered a success, maintaining the attendees' and participants' safety and well-being must remain a top priority. The organization of a festival presents substantial obstacles, including the management of huge people, the preparation for any emergencies, and the prevention of potential security concerns. A negative impact on the overall experience as well as a stain on the event's reputation can be caused by occurrences such as excessive

congestion, accidents, or acts of violence. For the purpose of preserving a safe and secure environment during a festival, it is very necessary to put in place stringent security precautions, crowd management tactics, and extensive emergency response plans.

4. **Economic Inequality and the Exploitation of People:**

Festivals and celebrations have the potential to deliver economic advantages to the communities in which they are held. However, they also have the potential to worsen existing economic imbalances and lead to the exploitation of local resources and labor.

In some instances, the inflow of tourists and attendees might cause costs to rise, which can create difficult financial circumstances for the local population. In addition, the employment of individuals in the event industry may involve exploitative practices such as low salaries and unsuitable working conditions. Moreover, the employment of individuals in the event business may involve exploitative practices. It is essential to strike a balance between the chances for economic growth, equitable distribution, and fair labor standards if one want to encourage inclusive and sustainable growth within the communities that are hosting the expansion.

5. **Accessibility and inclusiveness:**

For festival organizers, one of the most constant challenges is maintaining accessibility and inclusivity for all participants, including those with impairments. It's possible that many event facilities weren't intended to suit different people's needs, which could make it difficult for people with mobility, sensory, or cognitive impairments to take part in the activities. To effectively promote inclusivity, proactive steps are required, such as the provision of accessible facilities, the provision of experiences that are friendly to attendees' sensory experiences, and the implementation of complete accessibility policies that give priority to the requirements of all attendees.

6. **Compliance with Regulatory Requirements and Permitting:**

It can be a challenging undertaking for event planners to navigate the complicated regulatory landscape and secure the appropriate permits in order to organize festivals and celebrations because of the need to comply with those regulations. The enforcement of municipal legislation, such as zoning regulations, noise ordinances, and health and safety requirements, can frequently offer obstacles in terms of both administration and logistics. In the event that these requirements are not adhered to, legal issues, financial penalties, and even the postponement of events may result. It is absolutely necessary for the successful implementation of festivals to ensure that all regulatory standards are adhered to in an exacting manner and that open communication is maintained with the local authorities.

7. **The effect on the community's culture and heritage:**
   The commercialization and mass marketing of cultural events have the potential to water down or otherwise obscure a community's genuine local culture and tradition. It is possible for traditional celebrations to be altered or reinterpreted in order to appeal to a wider audience; however, this might result in the celebrations' original spirit and meaning being lost in the process. Finding a delicate balance that shows respect for the norms and principles of the community that is hosting an event is necessary in order to maintain the authenticity of the local culture and heritage while also catering to the interests of a wide range of attendees.

8. **Abuse of Alcohol and Other Substances:**
   Abuse of alcoholic beverages and other substances frequently presents considerable difficulties at parties and celebrations, which can result in serious dangers to one's health, accidents, and disruptive conduct. Drinking to excess and using illegal drugs both contribute to an environment that is not healthy for the participants as a whole and put their safety at risk. Such an environment is also detrimental to the attendees' ability to enjoy the event. In order to cultivate an environment that is safe and conducive to good health during a festival, it is vital to implement laws regarding the responsible delivery of alcohol, provide access to tools that reduce harm, and raise knowledge regarding the dangers associated with substance misuse.

9. **Differences of Opinion and Controversies Concerning Programming:**
   The selection of musicians, artists, and cultural programming at a festival can at times give rise to disagreements and controversies among the attendees and organizers of the event. Disagreements and rifts among stakeholders are possible outcomes of debates that involve the representation of various viewpoints, the admission of controversial artists, or the allocation of money for certain programs. It is essential, if the festival is to keep its integrity and credibility, that these issues be navigated with transparency, open communication, and a commitment to diversity and artistic expression.

10. **Sensitivities Regarding Sociopolitical Issues and Public Discussion:**
    In a social and political atmosphere that is becoming increasingly politicized, festivals and celebrations frequently become the center of public discourse and debates on critical themes. It is possible for public rallies, protests, or ideological confrontations to occur inside the context of the event, which might lead to potential interruptions and difficulty in maintaining a calm atmosphere. For the purpose of fostering a feeling of community and collective understanding within the festival space, it is necessary to cultivate an atmosphere that encourages mutual respect, open discourse, and tolerance for a variety of opinions.

11. **Issues Relating to the Public's Health and the Spread of Disease:**
    Recent crises in health around the world have brought to light the necessity of

addressing issues of public health at meetings of a large scale, such as music festivals. Organizers of events have a substantial obstacle in the form of the danger of illness transmission, which is particularly high in settings that are crowded and communal. It is essential to provide good sanitation, put in place health and safety standards, and make sure that participants have access to medical services in order to protect the health of attendees and reduce the likelihood of the transmission of infectious diseases.

12. **Behavior on Social Media Platforms and Online:**
The ubiquitous influence of social media and online communication can simultaneously improve and complicate one's experience at a festival. Even though social media platforms are a strong tool for marketing events and communicating with attendees, they also have the potential to accentuate unpleasant incidents and controversies, which may quickly lead to the spread of false information and increased scrutiny from the public. The maintenance of a healthy and courteous online environment that reflects the festival's core values and ethos is dependent on a number of factors, including the management of online conduct, the moderation of digital content, and the promotion of responsible digital citizenship.

13. **Relationships with the Community and Engagement of Stakeholders:**
It is crucial for the long-term survival of festivals to build and maintain positive relationships with the local communities, stakeholders, and inhabitants. Community ties can be strained, and resistance to future events can be prompted as a result of disagreements regarding the volume of noise, the volume of traffic, or the perceived interruptions to the local way of life. The development of open lines of communication, the solicitation of community feedback, and the addressing of the concerns of local residents are essential techniques for gaining support for the festival within the community that will be hosting it.

14. **Preparedness for Emergencies and Resilience in the Face of Adversity:**
Unforeseen natural disasters, harsh weather events, or emergency situations can all provide substantial hurdles to the safety and continuance of festivals. In order to ensure the resilience of festivals in the face of potential crises, it is vital to develop complete disaster preparedness plans, implement evacuation protocols, and undertake risk assessments. It is essential to work together with local emergency response organizations and put good crisis management techniques into action if one wishes to minimize the impact that unforeseen events will have on the festival and the attendees who will be attending.

15. **Maintaining a Viable and Sustainable Financial Position:**
Especially in the light of shifting market trends and economic unpredictability, festival organizers face an ongoing problem in ensuring the events' financial sustainability and viability. It might be difficult to maintain financial stability, obtain sponsorships, and effectively manage operating costs while still providing

attendees with a high-quality and interesting event experience. It is vital, in order to ensure the continuous success of festivals, to develop a sound financial strategy, to diversify the sources of revenue, and to establish long-term partnerships with sponsors.

16. **Concerns Regarding Intellectual Property and Copyright:**
Legal issues may arise if festivals make use of intellectual property like as music, photographs, and brand assets that are protected by copyright. Using someone else's intellectual property without their permission can lead to legal conflicts as well as financial consequences. In order to avoid potentially expensive legal penalties, festival organizers need to master the intricacies of copyright restrictions, obtain the appropriate permissions, and comply with intellectual property laws.

17. **Scalability and the Dangers of Overcommercialization:**
The difficulty that comes with striking a balance between a festival's size and its level of commercialization is becoming more and more importance. There is a risk that certain celebrations will become excessively commercialized, putting the pursuit of profit ahead of the event's founding principles and ethos. It is essential for the long-term viability of festivals to find the optimal compromise between expanding their attendance and preserving the original spirit and character of the event.

18. **Managing One's Image in the Public Eye and Public Opinions:**
Festivals are frequently susceptible to public views, which are susceptible to being impacted by media coverage, public relations, and the experiences of festival attendees. A festival's attendance and reputation can be negatively impacted by unfavorable incidents or controversies, which can have a lasting effect on the festival's image. It is absolutely necessary to have crisis communication plans, proactive image management, and honest reactions to obstacles in order to maintain the positive image of the event and the trust of the people.

19. **Innovation and the Preservation of Cultural Objects:**
It can be difficult to find a balance at festivals between the competing goals of conserving cultural traditions and encouraging creative experimentation. For festivals to continue to have cultural significance, it is imperative that they find a way to strike a balance between respecting long-standing traditions and welcoming novel forms of creative expression. To achieve a state of peaceful equilibrium, it is essential to promote artistic exploration while simultaneously honoring cultural legacy.

20. **The Importance of Technology in Today's Digital Culture:**

While technology does offer a number of advantages, it also creates obstacles for festival organizers in terms of preserving the genuine experience and human dynamics of their events. Because of the proliferation of cellphones, social media, and virtual experiences, there may be less emphasis placed on actual human interaction and connection. The utilization of technology for the purpose of increasing the festival experience while still conserving the inherent importance of human interaction is a delicate balancing act that must not be neglected.

Even while they are often filled with delight and have significant meaning, cultural celebrations, festivals, and events are not immune to the myriad of difficulties and debates that can surround them. To ensure the ongoing success of these gatherings and the beneficial impact they have, it is essential to have a solid understanding of these concerns and to work to address them. Event organizers can work toward the goal of creating meaningful and inclusive celebrations that resonate with a variety of communities and promote positive societal values by navigating the complexities of cultural appropriation, environmental sustainability, safety, economic disparities, inclusivity, and regulatory compliance, among other factors. In order to find solutions to these problems, rigorous planning, transparency, and a dedication to protecting the cultural, environmental, and social integrity of major events are required. In the end, if we acknowledge these problems and do our best to overcome them, we will be able to better appreciate and cherish the rich tapestry that is human culture and the experiences that we all have in common.

11.1 The tension between tradition and modernity

The constant interplay that exists between modernity and tradition is something that has been defining of human communities for hundreds of years. This complicated relationship is a reflection of the continuing conflict that exists between preserving long-standing cultural norms, practices, and beliefs (traditionally referred to as "tradition") and adapting to new ideas, technology, and societal shifts (often referred to as "modernity"). This tension is an essential component of the human experience and may be found in many other parts of life, such as identity, culture, religion, and politics. During this investigation, we will delve into the complexities of this ongoing battle, investigating its expressions, repercussions, and techniques for negotiating cultural transformation. This conflict has persisted for a long time.

1. **The Role of Tradition in Maintaining Order:**
   Within human civilizations, tradition functions as a moderating and balancing influence. It helps individuals and groups anchor themselves in a world that is constantly changing by providing a sense of continuity, identity, and belonging to those involved. Traditions, whether they pertain to customs, rituals, or values, frequently have deep historical roots and are passed down through generations. This is true whether or not the tradition is about values. They provide a feeling of regularity, a means of celebrating heritage, and a connection to the sage advice of people from the past.

For instance, cultural festivals such as Diwali in India, Thanksgiving in the United States of America, or Hanukkah in Jewish communities serve as cultural touchstones that bring families and communities together. These traditions help to instill a sense of solidarity, provide reassurance in the face of uncertainty, and strengthen the values that the community holds dear.

2. **The Role of Modernity as a Driving Force Behind Progress:**
On the other side, modernism is synonymous with advancement, transformation, and flexibility.
It is propelled by advances in science as well as innovative methods of thinking. The advent of modernity posed a threat to long-standing customs and practices, which frequently compelled communities to accept change and adjust to newly emerging conditions. It is distinguished by a forward-looking and active spirit that strives to improve the quality of life, advance technology, and increase human understanding.
Significant advances have been made in a variety of sectors as a direct result of modernity, including science, technology, and medicine. For example, internet use has fundamentally altered the ways in which people connect with one another, obtain information, and do business. These technological advancements have made previously inconceivable things possible and brought the entire world closer together.

3. **The Confrontation of Divergent Values:**
The struggle that exists between modernity and tradition frequently results in a collision of different values, beliefs, and worldviews. Traditional values frequently have their origins in religious, cultural, or historical roots, and they have a tendency to be resistant to new arguments that contradict the norms that have been established. On the other hand, modernity has a propensity to promote independence, innovation, and progress, which can be in direct opposition to the traditional communal ideals that people hold dear.
One prominent illustration of this conflict can be seen in the discussion that is taking place in many parts of the world around same-sex marriage. These unions are frequently opposed by traditional views on the basis of religious or cultural reasons, whilst modern views tend to argue for equal rights and inclusiveness. This conflict in values has led to changes in law and society in various regions, including the legalization of same-sex marriage as a reflection of the modern ideals that have prevailed in society.

4. **Striking a Balance Between the Preserving of Culture and Adapting to Change:**
When managing the tension between tradition and modernity, one of the most important challenges is to discover the sweet spot that allows for the preservation of cultural legacy while also welcoming in societal progress. As a result of shifting cultural norms and expectations, communities have the challenge of

deciding which traditions to preserve and which ones to modify or abandon altogether.

The celebration of cultural festivals all over the world is a good example of a situation in which this balancing act has been successfully performed. These festivals frequently combine modern aspects, such as music, art, and cuisine, in addition to their basic traditions.

The goals of doing so are to attract a wide audience and to ensure that the traditions continue to be relevant to future generations. For instance, the Chinese New Year celebration, which is based on long-established traditions, has developed to incorporate more modern aspects such as parades and fireworks.

5. **Conflicts between Different Generations:**

The friction that can develop between members of different generations within a society is one of the clearest examples of the conflict that can result when tradition and modernity coexist in a society. Older generations have a greater propensity to highlight the significance of upholding traditions and values that have been formed throughout time. They see these aspects as the foundation upon which society is built. Younger generations, on the other hand, typically have a more open attitude toward embracing change and innovation as they seek to adapt to the demands of modern life.

These clashes between generations occur regularly in the context of shifting gender roles, perspectives on marriage and family, and preferences on technology advancement. Conflicts that arise between parents and their children over topics such as the appropriate use of social media or the acknowledgment of gender identities that deviate from the norm are one manifestation of this tension.

6. **The Function of Religious Beliefs:**

Religion frequently occupies a pivotal position in the dynamic that exists between tradition and modernity. Religious customs are strongly embedded in many different cultures and have a tendency to be resistant to change, particularly in situations in which traditional interpretations of religion come into conflict with contemporary values or scientific discoveries. This conflict is frequently present in discussions about contentious topics like evolution, gender equality, and reproductive rights, among others.

On the other hand, there are religious communities and leaders that are willing to be open to reinterpretation and adaptation, looking for ways to create common ground between traditional beliefs and modern understandings. Within the context of religion, this adaptability can serve to facilitate the creation of a bridge between modernity and tradition.

7. **The influence on one's cultural identity**

The struggle that exists between modernity and tradition has a considerable bearing on the cultural identity of a people. In the face of societal shifts, people and communities frequently find themselves struggling with issues pertaining to their identities. The process of constructing an individual's sense of self-identity entails conducting research into one's family history and negotiating one's place in the world in terms of contemporary norms and customs.

People who live in countries that are multicultural may have to navigate the junction of various cultural identities, which can make their sense of who they are more complicated. A rich tapestry of identities that represent the varied and ever-evolving nature of contemporary culture can be produced as a result of the friction that exists between modernity and tradition.

8. **Misrepresentation of culture and appropriation of culture:**
The process of modernization can result in cultural appropriation and misrepresentation, in particular when elements of one culture are reduced to a commodity and appropriated by another culture for the purpose of making monetary benefit or for reasons that are only cosmetic. This phenomena frequently gives rise to conflicts that center on questions of authenticity, respect, and the commercialization of traditional traditions and symbols.

These debates are often made more contentious by the conflict that exists between modernity and tradition. While modernity may facilitate interactions between people of different cultures, it also begs the question of how cultural components should be used ethically. Finding a happy medium between appreciating different cultures and taking elements of those cultures for one's own ends is a difficult task that calls for sensitivity and respect.

9. **Techniques for Dealing with the Tension:**

Conversation and Open Communication: Encourage open conversation amongst people of different generations, cultures, and belief systems. Understanding and bridging differences in perspectives can be facilitated via respectful communication.

Education and Awareness: It is important to spread awareness about the importance of preserving cultural traditions and history by educating people about these topics. Education of this kind can assist individuals in appreciating the relevance of traditions and in making judgments on cultural adaptation that are based on accurate information.

Adaptation and Innovation: Embrace the possibility that a tradition will develop and change so that it can meet the demands of the modern world. Taking this method can be helpful in ensuring that traditions continue to have relevance and significance in a changing world.

Integration and Cultural interchange: One way to encourage cultural interchange and integration is to hold events that celebrate the various traditions practiced within a culture. This can help contribute to the creation of a good balance between modernity and tradition.

When incorporating aspects of other cultures into your own, it is important to give thought to both the ethical considerations involved and the possibility of engaging in cultural appropriation. Exhibit respect for the histories and connotations associated with these components.

The inherent conflict that arises from the clash of modernity with tradition is an essential component of human culture and civilization. It exemplifies the constant challenge of striking a balance between the protection of cultural assets and the requirement for adaptation in a world that is undergoing fast change. This tension is a dynamic force that has changed societies in the past and continues to shape societies today, having an influence on individual identity, the values of communities, and the path that human progress will take. Understanding this tension and navigating it with sensitivity, dialogue, and a dedication to cultural preservation can assist communities in finding a harmonic balance that embraces both tradition and modernity, so preserving a dynamic and inclusive cultural environment. This equilibrium can be achieved by helping societies discover a harmonious balance that embraces both tradition and modernity.

11.2 Cultural appropriation and respect for traditions

Cultural appropriation is a contentious and complex problem that has gained importance in recent years, provoking arguments in all facets of culture, from fashion and entertainment to art and gastronomy. This issue has been at the center of discussions in all of these areas. At its heart, the concept of cultural appropriation refers to the act of individuals or groups belonging to one culture borrowing, imitating, or adopting elements from another culture, frequently without a proper understanding, respect, or concern for the cultural value of those elements. This phenomena poses important problems regarding the proper observance of customs as well as the moral implications that accompany cross-cultural interactions. During this investigation, we will look into the complexities of cultural appropriation and how it intersects with the requirement to respect traditions in order to have a better understanding of both concepts.

Comprehending the Concept of Cultural Appropriation:

The idea of "cultural appropriation" has strong ties to questions pertaining to power, privilege, and the way people are represented. It takes place when groups that are dominant or privileged borrow aspects from groups that are marginalized or minority cultures. These components can include a wide range of factors, such as customs pertaining to clothes, hairstyles, language, religious symbols, art, music, and even culinary practices. The absence of awareness, comprehension, or respect for the culture from which aspects are appropriated is frequently the defining characteristic that differentiates cultural appropriation from cultural exchange. [Cultural appropriation] is not to be confused with cultural exchange.

The following are important features of cultural appropriation:

1. **The dynamics of power:** Cultural appropriation frequently takes place within the context of power inequalities, in which a dominant culture appropriates

aspects from a marginalized culture. This has the potential to uphold a colonial, exploitative, and oppressive past that dates back through history.
2. **Misrepresentation:** One of the potential outcomes of cultural appropriation is the misrepresentation or distortion of the culture that has been appropriated. This kind of inaccurate portrayal can help perpetuate negative preconceptions and obscure the genuine nature of a society.
3. **Commodification:** A significant portion of incidents of cultural appropriation involve the commercialization of aspects of culture in order to generate financial gain. This can be an especially troublesome situation in the event that underrepresented populations do not benefit from the commercialization of their customs.
4. **Absence of Consent:** Cultural appropriation frequently takes place in the absence of either the consent or the approval of the culture whose elements are appropriated. This lack of permission can be extremely disrespectful, and it can also be contemptuous of the traditions and values that are important to the community.
5. Diminished meaning When components of a culture are appropriated, their meaning may be diluted or reduced to become fashion trends or novelties. This is one of the potential consequences of cultural appropriation. This has the potential to destroy the deeply ingrained meanings and symbolism that are embedded into the culture.

The Value of Honoring Our Traditions:

Recognizing, appreciating, and protecting the cultural history of various groups is an essential part of respecting the traditions of those cultures. It requires recognizing the value of conventions, practices, rituals, and symbols within a specific culture and exhibiting a true dedication to comprehending and appreciating the traditions that are upheld in that society. This regard should extend to the traditions that are practiced by underrepresented or minority communities, as it is imperative to acknowledge the significance of these traditions in maintaining cultural variety and promoting mutual understanding.

The following are important components of respecting traditions:

1. **Cultural Sensitivity:** Approaching traditions with empathy and a conscious knowledge of the cultural, historical, and social context in which they exist is an essential component of cultural sensitivity. It is necessary to acknowledge the relevance of these customs to the communities that carry them out in order to accomplish this.
2. **Cooperation and Education:** Encouraging and enabling opportunities for cultural exchange between other cultures, as well as fostering collaboration between those cultures, can help to promote mutual respect and understanding.

Education about other traditions can also encourage respect by providing insights into the cultural relevance of different practices. This can be accomplished through the dissemination of knowledge.
3. **Authentic Appreciation:** Authentic appreciation of traditions is valuing them for the value that they bring to the community rather than treating them as if they are merely surface-level commodities. It recognizes the richness of meaning that can be found within cultural activities.
4. **Empowerment** In order for communities to keep their cultural identities and their legacy intact, they must respect the traditions that have come before them. It encourages communities who are marginalized or minority to define and share their traditions, which in turn promotes the communities' right to exercise self-determination.
5. **Ethical Consumption:** Ethical consumption refers to the practice of making educated decisions regarding items, fashion, or art that has a significant cultural impact. Supporting artists, creators, and companies from the culture in question is given higher priority than taking elements of that culture for one's own use, which is known as cultural appropriation.

Finding Your Way Through the Intersection:

1. **Sensitization and Instruction:**
Education is a powerful instrument that can be used to encourage respect for traditions and prevent the appropriation of other cultures. Studying the background, philosophical underpinnings, and contemporary relevance of many traditions is beneficial to both individuals and societies. Empathy and respect can be fostered through the acquisition of knowledge on the cultural milieu in which these traditions are practiced.
2. **Free-Flowing Conversation:**
A free exchange of ideas across different cultures is absolutely necessary in order to construct bridges of understanding and respect for one another. The place for different cultures to speak with one another, share their knowledge, and work together should be made available. Creating avenues for conversation can be an effective way to address concerns about appropriation and encourage interaction that is respectful.
3. **Proprietary Rights and Consent:**
For the sake of respecting traditions, it is necessary to first acknowledge who the owners of cultural components are and then acquire their informed consent before dealing with those components. If a certain community is open to having its traditions shared with other communities, it is imperative to do so with that community's permission and in a way that honors the significance of those traditions while also respecting their values.

4. **Diversity in Representation and Inclusion:**
   It is absolutely necessary to encourage variety in all facets of society, including the arts, fashion, and the media, in order to cut down on cultural appropriation. Misrepresentation is something that can be helped along by ensuring that marginalized and minority cultures have a platform from which they may legitimately represent themselves and share their traditions with others.
5. **Consumption with a Conscious:**
   Consumers have the ability to make ethical decisions by lending their support to companies,
   artists, and innovators who engage with cultural traditions in a fair and respectful manner. The prevention of cultural appropriation requires a number of steps, one of which is to steer clear of products or behaviors that either exploit cultures or misrepresent them.
6. **Contemplation of Oneself:**
   Self-examination, in which one examines oneself in terms of one's actions and any possible biases, is something that individuals should do. This self-awareness can lead to decisions that are more conscious as well as relationships with many traditions that are more respectful.
7. **Self-Determination and Community Support:**

A significant part of showing respect for traditions is giving underrepresented groups the opportunity to speak about their customs and points of view. A demonstration of solidarity and support for these communities can help raise the voices of the members of those communities and safeguard the traditions of those communities from being appropriated.

Some Examples of Cultural Exchange That Are Respectful:

1. **Festivals of Culture** There are many festivals of culture held all over the world, and many of these festivals give opportunity for exchanges that are polite, where traditions are shared with excitement and understanding. Attendees will have the opportunity to fully engage in cultural activities while maintaining an awareness of the significance of the customs that are being honored.
2. **Collaborative Art Projects:** Collaborative art projects that engage artists coming from a variety of cultural backgrounds can be a source of cultural exchange that is respectful. The end result of these types of undertakings is frequently the production of art that acknowledges the roots of the numerous parts that it incorporates from different cultures.
3. **Cultural Workshops and courses** Educational programs that offer cultural workshops and courses can enhance respectful interchange by offering chances for individuals to learn about and participate with customs straight from the source.

This allows individuals to gain a deeper understanding of the traditions and to feel more connected to them.

4. Businesses That Participate in Fair Trade Practices and encourage Ethical Consumption:

Businesses that participate in fair trade practices and encourage ethical consumption place a priority on the respectful involvement of many cultures. They collaborate directly with communities to guarantee that their cultural practices are reflected accurately and that they are compensated appropriately for doing so.

The place that exists at the crossroads between cultural appropriation and respect for traditions is one that is both complicated and always changing. It brings up fundamental problems regarding ethics, power relations, and the significance of maintaining cultural diversity in the world. Exchange of cultures is a natural component of human interaction; nonetheless, it is important that this process be carried out with attention and respect, so that traditions are not inappropriately taken or commercialized. To successfully navigate this intersection, a commitment to mutual understanding, consent, and representation is required, with the end objective of cultivating a society in which cultures are recognized, shared, and respected for their distinctive contributions to our common history.

11.3 Environmental and social issues in festival organization

Festivals, with their exuberant atmosphere and the confluence of people from all origins, have the capacity to unify communities, celebrate culture, and generate experiences that will stick with people for a long time. However, they do not exist in a vacuum and do have certain social and environmental effects. Festivals are frequently large-scale events that result in the generation of waste, the use of resources, and the presence of social repercussions that require attention. During the course of this conversation, we are going to investigate the myriad of ecological and social problems that are associated with the planning of festivals, as well as investigate the tactics and procedures that can assist in striking a balance between celebration and responsibility.

Concerns Regarding the Environment When Organizing a Festival:

The Production of Waste:

Festivals have the potential to generate a significant amount of garbage, which may include reusable food containers, disposable cups, and other goods with a single use. The local waste management systems may become overburdened as a result of this garbage, which may also contribute to pollution.

In terms of energy consumption:

It may need a significant amount of power to run the stages, lighting, and sound systems at a festival, along with other festival infrastructure. If they are not properly managed, traditional sources of energy can have a substantial negative effect on the surrounding ecosystem.

Utilization of Water:

Water is typically needed in great quantities at festivals for a variety of reasons, including cleanliness and food preparation. An excessive use of water can put a strain on the available local water resources, which is especially problematic in areas where water is in short supply.

Emissions Caused by Transportation:
The process of getting to and from festivals can result in significant emissions of greenhouse gases. As a result of the necessary infrastructure improvements to accommodate the large number of visitors, there may be an increase in the amount of emissions produced.

The disturbance of habitats and the erosion of land:
Erosion, harm to local ecosystems, and disturbing of local species are all potential consequences of holding festivals in natural environments. The building of temporary infrastructure can have effects on the environment that continue for an extended period of time.

Concerns Regarding Social Aspects in the Organization of Festivals:
Ability to Participate and Accessibility:
It is essential to take measures to make certain that festivals are accessible and inclusive for all participants, including those who may have disabilities. It may be difficult for people to participate in an event if the facilities and accommodations are inadequate.

Peace of Mind and Protection:
The upkeep of a secure atmosphere is of the utmost importance at festivals. Accidents, injuries, and even, in the worst of all possible worlds, acts of violence can all be caused by insufficient security measures.

Relationships with the Community:
Festivals are frequently held within or in close proximity to villages. The disruptions caused by things like traffic congestion, noise, and other disturbances might result in strained ties with the neighboring population.

Achieving Social Equity:
The economic gains that festivals provide are not necessarily dispersed in an even manner. It's possible that local communities won't receive equitable gains, which will only make problems with economic inequality worse.

Abuse of Substances and Concerns Regarding Health:
In some cases, festivals can create an atmosphere in which substance misuse, such as drinking alcohol and using illegal drugs, is common. This can be harmful to one's health and contribute to a hazardous environment.

Finding a Happy Medium Between Celebration and Responsibility:
Initiatives Regarding Sustainability:
The environmental toll that festivals take can be reduced by the organizers through the use of sustainability strategies. This includes the utilization of programs

for recycling and composting, the utilization of renewable energy sources, and the adoption of behaviors that are beneficial to the environment.

Alternatives for Transportation:

In order to assist reduce the carbon footprint that is caused by visitors traveling to and from festivals, it is helpful to encourage people to use public transportation, carpool, or take advantage of shuttle services.

Participation in the Community:

It is crucial to develop strong relationships with the communities that are located nearby. The organizers of the festival can collaborate closely with the locals to address their concerns and make certain that the event will be an improvement to the neighborhood.

Ability to Participate and Accessibility:

The provision of adequate facilities, the provision of sign language interpreters, and the development of accommodations for those with disabilities are three ways that festivals can ensure that their events are accessible to all guests.

Precautions Taken for the Protection of Others:

For the protection of the attendees, it is necessary to take extensive precautions regarding safety and security. This includes the provision of medical services and the presence of security officers as well as the management of the crowd.

Various Lineups with a Focus on Inclusivity:

Festival organizers have the ability to prioritize diversity in their lineups by including performers hailing from a variety of genres and backgrounds. This encourages inclusivity and reflects a diverse collection of musical and cultural traditions from throughout the world.

Participation in Community Activities:

The involvement of the local community can be advantageous in a variety of ways, including the formation of economic partnerships and participation in the process of planning and decision-making. Residents of the surrounding area should have a say in how the festival will affect their community.

Education and a Consciousness of the Facts:

Creating a culture of responsibility among festivalgoers can be accomplished through the promotion of sustainable practices, environmental stewardship, and social awareness. Educational endeavors may include the dissemination of knowledge concerning the reduction of waste, the responsible consumption of alcohol, and the respect for local communities.

The Obstacles to Overcome and the Way Forward:

There are still considerable obstacles to overcome, despite the fact that many festivals are making progress in addressing environmental and social concerns. The financial and logistical hurdles that must be overcome in order to put sustainable principles into action might be intimidating. Maintaining a responsible management structure while satisfying the drive for expansion and profit is an ongoing problem.

In addition, tackling social issues such as public safety and substance misuse calls for constant awareness as well as coordinated efforts.

Growing awareness of the need to practice environmental and social responsibility is likely going to be a driving force in the evolution of festival organization in the years to come. As the effects of climate change and other critical social concerns become more apparent, festivals will come under growing pressure to embrace environmentally responsible practices and to promote inclusiveness. Solar-powered stages and other attempts to reduce waste are two examples of the kinds of innovations in environmentally friendly infrastructure and practices that are anticipated to play a key part in tackling these difficulties.

Chapter 12

Preserving and Documenting Festivals

Celebrations, with all their vivacity, variety, and significance to human society, are known as festivals. They provide venues for the celebration of local customs, religious practices, artistic expressions, and communities. Festivals frequently capture the essence of a society by encapsulating its identity, values, and history, which is why they are necessary components of cultural heritage. However, as a result of the rapid pace of change in the globe, a great deal of celebrations are in danger of being lost or watered down. It is impossible to overestimate the significance of conserving festivals and documenting their histories, as doing so protects cultural diversity, fosters stronger relationships between generations, and encourages greater understanding between different cultures. In this essay of 3,000 words, we will discuss the necessity of documenting and preserving festivals, as well as the obstacles that festivals confront and the numerous ways that are employed to preserve the life of festivals.

1. **The Importance of Celebrations Throughout Cultural Traditions**
   1.1. One's Sense of Self and Heritage
   Festivals are a reflection of the identity and legacy of the society that hosts them. In many cases, they involve the wearing of traditional garb, the performance of traditional music and dance, the preparation of traditional foods, and the performance of traditional rites. These aspects are guarded and handed down from one generation to the next, ensuring that there will always be a sense of continuity and a link to the past. For instance, the Chinese New Year, which is observed by millions of people all over the world, exemplifies the rich tapestry of Chinese culture by including components such as dragon and lion dances, red envelopes, and traditional foods.
   1.2. The Cohesion of Society
   Festivals are powerful tools that can be used to establish and strengthen social relationships between individuals. They facilitate the coming together of

FESTIVALS AND CELEBRATIONS

individuals and the development of a sense of community and belonging.

Festivals create chances for people of different ethnicities and religious backgrounds to interact with one another, share their traditions, and foster an atmosphere of mutual understanding in communities that are multicultural. For instance, the Diwali festival, which is observed by Hindus, Jains, and Sikhs, bridges the gap between different cultures and religious traditions, providing a venue for cross-cultural communication and collaboration.

1.3. Expression of One's Culture

Festivals serve as venues for artistic expression and provide communities with opportunities to exhibit their creative potential, innate abilities, and historical accomplishments. Festivals are a celebration of the arts and demonstrate the artistic vitality and inventiveness of a civilization. Examples of such festivals are the magnificent samba parades of the Rio Carnival and the ornate sugar skull decorations of the Mexican Day of the Dead.

1.4. The Effect on the Economy

Many festivals contribute significantly, both locally and nationally, to the economies of the places in which they are held. They have the potential to increase tourism, bring in revenue for local companies, and make employment possibilities available. For instance, Mardi Gras in New Orleans is not just a cultural spectacular but also a significant economic driver for the city. It brings in millions of people and generates employment opportunities across a variety of industries.

1.5. The Transmission from Generation to Generation

Festivals are an essential method of intergenerational transmission because they provide an opportunity for elder generations to teach younger generations about their knowledge, customs, and core values. This passing down of cultural traditions ensures that they will not be lost or forgotten and that future generations will maintain a connection to their ancestry. For instance, the Obon festival in Japan is a time for families to remember and celebrate their ancestors while also passing down knowledge about the culture's history and customs to future generations.

2. Obstacles to the Long-Term Survival of Festivals

2.1. The Process of Globalization

The march of globalization has presented festivals with a variety of new opportunities in addition to new obstacles. While it has the potential to make the exchange of cultural traditions easier, it also has the potential to result in the watering down or commercialization of traditional celebrations. It's possible that certain festivals have watered down their genuineness or diminished its original cultural importance in order to appeal to a wider audience or attract more tourists. This has the potential to result in the festival losing its distinctive character.

2.2. The Rise of the City

The process by which cultures become more urbanized frequently results in a disconnection from their rural or traditional roots. It is possible for people to lose contact with the celebrations and traditions of their ancestors as they relocate to urban areas. Living in an urban environment can make it more difficult to maintain the traditions that are connected with rural celebrations, which may ultimately contribute to the festivals' extinction.

2.3. Appropriation of Other Cultures

Festivals run the risk of cultural appropriation in some instances. Cultural appropriation occurs
when aspects of one culture are appropriated and distorted by another culture, frequently without the appropriate level of understanding or respect. This can lead to the commercialization of cultural activities and symbols, which can be extremely upsetting to the culture from which these practices and symbols originated.

2.4. The Passing of Generations

There may be a decline in interest in traditional celebrations among younger generations, particularly in regions that are more developed or urbanized. Many people believe that the impact of contemporary technologies, shifts in lifestyle, and a lack of exposure to the cultural significance of these events are to blame for this generational shift.

2.5. The Changing Climate

Festivals that are dependent on particular weather conditions could experience substantial disruptions as a result of climate change. For instance, celebrations that are tied to agricultural cycles, such as harvest festivals, are susceptible to changes in climate patterns, which can wreak havoc on the timing of these events as well as the traditions that are associated with them.

3. The Value of Keeping Alive Festivals

3.1. The Diversity of Cultures

The continuation of festivals is absolutely necessary for the protection of cultural diversity. The globe is becoming more interconnected, and as a result, there is a greater likelihood that distinct customs and rituals will be lost in the process of culture mixing and blending. By protecting festivals, we can make sure that a wide variety of cultural expressions will continue to exist in the future.

3.2 The Connectedness of Everything

People from different countries and cultural backgrounds can be brought together via the power of festivals. They act as conduits via which cross-cultural understanding and collaboration can be achieved. People of varying cultural origins are given the opportunity to become more familiar with the customs and beliefs of one another through the documentation and preservation of festivals.

3.3. The Historical Heritage

Festivals are an essential component of the cultural inheritance left behind by societies. They frequently contain profound meaning and are a reflection of the challenges, victories, and progression of a community's cultural traditions. Festivals should be preserved so that future generations can gain a better understanding of the historical context and evolution of their culture.

3.4. The Cohesion of Society

Festivals are great for fostering communal solidarity and cohesion among members of the community. When festivals are maintained, they continue to offer occasions for people to congregate, share experiences, and develop a sense of connection with one another. The social fabric of societies is thereby strengthened as a result.

3.5. The Benefits to the Economy

There are numerous festivals that can generate tourists and encourage local economies, both of which are beneficial to the economy. Communities can continue to improve their standard of living and their overall well-being by preserving these events so that they can continue to benefit economically from them.

4. Methods of Festival Archiving and Documentation

4.1. The Tradition of the Oral

Festivals have often been preserved by oral tradition, which is one of the oldest methods. Younger generations are taught about the history, customs, and stories associated with festivals by elders and storytellers who are part of the community. This ensures that both information and the cultural significance of events are passed along.

4.2. Documents That Are Written

It is important to maintain the history and value of festivals by documenting them through written records like books, articles, and academic study. This is a useful approach to do so. The documentation and dissemination of knowledge about festivals is significantly aided by the work of researchers and intellectuals.

4.3. Documentation in Both Audio and Visual Forms

In this day and age of digital technology, audio and visual documentation have become extremely useful tools for the preservation of festivals. This comprises still photographs, moving pictures, and audio and video recordings that document the sights and sounds of various events. These albums are able to be distributed worldwide, which opens up festival attendance to audiences all over the world.

4.4. Art Galleries and Other Cultural Establishments

Museums and other cultural institutes frequently play an important part in the process of preserving festival artifacts and communicating the value of festivals to the general public. They might be responsible for the curation of exhibitions, the hosting of events, and the provision of educational resources to the general public.

4.5. Support from the Government

There are a number of governments that acknowledge the significance of festival preservation and provide support in the form of financial assistance, cultural programs, and laws. With this support, communities will be better able to preserve and carry on their traditions.

4.6. Instruction and Community Participation

Programs and community outreach initiatives can be offered by educational institutions and other groups to increase people's knowledge of the significance of festivals. They are also able to offer information and training to those individuals who are interested in learning more about festivals and maintaining them.

4.7. Intercultural Communication

People from a variety of cultural backgrounds are able to participate in and get an understanding of one another's celebrations thanks to programs that facilitate cultural exchange. These interactions cultivate an increased capacity for comprehension and enjoyment of varied cultural manifestations.

4.8. Tourism in Cultural Areas

Festivals can be protected in large part through the use of cultural tourism as an effective instrument. Festivals can be a powerful tool for communities to use in their efforts to increase tourism and revenue. However, it is vital to establish a balance between the preservation of cultural authenticity and the economic gains that may be gained.

The process of documenting and preserving festivals is not only a nostalgic gesture; rather, it is a necessary activity that must be carried out in order to protect our shared cultural legacy. Festivals are live manifestations of our many different cultures, and they serve as a bridge to connect people of all different backgrounds and ways of life. They honor the past, give communities a sense of vitality, and provide motivation for the generations to come.

It is impossible to overestimate the significance of conserving festivals and documenting their history in a society that is marked by fast change and the standardization of cultures. These festivals are a testimony to the tenacity of human culture and the strength of traditions that have been passed down through the generations. By preserving festivals, we can make certain that the intricate pattern of our shared cultural history will continue to exist in its original form. Furthermore, we can offer future generations with a guide to their roots and a feeling of who they are.

It is necessary for individuals, communities, academics, and governments to collaborate in order to preserve and disseminate information regarding these celebrations. We can assure the continued success of festivals by maintaining oral tradition, keeping written records, creating visual and aural documentation, preserving this information in museums, and engaging in cultural exchange. When we do this, we encourage the development of many cultures, we strengthen social cohesion, and we celebrate the exquisiteness of human expression.

12.1 The importance of cultural preservation

Culture is the filter through which we see and make sense of the world around us. It incorporates our commonly held ideals, customs, artistic practices, linguistic heritage, and historical background. It plays a significant role in determining who we are, how we relate with others, and the goals we set for ourselves. It is of the utmost significance to maintain a culture since it contains a wealth of information and history that has been handed down from generation to generation. In this essay of 1000 words, we will discuss the relevance of cultural preservation, focusing on its role in protecting our identity, encouraging diversity, and developing understanding among people of other cultures.

1. **Maintaining One's Identity**
   1.1. Continuity of Culture
   The continuation of a community's sense of self can be safeguarded through the practice of cultural preservation. Every society has its own distinct set of norms, rituals, and practices that serve to define the way of life for its people. By bridging the gap between the past, the present, and the future, these traditions foster a feeling of continuity as well as a sense of belonging. It is possible to lose this link if cultural preservation is not practiced, which would leave individuals and groups adrift in a world that is always changing.
   1.2. The Historical Footprint
   The act of keeping a community's history and legacy documented is known as cultural preservation. The history of a people can be pieced together from the traditions, tales, and artifacts that have been passed down through the generations. They provide light on the challenges they faced, the victories they achieved, and the cultural shifts that contributed to the formation of their identity. We ensure that these historical legacies will be passed down to future generations by maintaining culture. This gives future people the opportunity to comprehend and value where they come from.
   1.3. Customs and Rites of Culture
   Protecting one-of-a-kind customs that can't be replicated elsewhere is one of the most important reasons why cultural preservation is so important. These customs frequently have deep origins in the past and the physical landscape of a particular location. Whether it's a specific type of cuisine, a religious rite, or a traditional dance, conserving these habits helps to maintain the genuineness and diversity of human civilization.
2. **Promoting the Richness and Diversity of Cultures**
   2.1. A Vibrant Sampler of Human Cultures
   The world is made up of a beautiful tapestry of unique civilizations, each of which contributes something unique to the overall human experience mosaic. The maintenance of cultural traditions ensures that this patchwork will always be rich in variety. When different cultures are maintained and appreciated, it

enriches the entire human experience by providing a wide variety of viewpoints, practices, and approaches to life.

2.2. Intercultural Communication and Exchange

Efforts to maintain cultural traditions foster increased intercultural communication and interaction. When we show appreciation for and respect for the culture of other people, we foster an environment that is conducive to mutual understanding. This, in turn, creates the path for people from different backgrounds to peacefully coexist with one another and work together. By participating in this exchange, not only do we gain knowledge about other cultures, but we also improve our own understanding of who we are as a people.

2.3. Resisting Homogenization of the Environment

There is a danger of cultural homogeneity in the society we live in today as a result of increased globalization. This happens when various cultures begin to blend together to establish a single, unified global culture. Globalization has brought about many positive changes, but it also poses a risk to the diversity of the world's cultures. The continuation of distinct customs and the encouragement of communities to conserve their individual identities are two important aspects of cultural preservation that contribute to the fight against homogenization.

3. Facilitating Relationships Between Different Generations

3.1. The Transmission of Knowledge

The transmission of experience and expertise from one generation to the next is an essential component of cultural preservation. In many different cultures, the older generation plays an essential part in passing down knowledge to the younger generation on the history, values, and traditions of the culture. The transmission of knowledge and experiences from one generation to the next helps ensure that important information and lessons are not lost.

3.2. Improving Relationships Within the Family and Community

The majority of the time, families and communities are the keepers of cultural traditions. Families and communities can enhance their ties to one another by taking part in shared cultural activities, such as attending events, telling stories, and performing rituals. Because of this sense of belonging and shared identity, there is greater unity and resilience inside the group, which is especially important in trying times.

3.3. Enhancing Community Integration and Cohesion

The preservation of cultural traditions also serves to strengthen communities on a broader scale. The coming together of entire communities for the purpose of celebrating their cultural history helps to build a sense of belonging as well as a sense of shared purpose. This, in turn, contributes to the overall cohesion and peace of the social community.

4. Benefits to the Local Economy and Tourism

4.1. Tourism in Cultural Institutions

The preservation of cultural traditions can result in considerable financial rewards, particularly when they are facilitated by cultural tourism. Destinations that provide guests with one-of-a-kind cultural opportunities attract a significant number of tourists. Communities have the ability to attract tourists, produce cash, and create jobs in the tourism industry if they take measures to preserve their cultural heritage.

4.2. The Economy of the Area

By bolstering historically significant artistic enterprises, culinary practices, and handicrafts, cultural preservation can help invigorate local economies. This commercial endeavor not only contributes to the maintenance of cultural traditions, but it also makes it possible for people to make a living from traditional occupations.

5. Techniques for the Conservation of Cultural Objects

5.1. Oral History and Tradition

One of the earliest ways in which a culture's history can be preserved is through oral tradition. Through the use of spoken word, elders and storytellers of a culture transmit its history, myths, and traditions to younger generations. This technique is still very important in many different countries since it ensures that knowledge and anecdotes are passed down from one generation to the next.

5.2. Documents That Are Written

The preservation of written records, such as books, manuscripts, and historical papers, is of the utmost importance for cultural traditions. These documents offer a documented account of a community's cultural norms and traditions, as well as its historical events and core values. They are a source of reference for the generations who will come after us as well as for researchers.

5.3. Documentation in Both Audio and Visual Forms

In this day and age of digital technology, visual and aural documentation are significant tools for the preservation of cultural heritage. The sights, sounds, and traditions of a culture can be captured in still photographs, motion pictures, and audio recordings. These records are able to be distributed globally, which makes the practice of cultural preservation accessible to people all over the world.

5.4. Museums and other types of Cultural Centers

The preservation of cultural traditions is significantly aided by museums and other cultural institutes. They preserve antiques, works of art, and historical records by collecting them, displaying them, and making them available to the public. Museums are also educational institutions that explain to a wider audience the significance of cultural heritage and place it within its historical context.

5.5. Support from the Government

Numerous governments acknowledge the need of preserving cultural traditions and offer their assistance in the form of financial assistance, cultural programs, and legislative initiatives. It is possible that with this support, communities and institutions will be better able to carry out preservation initiatives and protect their cultural heritage.

The protection of our cultural heritage is essential to the maintenance of the integrity of who we are as individuals and as communities. It is a method for insuring the continuation of our cultural identity while also cultivating diversity, boosting intercultural understanding, developing intergenerational relationships, and reaping economic benefits. In a world that is evolving at a quick pace and where different cultures frequently interact with one another and blend, conserving culture is a method to ensure that our individual histories, values, and traditions are not lost.

The duty for the maintenance of cultural traditions is shared. People on their own, as well as communities, governments, and educational institutions, all have a part to play in the success of this attempt. By recognizing the significance of cultural preservation, we not only enrich our own lives, but we also contribute to the collective legacy of humanity. This ensures that the treasures of culture are passed on to subsequent generations, providing those generations with a profound connection to their roots as well as a deep appreciation for the beauty of human diversity.

12.2 Efforts to document and protect endangered festivals

Festivals are the most dynamic representations of human culture, and they reflect the norms, customs, and history of communities all over the world. However, as the global environment continues to shift and cultures continue to interact in a world that is becoming increasingly interconnected, many festivals are in danger of going extinct. To maintain the continuity of cultural traditions and to foster an understanding between people of different backgrounds, it has become an urgent need to record and safeguard festivals that are in risk of disappearing. In this essay of 1000 words, we will investigate the efforts and tactics that are employed to preserve and maintain endangered festivals, as well as the relevance of these festivals in preserving cultural diversity and the difficulties that they face.

1. **The Importance of Gathering Information on, and Attempting to Preserve, Vulnerable Festivals**
   ### 1.1. The Protection of Cultural Assets
   The documentation and defense of at-risk festivals are absolutely necessary for the continuation of cultural traditions. Many times, a society's history, its ideals, and its identity may be summed up in its festivals. They play an essential role in the continuation of cultural traditions and contribute to the preservation of a feeling of communal identity. over the maintenance of these celebrations, we protect the cultural heritage as well as the information that has been handed down over the years.

1.2. Facilitating Mutual Comprehension Across Cultures
Festivals around the world that are in risk of disappearing offer priceless insights into their civilizations, their customs, and their worldviews. When we take the time to record and preserve these celebrations, we make it easier for people to comprehend other cultures. This, in turn, fosters tolerance and respect for various expressions of cultural diversity, which, eventually, contributes to the development of a global community that is more peaceful.

1.3. Cultivating Relationships Between Different Generations
The traditions celebrated at festivals are passed down from generation to generation. The elder generations can pass down their knowledge, customs, and values to the future generations by documenting and protecting these celebrations. This passing down of cultural traditions helps to ensure that they will not be lost or forgotten, which in turn helps to maintain connections between generations.

1.4. The Effect on the Economy
There are several festivals that have a big impact on the local economy. They have the potential to increase tourism, bring in revenue for local companies, and make employment possibilities available. By preserving these at-risk celebrations, we are helping to sustain the economies of the surrounding areas and enhancing the quality of life for individuals who make their living off of festival-related work.

2. The Obstacles That Threaten the Survival of Festivals

2.1. The Process of Globalization
Festivals have been presented with benefits as well as challenges as a result of globalization. While it has the potential to make the exchange of cultural traditions easier, it also has the potential to result in the watering down or commercialization of traditional celebrations.

Some festivals may water down their traditions or downplay their original cultural value in an effort to appeal to a more general audience or to attract more tourists. This can result in the festivals losing their distinctive character.

2.2. The Rise of the City
The process by which cultures become more urbanized frequently results in a disconnection from their rural or traditional roots. It is possible for people to lose contact with the celebrations and traditions of their ancestors as they relocate to urban areas. Living in an urban environment can make it more difficult to maintain the traditions that are connected with rural celebrations, which may ultimately contribute to the festivals' extinction.

2.3. Appropriation of Other Cultures
Festivals run the risk of cultural appropriation in some instances. Cultural appropriation occurs when aspects of one culture are appropriated and distorted by another culture, frequently without the appropriate level of understanding

or respect. This can lead to the commercialization of cultural activities and symbols, which can be extremely upsetting to the culture from which these practices and symbols originated.

2.4. The Passing of Generations

There may be a decline in interest in traditional celebrations among younger generations, particularly in regions that are more developed or urbanized. Many people believe that the impact of contemporary technologies, shifts in lifestyle, and a lack of exposure to the cultural significance of these events are to blame for this generational shift.

2.5. The Changing Climate

Festivals that are dependent on particular weather conditions could experience substantial disruptions as a result of climate change. For instance, celebrations that are tied to agricultural cycles, such as harvest festivals, are susceptible to changes in climate patterns, which can wreak havoc on the timing of these events as well as the traditions that are associated with them.

3. Efforts to Record and Conserve Threatened Celebrations

3.1 The Tradition of the Oral

The transmission of knowledge through oral tradition is still an effective means of documenting vanishing celebrations.

Through the use of spoken word, community elders and storytellers continue to play an essential part in the process of maintaining the history, traditions, and stories associated with various festivals. This ensures that both information and the value of cultural traditions are passed down from one generation to the next.

3.2. Documents That Are Written

It is important to maintain the history and value of festivals by documenting them through written

records like books, articles, and academic study. This is a useful approach to do so. When it comes to documenting and spreading knowledge about imperiled celebrations, the work of researchers and academics is of the utmost importance.

3.3. Documentation in Both Audio and Visual Forms

Since the advent of digital technology, the use of video and audio recording has developed into a strong instrument for the purpose of documenting and preserving events that are in risk of being lost. This comprises still photographs, moving pictures, and audio and video recordings that document the sights and sounds of various events. These albums are able to be distributed worldwide, which opens up festival attendance to audiences all over the world.

3.4. Art Galleries, Museums, and Other Cultural Centers

Museums and other cultural institutes frequently play an important part in the documentation and preservation of festivals that are in danger of extinction by collecting and showcasing artifacts and exhibits linked to these festivals. They are stewards of cultural heritage, acting as a forum for educational opportunities and the protection of cultural artifacts.

3.5. Support from the Government
Numerous governments acknowledge the need of archiving and safeguarding festivals that are in danger of extinction, and they provide help in the form of financial assistance, cultural policies, and legislative initiatives. With this support, communities will be better able to preserve and carry on their traditions.

3.6. Educational Programs and Community Outreach
Programs and community outreach initiatives can be offered by educational institutions and groups to promote awareness about the significance of documenting and protecting festivals that are in danger of disappearing. They are also able to offer information and training to those individuals who are interested in learning more about these festivals and preserving them.

3.7. Intercultural Communication
People from a wide variety of backgrounds are able to participate in and get an understanding of historically significant celebrations because to programs that facilitate cultural exchange. These exchanges encourage a knowledge and appreciation of a wide variety of cultural manifestations, and they frequently include hands-on experiences and connections with the communities in which they take place.

An important step in preserving cultural history, fostering intergenerational connections, and fostering cross-cultural understanding, the documentation and protection of festivals that are at risk of extinction is a crucial activity. The significance of preserving distinctive cultural practices is becoming increasingly obvious as globalization continues to increase the level of connectivity throughout the globe. We not only celebrate cultural diversity but also help to the preservation of the human cultural mosaic by lending our support to efforts to preserve and protect festivals that are in danger of being lost.

Significant obstacles, such as globalization and shifts in generational attitudes, threaten the survival of festivals around the world. However, these problems can be overcome by employing strategies such as oral tradition, written records, visual and aural documentation, museums, government backing, educational initiatives, and cultural exchange. It is necessary for individuals, communities, academics, and governments to collaborate in order to preserve and disseminate information regarding these celebrations. By working together in this way, we will be able to ensure those festivals that are in risk of extinction will continue to thrive, protecting the vibrant tapestry of our shared cultural heritage for the generations that will come after us.

12.3 The role of museums and institutions in preserving festival heritage
When it comes to the preservation of festival history, museums and other cultural organizations play a crucial role. They are the keepers of cultural traditions, serving as repositories for artifacts, documents, and the information that is associated with the many different celebrations. In this essay of 1500 words, we will investigate the varied

role that museums and other institutions play in the preservation of festival legacy, including how they contribute to the protection of cultural variety, teaching, and research, as well as the problems that they confront in order to achieve this extremely important obligation.

1. The Opening Statements

   Festivals are live representations of culture and play a crucial role in conserving and spreading cultural heritage. Festivals are held in many countries across the world. Because they are able to capture a society's identity as well as its values and its history, they are an essential component of cultural continuity. Nevertheless, the maintenance of festivals is a challenging job, and museums and other institutions play an essential role as stakeholders in this attempt. These organizations have the knowledge, resources, and infrastructure necessary to document, safeguard, and spread the word about the cultural value of festivals.

2. The Involvement of Museums and Other Institutions in the Conservation of Festival Heritage

   2.1. The Accumulation and Conservation of Artifacts

   Festival artifacts are an important category for museums and other types of institutions to collect and store, as this is one of their fundamental functions. Traditional garb and masks, musical instruments, paraphernalia associated with various religions, and festival decorations are all examples of the kinds of artifacts that fall under this category. These artifacts will be preserved for much longer thanks to the climate-controlled and secure setting that museums provide for them.

   2.2. The Process of Documenting and Archiving

   Festivals are frequently documented by museums and other types of institutions, utilizing a wide variety of different forms of media. They take pictures, movies, and audio recordings in order to preserve the memories of the sights, sounds, and stories that occurred during these events. For scholars, historians, and future generations who are interested in comprehending the cultural importance of celebrations, this record is a priceless resource.

   2.3. Exhibiting and Providing Interpretation

   Exhibits are created by museums and other cultural organizations based on their interpretation of festival-related objects and documents in order to illustrate the story of various cultural events. These exhibitions are not only informational but also experiential, providing guests with the opportunity to connect with the festivities via the use of displays, interactive features, and multimedia presentations. The public receives an education while also gaining a better understanding of other cultures thanks to these shows.

   2.4. Educational Programs and Opportunities

   There are several educational programs available at museums and other institutions that are tied to festival heritage. These activities may take the form of guided tours, workshops, lectures, or even school programs that are designed to educate children about the significance of festivals and their rich histories. They contribute to the maintenance of festival heritage by increasing the public's cultural literacy and appreciation of different traditions.

2.5. Research and Academic Achievement

The scholarly study of festival heritage is frequently supported by museums and other institutions. Researchers and academics work along with these groups to conduct in-depth studies of festivals. These studies involve doing ethnographic research, studying artifacts, and investigating the cultural, historical, and social aspects of the events. This research not only contributes to academic knowledge but also to our overall advancement in our understanding of festival history.

2.6. Cultural Preserving and Efforts to Promote It

Museums and other types of institutions play an important role in ensuring the continuity of festival traditions. They have the ability to push for government assistance, financial funding, and legal protections in order to preserve festivals that are in risk of extinction, which can play a role in increasing awareness about the significance of these traditions. They are making a contribution to the larger cultural preservation efforts on both the local and the international levels by doing so.

2.7. Shared Experiences of Other Cultures

Exchanges between different cultures frequently take place in museums and other types of institutions. In order to encourage people to share their festival legacy, they work together with local communities, artists, and cultural practitioners. As part of this effort, you might offer events, festivals, and performances that highlight the customs of a variety of different cultures. These interactions foster a better understanding and appreciation of different cultures.

3. Obstacles That Museums and Other Institutions Need to Overcome in Order to Preserve Festival Heritage

3.1. Restricted Access to Resources

A great number of museums and other cultural organizations are restricted in their capacity to collect, maintain, and display festival legacy as a result of resource limitations. This includes restrictions imposed by financing, staffing levels, available storage space, and technological capabilities. Their potential to carry out comprehensive preservation measures may be hindered as a result of these constraints.

3.2. Respect for Other Cultures and Appropriation of Their Art

Problems of cultural insensitivity and the possibility of appropriation must be navigated by museums and other types of institutions. They need to find a way to educate the general public about the history of the event while also showing respect for the cultures from whom these customs originated. Misrepresentation or the incorrect use of festival objects and documentation can lead to cultural insensitivity, which in turn can lead to disputes.

3.3. Legality and Return to Your Country

The question of who owns cultural items and where they should be repatriated can be a difficult and controversial one. When it comes to the legitimacy of their collections, museums and other types of organizations frequently run into difficulties, particularly in cases where cultural relics may have been obtained through colonial practices or other immoral ways. The demand for repatriation made by communities or countries of origin offers a conundrum for institutions that need to negotiate the ethical and legal factors that come into play.

3.4. The Evolution of Traditional Practices

Alterations to or elimination of certain festival customs are possible when cultural practices progress over time. The documentation of these shifts presents a problem for museums and other types of organizations, as they must do so without compromising the original customs' cultural relevance or their validity. It is a difficult challenge to achieve a balance between documenting emerging customs and conserving the cultural character of festivals.

3.5. Accessibility and inclusivity

The difficulty that museums and other types of organizations have is making certain that the heritage of festivals can be accessed by everyone. They are obligated to give thought to the means by which they can make their displays and programs accessible to a wide variety of audiences, such as those with varying levels of cultural literacy, different linguistic backgrounds, and different types of disabilities. The removal of accessibility barriers can require a significant investment of resources.

By collecting and preserving artifacts, documenting traditions, interpreting and exhibiting festival heritage, providing educational programs, supporting research, advocating for cultural preservation, fostering intercultural exchange, and promoting cross-cultural understanding, museums and cultural institutions play an essential role in the preservation of festival heritage. They are vital players in the fight to preserve cultural variety and make certain that festival legacy will continue to enrich our global cultural fabric in the future.However, these establishments are also confronted with a plethora of issues, such as the management of limited resources and the balancing of cultural appropriation and sensitivity. To be successful in overcoming these obstacles, you will need to demonstrate a dedication to ethical practices, a respectful engagement with communities, and a commitment to accessibility and diversity.

www.ingramcontent.com/pod-product-compliance
Lightning Source LLC
LaVergne TN
LVHW011934070526
838202LV00054B/4636